SPSS for Windows: An Introduction to Use and Interpretation in Research

George A. Morgan
Orlando V. Griego[1]
Gene W. Gloeckner

In Collaboration with
Nancy L. Leech
James M. Lyall
Don Quick
Mei-Huei Tsay[2]
Lisa M.Vogel

Colorado State University

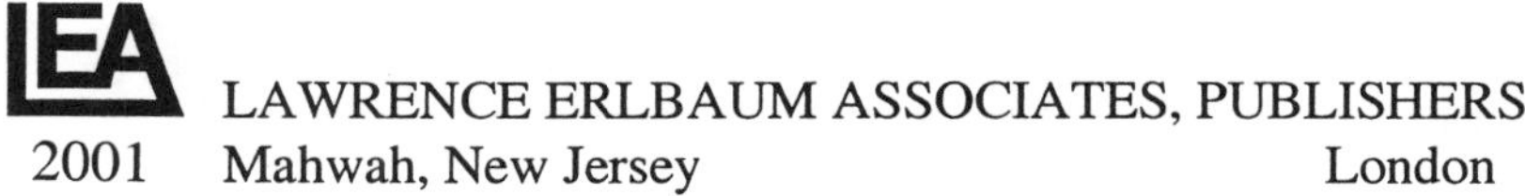

LAWRENCE ERLBAUM ASSOCIATES, PUBLISHERS
2001 Mahwah, New Jersey London

[1] Now at Azusa Pacific University
[2] Now at Chung Tai Institute of Health Sciences and Technology, Taiwan

Copyright © 2001 by Lawrence Erlbaum Associates, Inc.
All rights reserved. No part of this book may be reproduced in any form, by photostat, microform, retrieval system, or any other means, without the prior written permission of the publisher.

Lawrence Erlbaum Associates, Inc., Publishers
10 Industrial Avenue
Mahwah, New Jersey 07430

Library of Congress Cataloging-in-Publication Data

Morgan, George A.
SPSS for Windows : an introduction to use and interpretation in research / George A. Morgan, Orlando V. Griego, Gene Gloeckner ; in collaboration with Nancy L. Leech ... [et al.].
p. cm.
Includes index.
ISBN 0-8058-3584-9 (pbk.: alk. paper)
1. SPSS for Windows. 2. Social sciences–Statistical methods–Computer programs. I. Griego, Orlando V. II. Gloeckner, Gene. III. Title.

HA32.M667 2000
300'.285'5369–dc21

00-042670

Books published by Lawrence Erlbaum Associates are printed on acid-free paper, and their bindings are chosen for strength and durability.

Printed in the United States of America

10 9 8 7 6 5 4 3 2 1

Table of Contents

Appendices

PREFACE

This book is designed to help students learn how to analyze and interpret research data. It is intended to be a supplemental text in an introductory (undergraduate or graduate) research methods or statistics course in the behavioral sciences or education. We have found that the book makes SPSS so easy to use that it is not necessary to have a formal lab, except perhaps for the first couple of assignments (Lab A and B in chapters 1 and 5). Access to SPSS and some familiarity with Windows is all that is required.

We use SPSS 10 for Windows in this book; however, there are only minor differences from versions 7, 8, and 9. In fact our students have used this book or earlier drafts with all of these versions of SPSS. Both the procedures and outputs are quite similar, and we expect future Windows versions to be very similar, so you should have little difficulty if you have access to versions 7 through 9 or, we anticipate, versions 11 and 12. We will point out some of the changes at various points in the text.

SPSS for Windows is quite easy to use, especially in contrast to earlier mainframe and DOS versions, but SPSS provides such a wide variety of options and statistics that the printouts can be difficult to interpret. This book demonstrates how to produce a variety of statistics that are usually included in basic statistics courses. Our goal has been to describe the use and interpretation of these statistics as much as possible in nontechnical, jargon-free language. Also, at the end of this book we have provided a bibliography of some of the books we have found useful. You will find it helpful to read about each statistic before doing the lab assignments in this book.

Helping you learn how to choose the appropriate statistics, interpret the outputs, and develop skills in writing about the meaning of the results are the main goals of this book. Thus, we have combined material on a) how the appropriate choice of a statistic is based on the design of the research, b) how to use SPSS to answer a number of research questions mainly about one realistic data set, and c) how to interpret SPSS outputs. This will help you develop skills that cover the whole range of the design, data collection, data entry, analysis, and interpretation process. The high school and beyond data set (HSB) used in this book is similar to what you might have for a thesis, dissertation, or research project. Therefore, we think it can serve as a model for your analysis. The compact disk packaged with the book contains the HSB data file.

There are several unusual features of this book that we and our students think make it especially user friendly. First, we have included the key SPSS windows that you see when performing the statistical analyses. This has been helpful to "visual learners." Second, we have included the complete outputs for the analyses that we have done so you can see what you will get, after some editing in SPSS to make the outputs fit better on the pages. In chapter 1 we tell you how to do this. Third, we have included call-out boxes on the outputs that point out parts of the output on which to focus and indicate what they mean. Fourth, for each output, we have provided an interpretation section that should help you understand the output. Fifth, we have provided interpretation questions that stimulate you to think about the chapters and outputs and their meaning. Sixth, each chapter ends with several extra problems for you to run with SPSS and discuss. Seventh, the first five appendixes provide examples of how to write research problems and questions, develop a questionnaire, make a code book, make tables and figures, and write the method, results, and discussion of a research paper. Finally, several other appendixes provide information and examples of other useful features of SPSS: how to import and export SPSS files, how to use some other SPSS commands, how to create 3-D figures with SPSS, and how to use SPSS log or syntax commands. The answers to the interpretation questions are provided in the last appendix.

Our approach in this book is to present the concept of how to use and interpret SPSS in the context of actually proceeding as if these were the data from your research project. Thus, before starting the SPSS assignments, we have three introductory chapters. In chapter 1, we provide an overview of SPSS 10 and some of the many statistics and other manipulations possible with this sophisticated package. The second chapter describes research problems, variables, and questions and hypotheses, and it identifies a number of specific research questions related to the HSB data. The goal is to use SPSS as a tool to help you answer the research questions. Appendix A provides some guidelines for phrasing or formatting research questions. Chapter 3 discusses measurement and its relation to the appropriate use of statistics. This chapter also includes a brief review of descriptive statistics.

Because many of you may have little experience with research methods, we have written chapters 4 and 5 to help you get started. Chapter 4 presumes that you will finalize the development of a questionnaire and collect data with it as part of a class activity. However, if you are not in a class or the instructor decides not to do the class activity, a sample questionnaire and data are provided in Appendix B. The data are available on the compact disk that is provided with the book. Chapter 5 provides you with experience entering data and doing basic descriptive statistics on a small sample of data whose variables should be easily understood. If you have experience with data collection and entry, it may be possible to skip chapters 4 and 5 and start in chapter 6 analyzing the high school and beyond (HSB) data set, which is more like one you might have for a thesis or research project.

Chapter 7 provides a brief overview of research designs (between groups and within subjects) and how to set up and enter data for each type of design. This chapter also describes a system for selecting an appropriate statistic and an overview of how to interpret the results of an inferential statistic. Our approach to design and statistics in chapters 2, 3, and 7 is somewhat nontraditional because we have found that students have a great deal of difficulty with some aspects of statistics but not others. Most can learn formulas and "crunch" the numbers quite easily and accurately with a calculator or with a computer. However, many have trouble knowing what statistics to use and how to interpret the results. They do not seem to have a "big picture" or see how research design influences data analysis. Part of the problem is inconsistent terminology. We are reminded of Bruce Thompson's frequently repeated, intentionally facetious remark at his many national workshops: "We use these different terms to confuse the graduate students." For these reasons we have tried to present a semantically consistent and coherent picture of how research design leads to three basic kinds of research questions (difference, associational, and descriptive) which, in turn, lead to three kinds or groups of statistics with the same names. We realize that these and other attempts to develop and utilize a consistent framework are both nontraditional and somewhat of an oversimplification. However, we think the framework and consistency pay off in terms of student understanding and ability to actually use statistics to answer their research questions. Instructors who are not persuaded that this framework is useful can skip chapters 2, 3, and 7 and still have a book that helps them and their students use SPSS.

Laboratory Assignments B and C (chapters 5 and 6) are organized in very much the way you might proceed to analyze the data if this were your project. For example, we start by labeling variables and entering data. Next, we examine and check the data for errors. Then, we calculate a variety of descriptive statistics, check certain statistical assumptions, and make a few data transformations. Much of what is done in these two assignments is preliminary analysis to get ready to answer the research questions that you might state in a report. Laboratory Assignments D through G (chapters 8-11) are designed to answer the research questions posed in chapter 1 as well as a number of additional questions that should give you a good idea of the key statistics that can be computed with SPSS.

Hopefully, seeing how the research questions and design lead naturally to the choice of statistics will become apparent after using this book. In addition, it is our hope that interpreting what you get back from the computer will become more clear after doing these assignments, studying the outputs, answering the interpretation questions and doing the extra problems.

Some parts of this book adapt information and graphics from Morgan and Griego (1998), our longer SPSS book, published by Lawrence Erlbaum Associates, that covers more complex statistics (e.g., factor analysis, discriminant analysis, and MANOVA) than this book. Both SPSS books are consistent with and could be used as supplements for Gliner and Morgan, (2000) *Research Methods in Applied Settings: An Integrated Approach to Design and Analysis,* also published by Erlbaum.

We would like to acknowledge the assistance of the students who have used earlier versions of this book and provided helpful suggestions for improvement. We could not have completed the task or made it look so good without our word processor, Linda White, and several capable work study students including Rae Russell. Bill Sears, LaVon Blaesi, Jenny Kou, and Mei-Huei Tsay assisted with classes and the development of materials for the DOS and earlier Windows versions of the assignments. The collaborating authors (Nancy Leech, Lisa Vogel, Don Quick, James Lyall, and Mei-Heui Tsay) plus Joan Anderson, Sue Doe, Mary Hart and Deena Koessl, helped with editing parts of the manuscript. Karen Barrett, Jeff Gliner, Heather Miles, and Jim zumBrunnen and several other reviewers provided editorial advice and suggestions about the selection and interpretation of statistics and options. Bart Beaudin, Bob Fetch, and Lillian Wehmeyer provided helpful feedback from an adult education point of view. We also acknowledge the financial assistance of two instructional improvement grants from the College of Applied Human Sciences at Colorado State University. Finally, the patience and help of our wives, Hildy, Lise, and Susan, enabled us to complete the task.

G. M., O. G. and G.G.
Fort Collins, Colorado
June, 2000

CHAPTER 1

Overview of SPSS for Windows

James M. Lyall and Nancy L. Leech

SPSS (Statistical Products and Service Solutions) is a powerful, easy to use statistical package designed in a Windows environment, which provides the social sciences professional with many options. Although SPSS is available for several different operating systems, version 10, and therefore this manual, is designed for use with Windows 95/98/NT. Although there are a few differences between SPSS version 10 and the earlier versions, the user interface, or desktop, is basically the same. Because the lab assignments in this manual are specifically for use with SPSS, differences in the Windows environment will not affect how the lessons are completed.

This manual is designed for use with the full version of SPSS 10, which is available at the many universities with a site license, and also for students who have the *Advanced Grad Pack.* The manual is also designed to be used with the less complete versions, the *Career Starter and Student Version,* available to students in classes that use SPSS.

It is not possible to compare and contrast each version of SPSS in this manual. It is, however, important to note some enhancements that have been made to the most recent version of SPSS. New for SPSS 10 is increased speed of data analysis. Also new is a search and replace in the data editor, including searching of variable and value labels. In terms of integration with other types of software, there have also been improvements. It is now possible to use SPSS to create graphics and then paste them into other applications to easily generate reports. However, SPSS 7, 8, 9, and 10 are very similar from the user's perspective. Most windows are the same and almost everything in this book applies to versions 7-9 and, probably, to future versions, at least for the next few years. From the students' point of view, there is one main difference between 7-9 and version 10 (i.e., how variables are defined and labeled). We will point out this difference in this chapter and in chapter 5.

In the assignments throughout this book, all menu or button options are displayed in **Bold** type. This will help users as they learn to navigate in the Windows environment.[1] This chapter is designed as an overview of SPSS to help you get started, to familiarize yourself with the many functions of SPSS, and to learn how to edit and print your outputs.

---

[1] In the chapters with lab assignments we have identified the variable names using italics (e.g., *math achievement).* Italics are also used for emphasis.

Copying the Data Files from the Compact Disk

For Lab Assignment A in this chapter, you will need the **Descriptives Output File** from the compact disk (CD) provided with this book. However, it is best to **copy** all of the files from the CD to a diskette *or* to a folder on your hard drive. Even though we have used a CD for these files, they are not very big and should fit on a blank diskette with plenty of room for the exercises in this book. The three files are:

Descriptives Output File.spo (11k)
hsbdata with errors.sav (5k)
May28thAppBdata.sav (4k)

Note: you may not see the file extensions (.spo and .sav) depending on your computer setup.

There are several ways to copy the files. Also our letters for the computer drives may not be the same on your computer. The method described below assumes that your CD drive is F: (some systems use E: or D:) and you will be copying to a blank diskette in drive A:. Insert the compact disk found with this book in your CD drive and a blank diskette into your A: drive.

- Point at the **Start** button in the lower left corner of your screen and click the **right** button (not the left) on your mouse.
- Click **Explore** with the **left** button.
- On the left side of the Window click the **CD icon SPSS Data (F:).**
- The display should look something like Figure 1.1

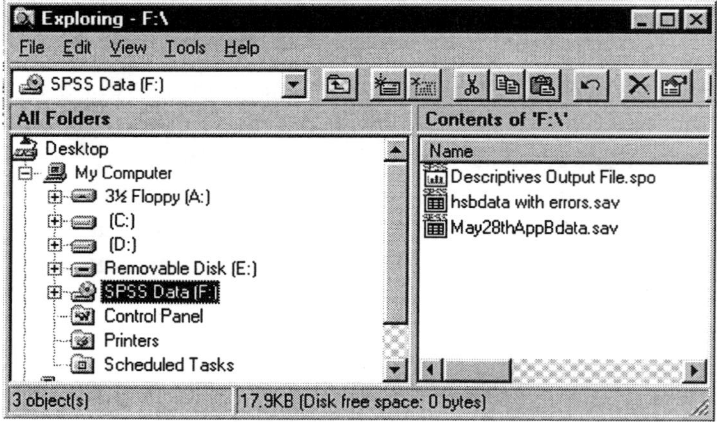

Fig. 1.1. Copying the SPSS files using the exploring window

- Click and drag each of the **three files** in the right column to the **3½ Floppy (A:) icon** on the left.
- Close the **Explore** window.

Lab Assignment A

Logon

There are several ways to open SPSS. One way is:

- Double click on the **SPSS icon** in Windows if it is available.

Note: If an icon is not available, you should begin at the **Start** button (bottom left of the Windows Desktop). Click the **Start** button; move up to **Programs**, then to **SPSS for Windows** (See Fig. 1.2). There may be some variation as to the location of the **SPSS 10 for Windows** icon depending on how your computer is configured.

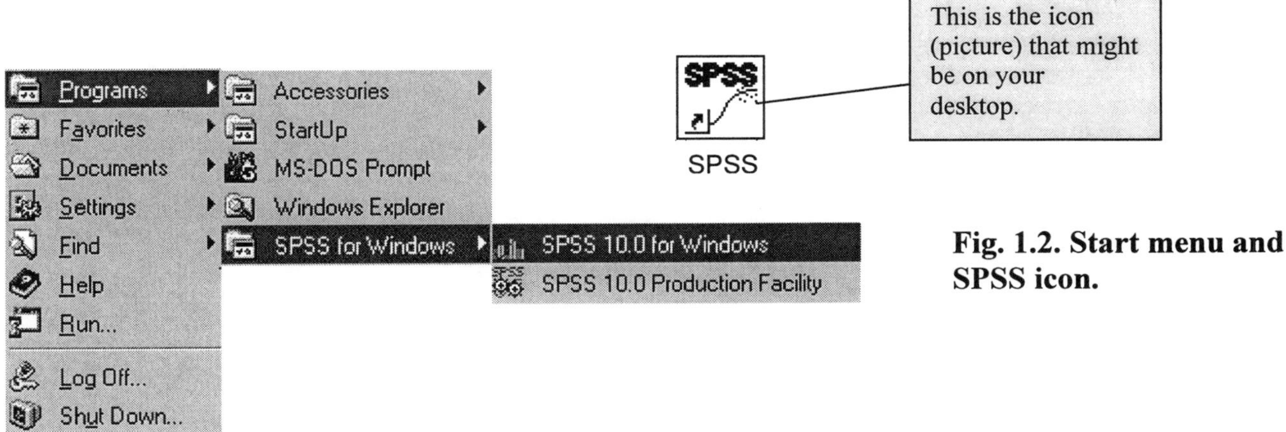

Fig. 1.2. Start menu and SPSS icon.

After you have successfully started SPSS you will see the SPSS Startup screen shown in Fig. 1.3. Notice that in the Startup screen there is a list of all SPSS files available.

- Click the **Cancel** button shown in Fig. 1.3 or, in the future, you can click on the SPSS file you wish to use.

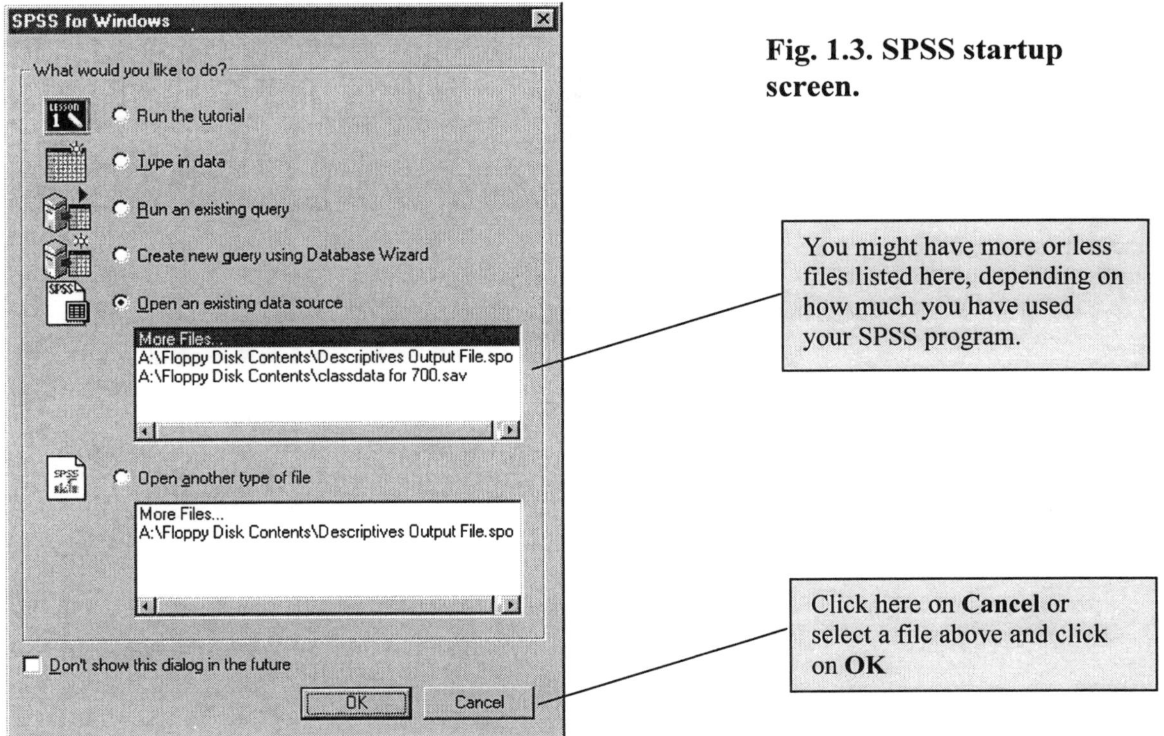

Fig. 1.3. SPSS startup screen.

After clicking cancel, you will see the SPSS desktop, called the SPSS Data Editor as shown in Fig 1.5 and 1.6.

The SPSS Data Editor

There are two tabs at the bottom left side of the **SPSS Data Editor** (Fig. 1.4). The **Data View** tab and the **Variable View** tab. It is important to notice the *subtle* difference in the desktop between these two views (compare Fig. 1.5 and Fig. 1.6). The toolbar at the top of the screen is the same for both the Variable and Data View screens. Notice that when you click on the **Variable View** tab the column names are like those in Fig. 1.5. It is easiest to create new variables by clicking on the Variable View tab, as we will do in chapter 5. When you click on the **Data View** tab, the columns change to **var** or to the names of your variables if you have already entered them. (See Fig. 1.6.) When you are inputting new data, be sure you have clicked on the Data View tab.

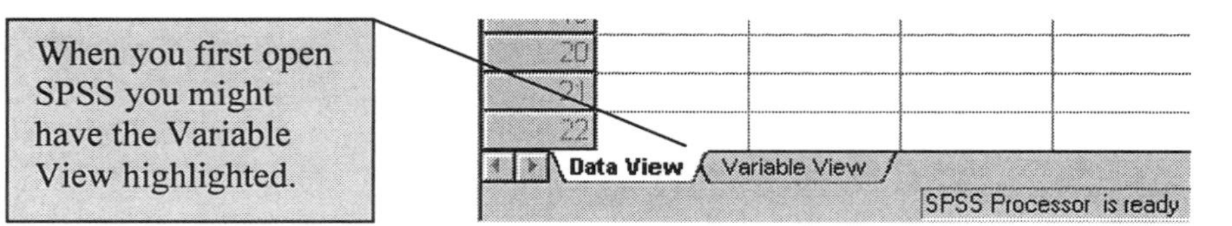

Fig. 1.4. View tabs.

Important: The **Variable View** and **Data View** tabs are new to SPSS 10. If you have an SPSS 9.0 or lower version, you will not have the Variable View screen option and will have to enter the variable information differently. Please refer to your SPSS Help menu for further information in earlier versions.

- If you have not done so already, click on **Variable View** to produce Fig. 1.5.

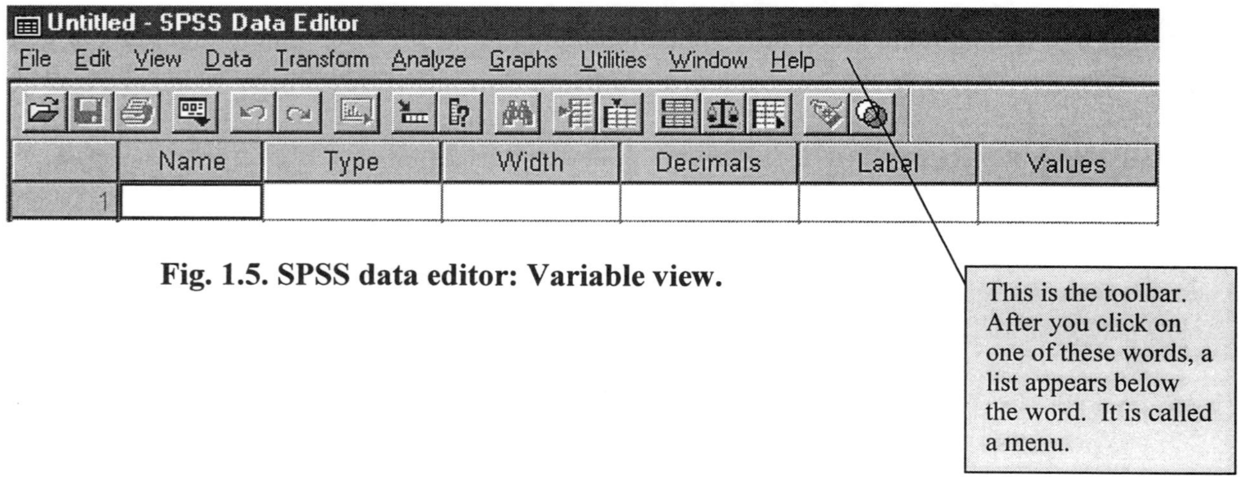

Fig. 1.5. SPSS data editor: Variable view.

- Now click on the Data View tab to produce Fig. 1.6.

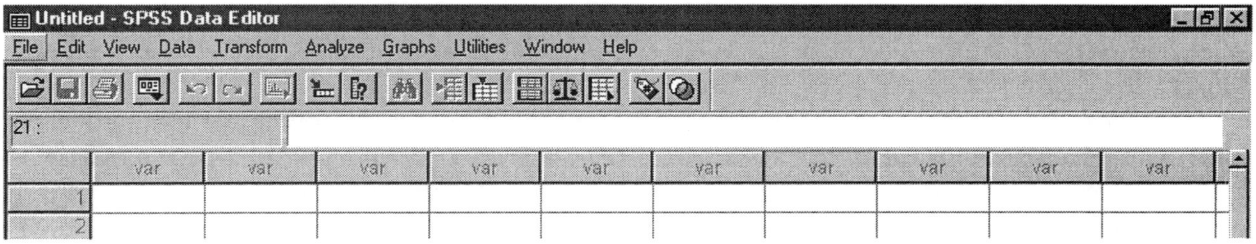

Fig. 1.6. SPSS data editor: Data view.

Menu overview. There are ten menu options available for both the Variable View and the Data View screens (see Fig 1.5 and 1.6). These include the common Windows menus of **File**, **Edit**, **View**, **Window**, and **Help**. You will find general commands, such as saving a file or printing that are available in all Windows applications.

The following exercise is meant to help you explore the SPSS menu options and become familiar with the desktop, not to explain each of the options. As the menu options are mentioned, *click on each one* to see what features are available under each.

- Under the **File** menu, for example, are the options for creating, opening, saving, and printing an SPSS file. Click on **File** now if you did not already.
- The **Edit** menu provides the options for moving data such as cut, copy, and paste. If data are wrongly inputted into a column, they can be selected, cut, and copied to the correct column without retyping. Edit commands are not in dark print because we have not opened a data file.
- To change the appearance of SPSS, the **View** menu offers options about which toolbars are visible as well as how the data is displayed.
- You will find functions that allow you to manipulate your data file under the **Data** menu. One feature found under this menu option is **Insert Variable.**
- The **Transform** menu provides options to change or redefine variables. You will, for example, **Recode** variables without re-entering data in chapter 6.
- The **Analyze** menu option contains the statistical analysis options in SPSS. You will become much more familiar with the options in this menu as you continue through this book.
- A variety of outputs can be generated from the **Graphs** menu. The functions under this menu are primarily used with data output files such as the one we will use in this chapter.
- There are several advanced options available under the **Utilities** menu. One of the key options is **File Info** used to create your codebook. See chapter 5 and Appendices B and C.
- The **Window** menu lists all the windows currently open *within* SPSS. If multiple SPSS files are open, this is helpful for easily switching between them.
- The **Help** menu in particular can be useful for finding answers to common questions about how to use SPSS. It can be especially convenient for helping with specific statistical functions.

Editing and Printing the Data Output File

You probably know that SPSS can be used for statistical analysis. It can also be used to create graphs, charts, and tables from your data. For this exercise, you will open, modify, and print an output file of descriptive statistics. The descriptive statistics in this output file were generated using the *visualization score* variable from HsbDataWithErrors file. You will learn the process for creating such outputs in chapter 5; this exercise will focus only on manipulating the output file to add your name and format it for printing. By manipulating the output file, you can print your outputs so they will fit better on the page.

Retrieve the data output file from your disk. There are many ways to retrieve data and output files. We will explain one of the easier ways.

- To open the output file, select **File => Open => Output...** (see Fig. 1.7). This will show you all the output files you have on your disk. Note, when you want to retrieve *data* from your disk, select **File => Open => Data**.

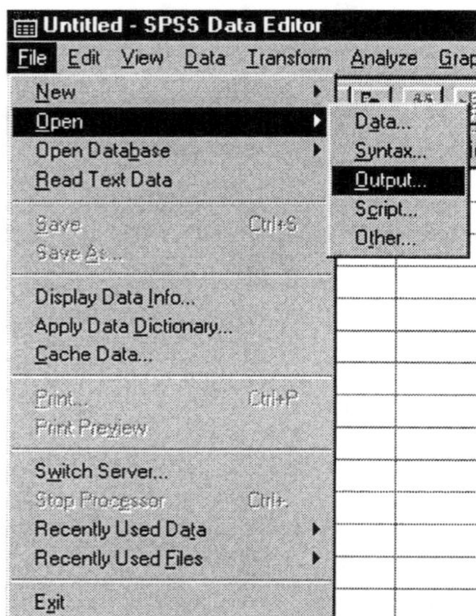

Fig. 1.7. File open output.

- You will see the **Open File** dialogue box (Fig. 1.8).
- Check to see what is shown in the **Look in** box. If it is not the **3 ½ Flop**py, then click on the arrow to the right of the box. By doing this you will see a list of places in your computer where the file might be (see Fig 1.8). Highlight and then click on **3 ½ Floppy.**

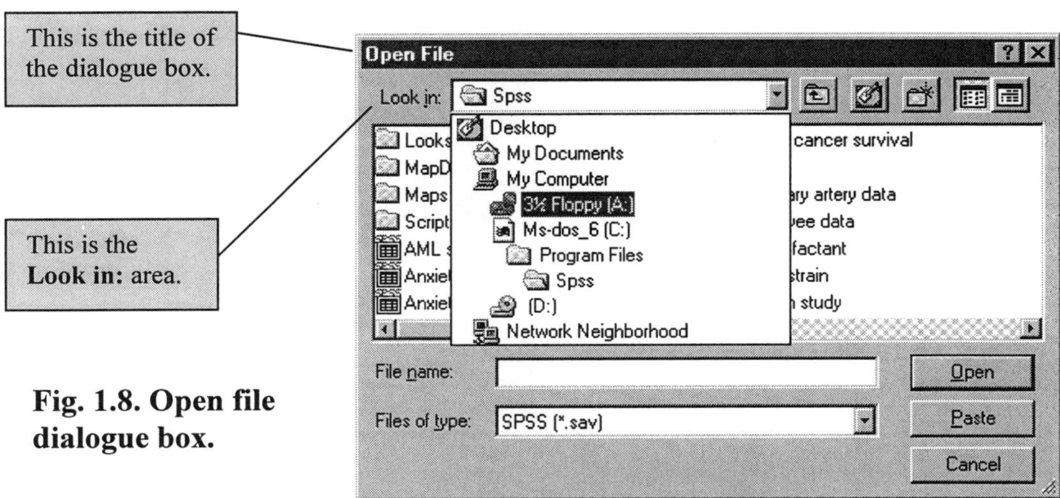

Fig. 1.8. Open file dialogue box.

- You should now see a window similar to Fig 1.9.
- Highlight **DescriptivesOutput.spo**.
- Click once on **Open** in Fig. 1.9.

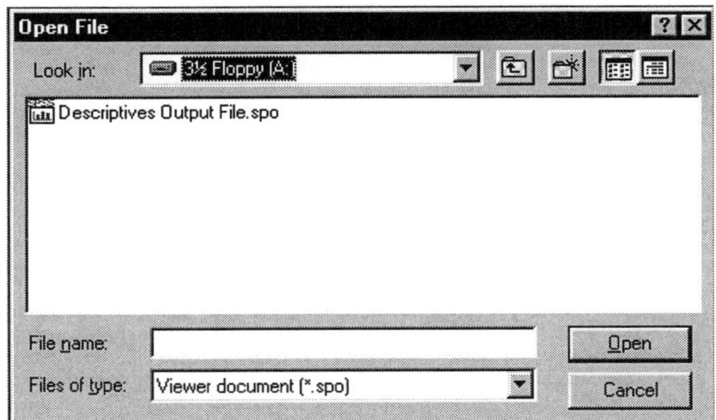

Fig. 1.9. Open output file.

You will see a table of descriptive statistics (see Fig 1.10) created by SPSS.

Adding information to your output. The first step will be to add your name to the chart. This may be important if you are in a lab classroom as there may be many people printing the same outputs and no way to determine who has created which output. You may also want to use this procedure to add titles or other information to your outputs.

Outputs are created after you input data, label variables, and have requested a statistical analysis to be done. Note that the output screen has a different toolbar. The output screen toolbar functions are described later in the book.

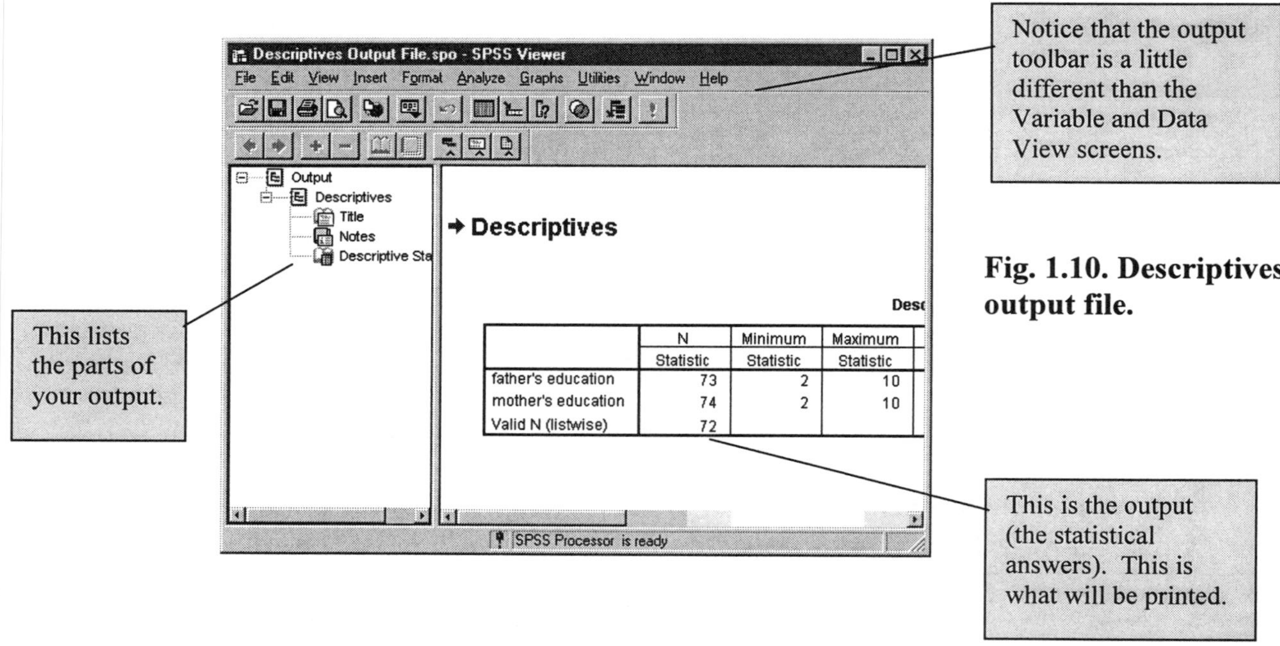

Fig. 1.10. Descriptives output file.

- Click **Insert => New Text** (See Fig 1.11).

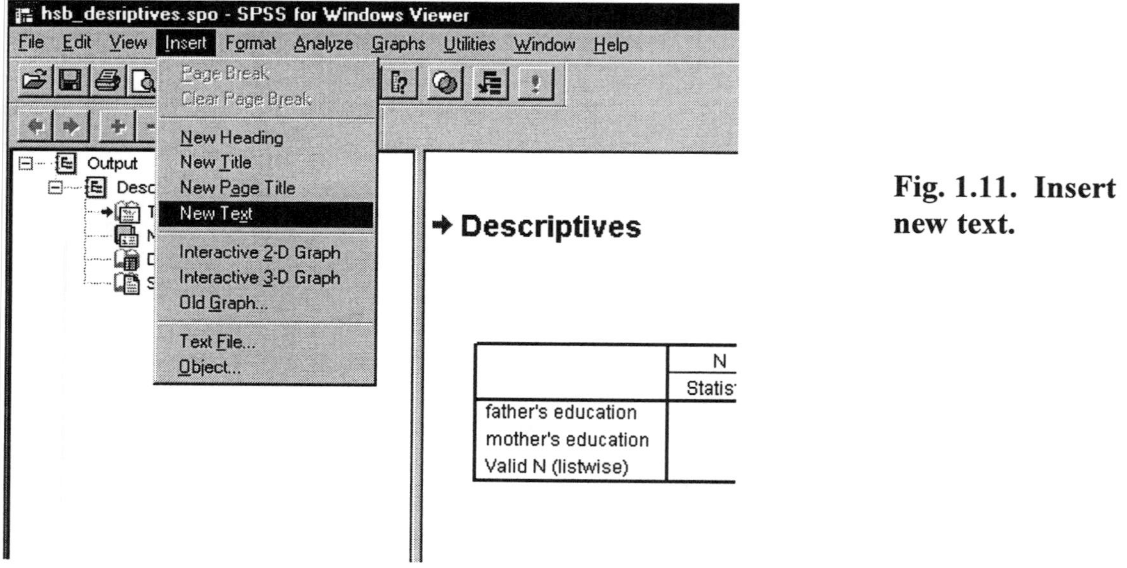

Fig. 1.11. Insert new text.

- A box with fuzzy lines will appear with a cursor prompting you to type (See Fig 1.12). You are now in the editing mode.
- Type your name in the box and then click anywhere else on the table to exit the editing mode.

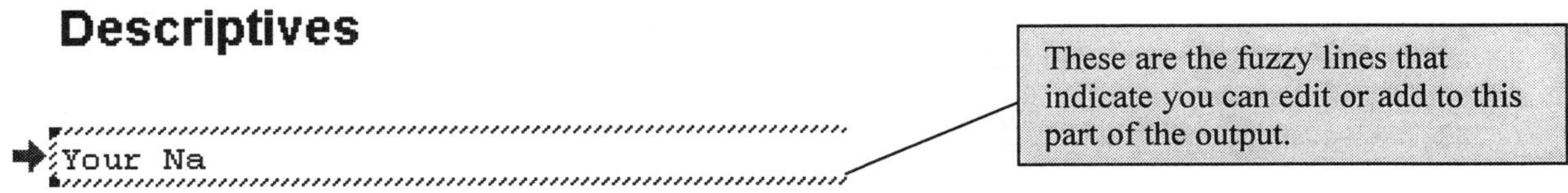

	N	Minimum	Ma
	Statistic	Statistic	St
father's education	73	2	

Fig. 1.12. Text box.

Print preview and printing the output. On the left side of the output screen, there is a list of words (Output, Descriptives, Title, etc.).

- Click once on the word **Descriptives.** This will make the words **Descriptives**, **Title**, **Notes**, **SPSS Text**, and **Descriptive Statistics**, turn dark. (Do not click on the right side of the window, which is your output). Be sure all the words are dark *exactly* like in Fig. 1.13.

By selecting the **Descriptives**, not descriptive statistics, (See Fig. 1.13) you are choosing what part of the output file you will be viewing in the print preview, which in this case is the whole output file. This step will be helpful with future outputs. When doing several statistical analyses at one sitting, all of the outputs will be in the same file. With this step you can select which parts of the output file you want to print so you do not have to print the entire file.

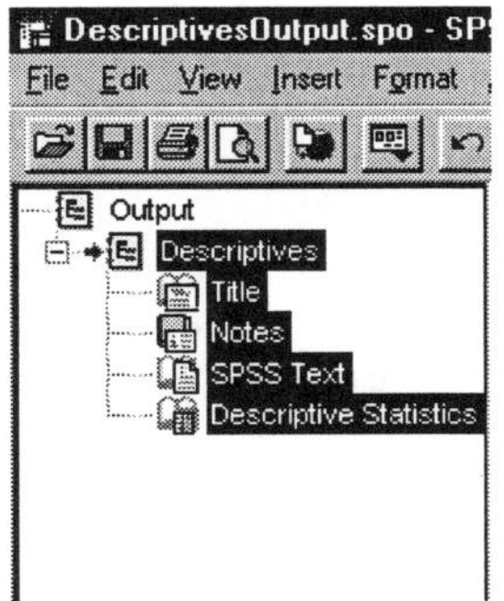

Fig 1.13. Descriptives.

Now we will use the print preview option to verify how the table will appear on the printed page:

- Choose **File => Print Preview** from the main menu bar (See Fig. 1.14). You will see what will be printed.

Notice that the output is not all on one line. Having an output like this can be confusing and difficult to read and understand. With SPSS 10 (but *not* earlier versions) you can rescale, or shrink the output, so that it will better fit on the page.

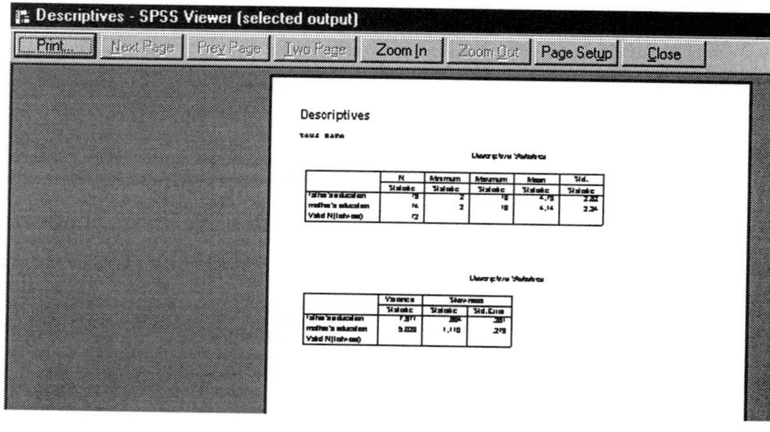

Fig. 1.14. Menu for print preview and print preview screen.

- Click on Close in the upper right to close print preview.

Rescaling the output. Be sure that the print preview window is closed.

- *Double*-click on the table to enter the editing mode to make sure this table will print correctly. You can verify that you are in this mode (and that you successfully double clicked) by the fuzzy border that appears around the table (see Fig. 1.15) as well as the appearance of two different toolbars: Pivoting Trays 1 and Formatting Toolbar 1. You will not use either of these toolbars now; they will automatically disappear when you finish editing the table. If the table border does not become fuzzy or the pivoting trays and formatting toolbar do not appear, try double clicking on the table again.

- Select the **Format => Table Properties** (See Fig. 1.15).

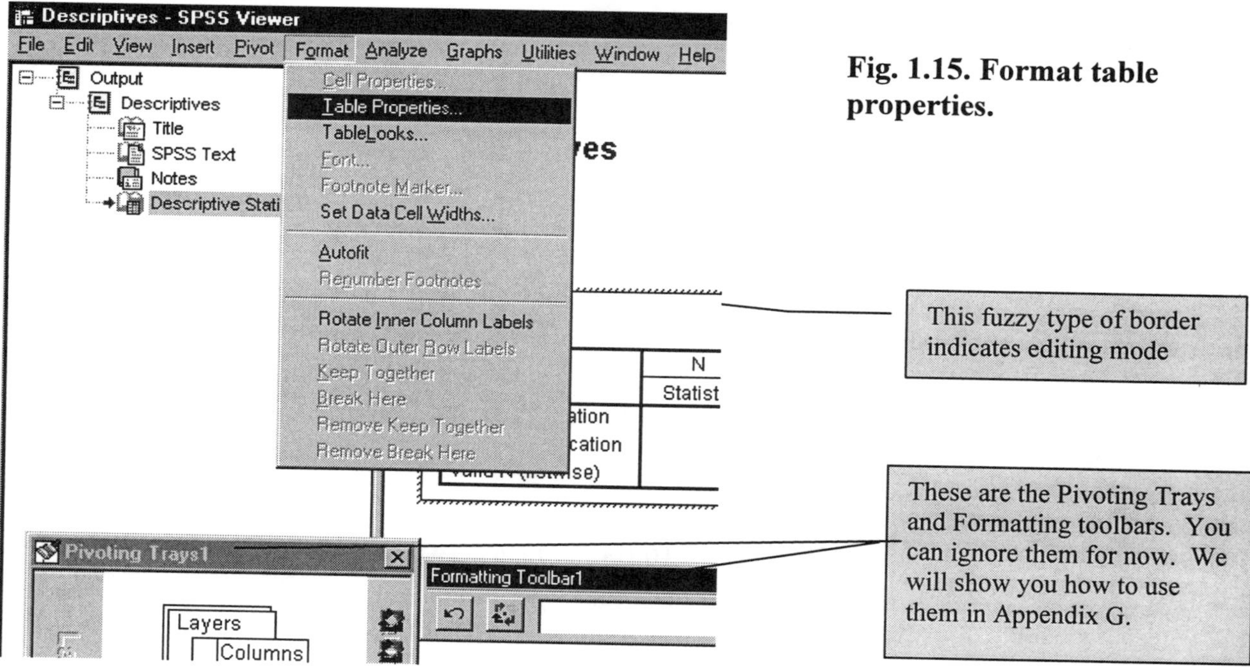

Fig. 1.15. Format table properties.

The Table Properties dialogue box will appear (See Fig. 1.16).

- Choose the **Printing** tab on the top of the **Table Properties** window.
- Check the box for **Rescale wide table to fit page**.
- Click **OK** at the bottom of the window.
- Click anywhere on the output screen under **Sample** to exit editing mode.

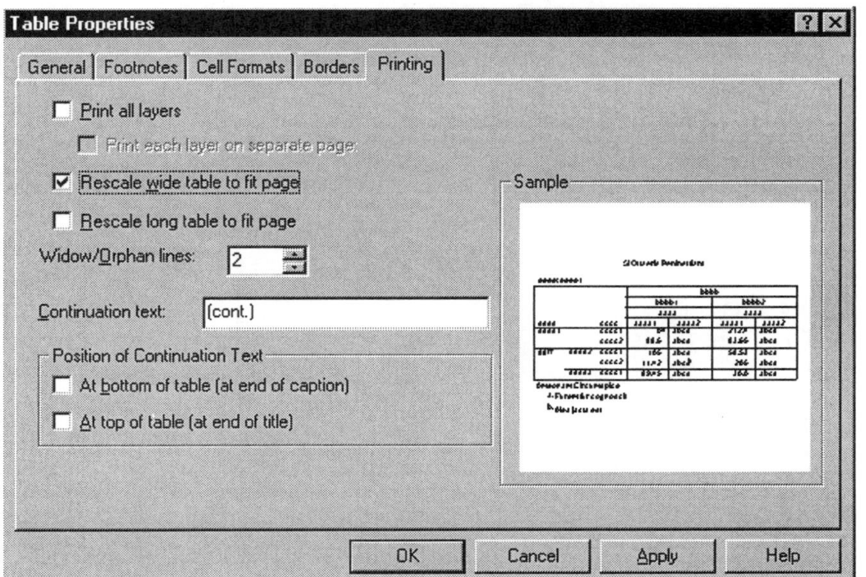

Fig. 1.16. Table properties.

Before continuing, you should click on print preview again to be sure that the rescaling of your output worked (See Fig. 1.17). If you do not remember how, turn back to the Print Preview section earlier in this chapter. Below is what your print preview screen should look like after you have rescaled it.

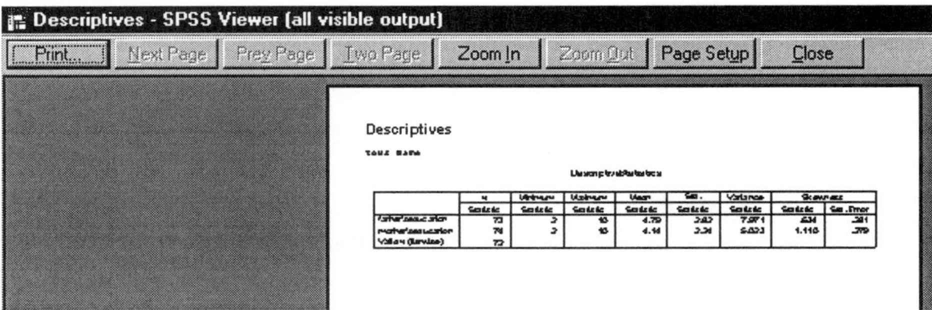

Fig 1.17. Print preview of your rescaled output.

Printing. Now that the chart has been labeled with your name, formatted to fit the page, and you have previewed what will be printed, you can print it. You do not have to preview every time you print. You can do print preview when you want to see what the printed pages will look like, before printing.

- Using the **File => Print** menu option, print out the table to determine how the on-screen format compares with a printed version. You have several options available from the Print menu. You can choose to print all visible output, which is the entire output file, or only print the selected tables and charts (See Fig. 1.18).

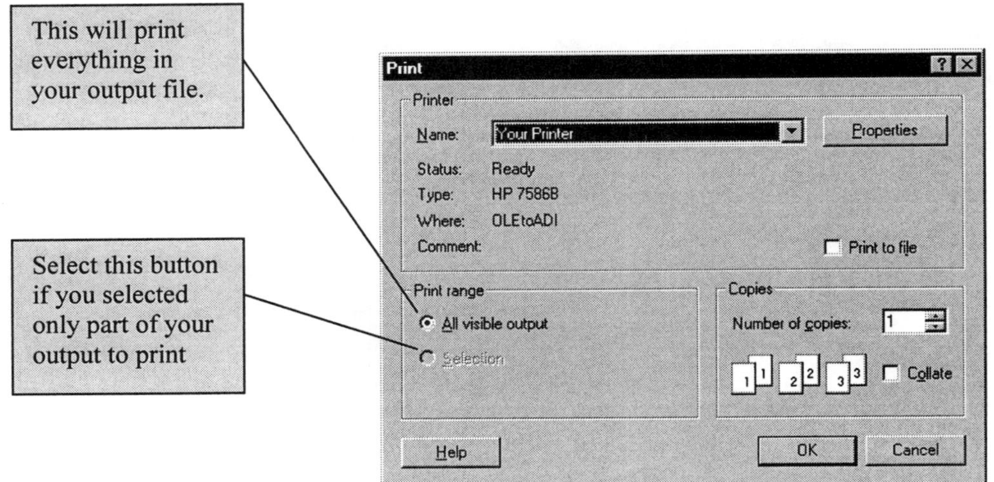

Fig. 1.18. Printing.

- Click **OK.** This will print your file.

Exit

- Click **File => Exit**. This will close the SPSS program.

Interpretation Questions

1. Why should you generally put a) your name on your output, b) longer titles on the output tables, and c) the date on the output?

2. What menu contains the available statistical analysis functions?

3. If you wanted to recode your data, what menu would you use?

Extra Problems

1. To practice what you have just done, logon to SPSS again, get the output file, and insert information displaying the today's date and your instructor's name. Also, expand the title of the output to Descriptives for Lab Assignment A. Print the revised output.

2. Use the SPSS **Help => Topics**; read about Pivot Tables.

CHAPTER 2

Research Problems and Questions

Research Problems

The research process begins with a problem. A *research problem* is a statement that asks about *the relationship between two or more variables*. Note that almost all research studies have *more* than two variables. Appendix A provides templates to help you phrase your research problem, and provides examples from the high school and beyond (HSB) data set that will be described briefly at the end of this chapter and in more detail in chapter 6. The process of moving from a sense of curiosity, or a feeling that there is an unresolved problem, is a complex and sometimes long one. That part of the research process is beyond the scope of this book, but it is discussed in most books about research methods and books about completing a dissertation or thesis.

Variables

A *variable* has one defining quality. *It must be able to vary or have different values*. For example, *gender* is a variable because it has two values, female or male. *Age* is a variable that has a large number of values. *Type of treatment/intervention* (or *type of curriculum*) is a variable if there is more than one treatment or a treatment and a control group. *Number of days to learn something or to recover from an ailment* are common measures of the effect of a treatment and, thus, are also variables. Similarly, *amount of mathematics knowledge* is a variable because it can vary from none to a lot. If a concept has one value in a particular study it is not a variable, e.g., ethnic group is not a variable if all participants are Caucasian.

Definition of a variable. We can define the term *variable* as a characteristic of the participants or situation of a given study that has different values in that study. In quantitative research, variables are defined operationally and are commonly divided into independent variables (active or attribute), dependent variables, and extraneous variables. Each of these topics will be dealt with in the following sections.

Operational definitions of variables. An operational definition describes or defines a variable in terms of the operations or techniques used to elicit or measure it. When quantitative researchers describe the variables in their study, they specify what they mean by demonstrating how they measured the variable. Demographic variables like age, gender, or ethnic group are usually measured simply by asking the participant to choose the appropriate category from a list. Types of treatment (or curriculum) are usually described/defined much more extensively so the reader can understand what the researcher meant by, for example, a cognitively enriching curriculum or sheltered work. Likewise, abstract concepts like mathematics knowledge, self-concept, or mathematics anxiety need to be defined operationally by spelling out in some detail how they were measured in a particular study. To do this, the investigator may provide sample questions, append the actual instrument, or provide a reference where more information can be found.

Independent Variables

Active or manipulated independent variables. A frequent goal of research is to investigate the effect of an intervention. An example might be a new kind of therapy compared to the traditional treatment. A second example might be the effect of a new teaching method, such as cooperative learning, on student performance. In the two examples provided above, the variable of interest was something that was *given to* the participants. Therefore, an *active independent variable* is a variable, such as a workshop, new curriculum, or other intervention, one level of which *can be given to a group of participants*, usually within a specified period of time *during the study*. Thus, active independent variables are *given* to the participants in the study but are not necessarily manipulated by the experimenter. They may be given by a clinic, school, or someone other than the investigator, but from the participants' point of view the situation was manipulated.

Attribute or measured independent variables. Like SPSS but unlike authors of some research methods books, we do not restrict the term *independent variable* to those variables that are manipulated or active. We define an independent variable more broadly to include any predictors, antecedents, or *presumed* causes or influences under investigation in the study. Attributes of the participants as well as active independent variables fit within this definition. For the social sciences and education, attribute independent variables are especially important. Type of disability or level of disability is often the major focus of a study. Disability certainly qualifies as a variable since it can take on different values even though they are not *given* during the study. For example, cerebral palsy is different from Down syndrome, which is different from spina bifida, yet all are disabilities. Also, there are different levels of the same disability. People already have defining characteristics or *attributes* that place them into one of two or more categories. The different disabilities are already present when we begin our study. Thus, we are also interested in studying a class of variables that are not given or manipulated *during the study*, even by other persons, schools, or clinics.

A variable which cannot be given, yet is a major focus of the study, can be called an attribute independent variable. In other words, the values of the independent variable are attributes of the persons or their ongoing environment that are not manipulated during the study. For example, *gender*, *age*, *ethnic group*, *IQ*, and *self-esteem* are attributes of a person.

Other labels for the independent variable. SPSS uses a variety of terms such as *factor* (chapters 10 and 11), and *grouping variable* (chapter 10). In other cases, (chapter 9) SPSS and statisticians do not make a distinction between the independent and dependent variable; they just label them *variables*. Strickly speaking, there is no independent variable for a correlation or chi-square. However, we think it is educationally useful to think of one variable as the predictor (independent variable) and the other as the outcome (dependent variable) even when discussing correlation.

Type of independent variable and inferences about cause and effect. When we analyze data from a research study, the statistical analysis does not differentiate whether the independent variable is an active independent variable or an attribute independent variable. However, even though SPSS and most statistics books use the label independent variable for both active and attribute variables, there is a crucial difference in interpretation.

A major goal of scientific research is to be able to identify a causal relationship between two variables. For those in applied disciplines, the need to demonstrate that a given intervention or treatment causes change in behavior or performance is extremely important. Only the approaches that have an active independent variable (the randomized experimental and to a lesser extent the quasi-experimental) can be successful in providing data that allow one to infer that the independent variable caused the dependent variable.

However, a significant difference between or among persons with different values of an attribute independent variable should *not* lead one to conclude that the attribute independent variable caused the dependent variable to change. Thus, this distinction between active and attribute independent variables is important because terms such as *main effect* and *effect size* used by SPSS and most statistics books might lead one to believe that if you find a significant difference the independent variable *caused* the difference. These terms are misleading when the independent variable is an attribute.

Although studies with attribute independent variables are limited in what can be said about causation, they can lead to solid conclusions about the differences between groups and about associations between variables. Furthermore, they are the *only* available approach if the focus of your research is on attribute independent variables.

Values of the independent variable. We said that it must have more than one value. Logically, SPSS uses the term "values" to describe the several options or values of a variable. These values are *not* necessarily ordered, and several other terms *categories, levels, groups,* or *samples* are sometimes used interchangeably with the term values, especially in statistics books. Suppose that an investigator is performing a study to investigate the effect of a treatment. One group of participants is assigned to the treatment group. A second group does not receive the treatment. The study could be conceptualized as having one independent variable (*treatment type)*, with two values or levels (treatment and no treatment). The independent variable in this example would be classified as an active independent variable. Now suppose instead, that the investigator was interested primarily in comparing two different treatments but decided to include a third no-treatment group as a control group in the study. The study still would be conceptualized as having one active independent variable (treatment type), but with three values (the two treatment conditions and the control condition). This variable could be diagrammed as follows:

Variable Label	*Values*	*Value Labels*
	1	= Treatment 1
Treatment type	2	= Treatment 2
	3	= No treatment (control)

As an additional example, consider gender, which is an attribute independent variable with two values, male and female. It could be diagrammed as follows:

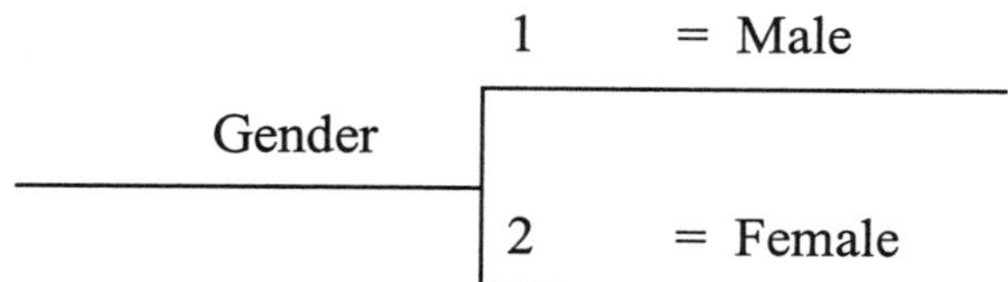

Note that in SPSS each variable is given a label; the values, which are usually numbers, may also have labels. It is especially important to know the value labels when the variable is nominal; i.e., when the values of the variable are just names and, thus, are not ordered.

Dependent Variables

The dependent variable is the presumed outcome or criterion. It is assumed to measure or assess the effect of the independent variable. Dependent variables are often test scores, ratings on questionnaires, readings from instruments (electrocardiogram, galvanic skin response, etc.), or measures of physical performance. When we discuss measurement in chapter 3, we are usually referring to the dependent variable. Dependent variables, like independent variables must have at least two values; most dependent variables have many values, varying from low to high so they are not easy to diagram as shown above.

SPSS also uses a number of other terms for the dependent variable. *Dependent list* is used in cases where you can do the same statistic several times, for a list of dependent variables (e.g., in chapter 10 with one-way ANOVA). The term *test variable* is used in chapter 10 for the *t* test.

Extraneous Variables

These are variables that are *not* of interest in a particular study but could influence the dependent variable. Environmental factors (e.g., temperature or distractions), time of day, and characteristics of the experimenter, teacher, or therapist are some possible extraneous variables that need to be controlled. SPSS does not use the term *extraneous variable.* However, sometimes such variables are controlled using statistics that are available in SPSS.

Research Questions

Hypotheses are *predictive statements about the relationship between variables.* Research questions are similar to hypotheses in question format. We divide research questions into three broad types: *difference, associational,* and *descriptive.* For the difference type of question, we compare groups, derived from values of the independent variable, on their scores on the dependent variable. This type of question typically is used with the randomized experimental, quasi-experimental, and comparative approaches. For an associational question, we associate or relate the independent and dependent variables. Descriptive questions are not answered with inferential statistics; they merely describe or summarize data. Figure 2.1 shows that both difference and associational questions or hypotheses have as a *general purpose* the exploration of relationships between variables. This similarity is in agreement with the statement by statisticians that all common parametric inferential statistics are relational.[1] However, we believe that the distinction between these two types of questions is educationally useful. Note that difference and associational questions differ in specific purpose and the kinds of statistics they use to answer the question.

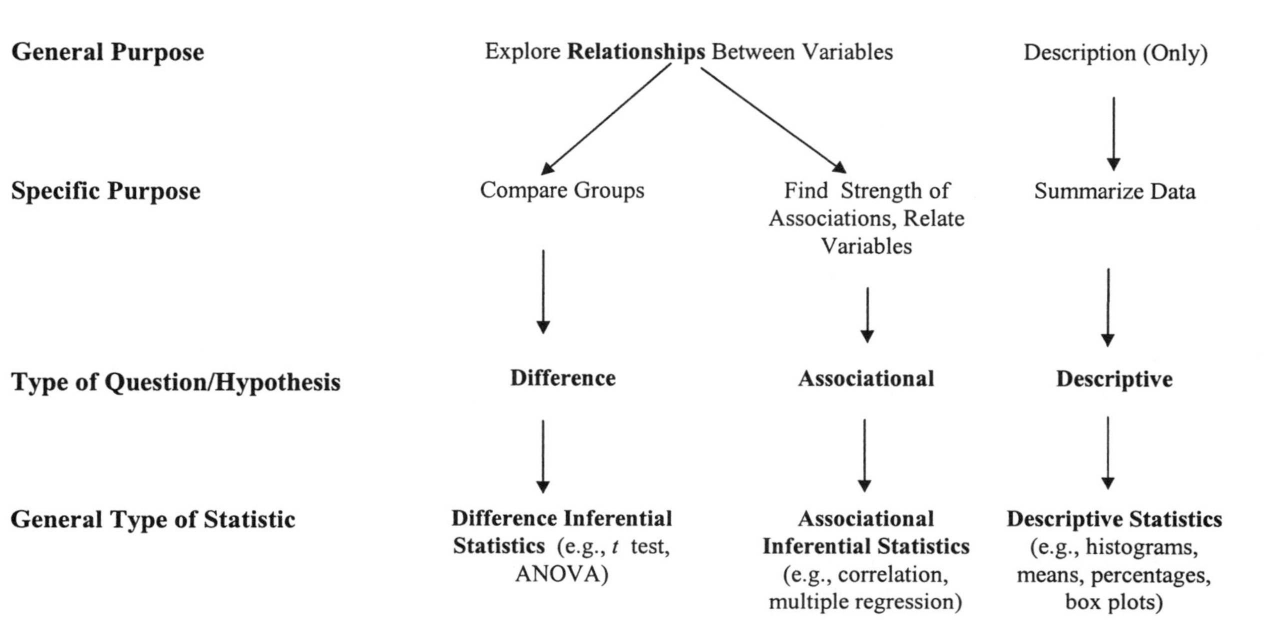

Fig. 2.1. Schematic diagram showing how the purpose and type of research question correspond to the general type of statistic used in a study.

Difference versus associational inferential statistics. We think it is educationally useful, although not common in statistics books, to divide inferential statistics into two types corresponding to difference and associational hypotheses or questions[2]. Difference inferential statistics (e.g., *t* test or analysis of variance) are used for approaches which test for *differences between groups* (e.g., using analysis of variance). Associational inferential statistics test for *associations or relationships between variables* and use correlation or multiple regression

[1] We use the term *associational* for the second type of research question,and statistics rather than relational or correlational to distinguish them from the *general purpose* of both difference and associational questions/hypotheses. Also we wanted to distinguish between correlation, as a specific statistical technique, and the broader types of question and group of statistics.

[2] We realize that all parametric inferential statistics are relational so this dichotomy of using one type of data analysis procedure to test for differences (when there are a few values or levels of the independent variables) and another type of data analysis procedure to test for associations (when there are continuous independent variables) is somewhat artificial. Both continuous and categorical independent variables can be used in a general linear model approach to data analysis. However, the practical implication is that most researchers utilize the above dichotomy in data analysis.

analysis. We will utilize this contrast between difference and associational inferential statistics in chapter 7 and later in this book.

Table 2.1 provides the general format and one example of a basic *difference question,* a basic *associational question,* and a basic *descriptive question*. Remember that research questions are similar to hypotheses, but they are stated in question format. We think it is advisable to use the question format when one does not have a clear directional prediction and for the descriptive approach. More details and examples are given in Appendix A. As implied by Fig. 2.1, it is acceptable to phrase any research question that involves two variables as whether or not there is a relationship between the variables (e.g. is there a relationship between anxiety and GPA?). However, we think that phrasing the question as a difference or association is desirable because it helps one choose an appropriate statistic and interpret the result.

Table 2.1. ***Examples of Three Kinds of Research Questions/Hypotheses***

1. ***Difference (group comparison) Questions***

    - Used usually for Randomized Experimental, Quasi-Experimental, and Comparative Approaches
    - For this type of question, values or categories of the independent variable (e.g., anxiety) are used to split the participants into groups (e.g., high and low) which are then compared to see if they differ in respect to the average scores on the dependent variable (e.g., GPA).
    - An example. Do persons with low and high anxiety differ on their average grades? In other words, will the average GPA of the high anxiety persons be significantly different from the average GPA for low anxiety persons?

2. ***Basic Associational (relational) Questions***

    - Used for the Associational Approach in which the independent variable is usually continuous, (i.e., has many ordered levels)
    - For this type of question, the scores on the independent variable (e.g., anxiety) are associated with or related to the dependent variable scores (e.g., GPA).
    - An example. There will be a negative association (correlation) between anxiety scores and grade point average. In other words, those persons who are high on anxiety will tend to have low GPAs, those with low anxiety will tend to have high GPAs, and those in the middle on the one variable will tend to be in the middle on the other variable.

3. ***Basic Descriptive Questions***

    - Use for Descriptive Approach
    - For this type of question, scores on a single variable are described in terms of their central tendency, variability, or percentages in each category/level.
    - Example. The average GPA was 2.73, or 30% had high anxiety.

Complex Research Questions

Some research questions involve more than two variables at a time. We call such questions and the appropriate statistics complex. Some of these statistics are called "multivariate" in other texts, but there is not a consistent definition of multivariate in the literature. We provide examples of how to write complex research questions in Appendix A, and show you how to compute two of the most common complex statistics (factorial ANOVA and multiple regression) in chapter 11.

A Sample Research Problem - The High School and Beyond (HSB) Study

Imagine that you are interested in the general problem of what factors influence mathematics achievement at the end of high school. You might have some hunches or hypotheses about such factors based on your experience and your reading of the research and popular literature. Some factors that might influence mathematics achievement are commonly called demographics; e.g., gender, ethnic group, and mother's and father's education. A probable influence would be the mathematics courses that the student has taken. We might speculate that grades in math and in other subjects could have an impact on math achievement.[3] However, other "third" variables, such as students' IQ or parent encouragement and assistance, could be the actual causes of both high grades and math achievement. Such variables could influence what courses one took, the grades one received, and might be correlates of the demographic variables. We might wonder how spatial performance scores such as pattern or mosaic test score and visualization score might enter into a more complete understanding of the problem and whether these skills seem to be influenced by the same factors as math achievement.

Before we state the research problem and questions in more formal ways, we need to step back and discuss the types of variables and the approaches that might be used to study the above problem. What are the *independent/antecedent* (presumed causes) *variables* and what are the *dependent/outcomes variable(s)* in the above problem? Hopefully, it is obvious that math achievement is the primary dependent variable.

Given the above research problem, which focuses on achievement tests at the end of the senior year, the number of math courses taken is best considered to be an antecedent or independent variable in this study. What about father's and mother's education and gender? How would you classify gender and parents education in terms of the type of variable? What about grades? Like the number of math courses they would be independent variables because they occurred before the math achievement test. Visualization and mosaic pattern scores probably could be either independent or dependent variables depending upon the specific research question because they were measured at approximately the same time as math achievement, at the end of the senior

[3] We have decided to use the short version of mathematics (i.e., math) throughout the book to save space and because it is used in common language.

year. Note that student's class or grade level is not a variable in this study because all the participants are high school seniors (i.e., it does not vary; it is the population of interest).

As we discussed previously, independent variables can be *active* (given to the participant or manipulated by the investigator) or *attributes* of the participants or their environments. Are there any *active* independent variables in this study? No! There is no intervention, new curriculum, or something similar. All the independent variables, then, are attribute variables because they are attributes or characteristics of these high school students. Given that all the independent variables are attributes, the research approach *cannot be experimental*. This means that we will *not* be able to draw definite conclusions about cause and effect (i.e., we will find out what is related to math achievement, but we will not know for sure what *causes* math achievement).

Research Questions for the Modified HSB Study[4]

We will generate a large number of research questions from the modified HSB data set for Assignments C, D, E, F and G. Assignment B uses a different data set based on data collected from your class that you will enter into SPSS. In this section, we will list some research questions to be answered with the HSB data to give you an idea of the range of types of questions that one might have in a typical research project like a thesis or dissertation. In addition to the *difference* and *associational questions* that are commonly seen in a research report, we have asked *descriptive questions* and questions about assumptions in the early assignments. Templates for writing the research problem and research questions/ hypotheses are given in Appendix A, which should help you write questions for your own research. The questions below correspond to the lab assignments in Chapters 6, 8, 9,10, and 11.

1) Often, we start with basic *descriptive questions* about the demographics of the sample. Thus, we could answer, with the results of Assignment C, the following basic descriptive question: "What is the average educational level of the fathers of the students in this sample?" "What percentage of the students are male and what percentage are female?"

2) In Assignment C, we also will examine whether the dependent and continuous independent variables (those that might be used to answer associational questions) are distributed normally, an *assumption* of many statistics. One question is, "Are the frequency distributions of the math achievement scores markedly skewed; i.e., different from the normal curve distribution?"

3) Tables crosstabulating two categrical variables (ones with a few values or categories) will be computed in Assignment D. Crosstabulation and the chi square statistic can answer research questions such as "Is there a relationship between gender and math grades (high or low)?

---

[4] The High School and Beyond (HSB) study was conducted by the National Opinion Research Center (1980). The example, discussed here and throughout the book, is based on 13 variables obtained from a random sample of 75 out of 28,240 high school seniors. These variables include achievement scores, grades, and demographics. The raw data for the 13 variables were slightly modified from data in an appendix in Hinkle, Wiersma, and Jurs (1994). That file had no missing data, which is unusual in behavioral science research.

4) In Assignment E, we will answer basic *associational* research questions (using Pearson product-moment correlation coefficients) such as, "Is there a positive association/relationship between grades in high school and math achievement?" Correlation can also be used to assess several types of reliability. This assignment also will produce a correlation matrix of all the correlations among several key variables including math achievement. Similar matrixes will provide the basis for computing multiple regression in Assignment G.

5) Several *difference questions* will be asked in Assignment F. For example, "Do males and females differ on math achievement?" *Basic difference questions* in which the independent variable has three or more values will be asked also in Assignment F. For example, "Are there differences among the three father's education groups in regard to average scores on math achievement?"

6) *Complex difference questions* will be asked in Assignment G. One *set* of three questions is as follows: (1) "Is there a difference between students who have fathers with no college, some college, and a BS or more with respect to the student's math achievement?" (2) "Is there a difference between students who had a B or better math grade average and those with less than a B average on a math achievement test at the end of high school?" and (3) "Is there an interaction between father's education and math grades with respect to math achievement?"

7) Assignment G also poses *complex associational questions* such as "Is there a combination of variables that predicts math achievement?"

This introduction to the research problem and questions raised by the HSB data set should help make the assignments meaningful, and it should provide a guide and examples for your own research.

Interpretation Questions

1. Compare the terms *active independent variable* and *attribute independent variable*. What are the similarities and differences?

2. What kind of independent variable is necessary to infer cause?

3. What is the difference between the independent variable and the dependent variable?

4. Compare and contrast associational, difference, and descriptive types of research questions.

CHAPTER 3

Measurement and Descriptive Statistics

Measurement

Measurement is the assignment of numerals to behaviors or events according to rules. As we have seen in chapter 2, the process of research begins with a problem that is a statement about the relationship between two or more variables. Measurement is introduced when these variables are operationally defined by certain rules that determine how the participants' responses will be translated into numerals. It is common to discuss four scales or levels of measurement: *nominal, ordinal, interval,* and *ratio*, which vary from the unordered (nominal) to the highest level (ratio). However, because these four terms are not the same as those used in SPSS and are not the most useful for determining what statistics to use, we will provide only a brief discussion of them.

SPSS Measurement Terms

SPSS uses three terms (*nominal, ordinal,* and *scale*) for the types or levels of measurement. When you name and label the variables you use in a research study, SPSS gives you the opportunity to select one of these three types of measurement. Although what you choose does not affect what SPSS does, an appropriate choice indicates that you understand your data and should help guide your selection of a statistic. Table 3.1 is a summary description of our definitions of these three measurement terms intended to help you select the correct one for each of your variables.

Table 3.1. ***Descriptions of SPSS Measurement Terms and How We Use Them***

SPSS Term	Our Description
Nominal	Three or more *unordered* or qualitative categories. Also usually dichotomous (two category) variables are considered nominal.
Ordinal	Three or more *ordered* categories, but the responses are not normally distributed among the categories, or they are *ranks.*
Scale	Three or more *ordered* categories, and the responses are approximately normally distributed among the categories.

Nominal variables. These are the most basic or lowest level in which the numerals assigned to each category stand for the *name* of the category, but they have no implied order or value. For example, in a study males may be assigned the numeral 1 and females may be coded as 2. This does not imply that females are higher than males or that two males equal a female or any of the other typical mathematical uses of the numerals. The same reasoning applies to many other true categories such as ethnic groups, type of disability, or section number in a class schedule. In each of these cases the categories are distinct and non-overlapping, but not ordered, thus each category in the variable ethnic group is different from each other but there is no necessary order to the categories. Thus, the categories could be numbered 1 for Asian American, 2 for Latin American, 3 for African American, and 4 for European American or the reverse, or any combination of assigning a number to each category. What this implies is that you must *not* treat the numbers used for identifying the categories in a nominal scale as if they were numbers that could be used in a formula, added together, subtracted from one another, or used to compute an average. Average ethnic group makes no sense. However, if you ask a computer to do average ethnic group, it will do so and give you meaningless information. The important thing about nominal scales is to have clearly defined, non-overlapping or mutually exclusive categories that can be coded reliably by observers or by self-report.

It should be pointed out that qualitative or constructivist researchers rely heavily, if not exclusively, on nominal variables and on the process of developing appropriate codes or categories for behaviors, words, etc. Qualitative coding may seem different because often it is much more detailed and sophisticated, and because it is unusual to assign numerals to the various categories. Although using qualitative/nominal scales does dramatically reduce the types of statistics that can be used with your data, it does not altogether eliminate the use of statistics to summarize your data and make inferences. Therefore, even when the data are nominal or qualitative categories, your research may benefit from the use of appropriate statistics. We will return shortly to discuss the types of statistics, both descriptive and inferential, that are appropriate for nominal data.

Ordinal variables. In ordinal measurement there are not only mutually exclusive categories as in nominal scales, but the categories are ordered from low to high in much the same way that one would *rank* the order in which horses finished a race (i.e., first, second, third, ...last). Thus in an ordinal scale one knows which participant is highest or most preferred on a dimension but the intervals between the various ranks usually are not equal. For example, the second place horse may finish far behind the winner but only a fraction of a second in front of the third place finisher. Thus, in this case there are unequal intervals between first, second, and third place with a very small interval between second and third and a much larger one between first and second. More importantly, for the selection of appropriate statistics, the responses to each category or value are not distributed like the bell shaped normal curve with more responses in the middle categories and fewer in the lowest and highest categories.

Scale variables. Scale variables not only have mutually exclusive categories that are ordered from low to high, but also, as stated in Table 3.1, the responses to the ordered categories are approximately normally distributed. That is, most scores are somewhere in the middle with fewer very low and very high scores. Thus a Likert scale, such as strongly agree to strongly disagree, could be ordinal or scale depending on whether the distribution was approximately normal or not.

Interval and ratio variables. SPSS does not use these terms, but because they are common in the literature and overlapping with the term scale, we will describe them briefly. *Interval* variables have ordered categories that are equally spaced (i.e., have equal intervals between them). Most physical measurements (length, weight, money, etc.) have equal intervals between the categories and, in fact, are called *ratio* scales because they have, in addition, a true zero, which means in the above examples, no length, no weight or no money. Few psychological scales have this property of a true zero and thus even if they are very well constructed equal interval scales, it is not possible to say that one has no intelligence or no extroversion or no attitude of a certain type. The differences between interval and ratio scales are not important for us because we can do all of the types of statistics that we have available with interval data. SPSS terminology supports this non-distinction by using the term *scale* for both interval and ratio data.

Distinguishing Between Levels of Measurement

Distinguishing between nominal and ordinal variables. When you label variables in SPSS it asks you whether the variable is nominal, ordinal, or scale. We suggest that *if the variable* has only two levels, you call it nominal even though it is often hard to tell whether such a *dichotomous* variable, (e.g., Yes or No, Pass or Fail), is nominal or ordered. We argue that, although some such dichotomous variables are clearly nominal (e.g., gender) and others are clearly ordered (e.g., math grades--high and low), all dichotomous variables form a special case. For most purposes, it is best to use the same statistics for dichotomous and nominal variables. *However,* statistics such as the mean that would be meaningless for a three or more category nominal variable (e.g., ethnic group) do have meaning when there are only two categories. For example, in the HSB data the average gender is 1.55 (with males = 1 and females = 2). This means that 55% of the participants were females. Furthermore, we will see in chapter 11, on multiple regression, that dichotomous variables, called dummy variables, can be used as independent variables along with other variables that are scale. Thus, although we label a dichotomous variable as nominal, they are really a special case and for some purposes they can be treated as if they were *scale* data.

If there are three or more categories, it is usually fairly easy to tell whether the categories are ordered or not, so students and researchers can distinguish between nominal and ordinal data. That is good because this distinction makes a lot of difference in choosing appropriate statistics, as we shall see.

Distinguishing between ordinal and scale variables. Fortunately, there is a way to test variables to see whether it is more reasonable to treat them as *scale* variables or *ordinal* variables. Unfortunately, you will not know for sure until after the data have been collected and preliminary analyses are done. One of the assumptions of most of the statistics (e.g., *t* test) that you will compute with SPSS is that the variable must be at least approximately normally distributed. The way we define the SPSS term, scale variable, is that in addition to having ordered categories, the frequency distribution of scores or responses is similar to the normal curve. (See Fig. 3.1.)

Confusing Terms

Unfortunately, the literature is full of confusing terms to describe the measurement aspects of variables. *Categorical* and *discrete* are terms sometimes used interchangeably with nominal, but we think that nominal is better because it is possible to have *ordered*, discrete categories. *Continuous, dimensional*, and *quantitative* are terms that you will see in the literature for variables that vary from low to high, and are assumed to be normally distributed. SPSS uses *scale* as previously noted.

Review

Most of the above information is summarized in the top part of Table 3.2. This should provide a good review of the concept of type of measurement of a variable. The bottom section of Table 3.2 provides some additional information and examples about the appropriate use of various kinds of descriptive statistics given nominal, ordinal, or scale data.

Table 3.2. ***Selection of Appropriate Descriptive Statistics for One Dependent Variable***

	TYPE OF MEASUREMENT OF A VARIABLE		
	Nominal	**Ordinal**	**Scale**
Characteristics of the Variable	- Qualitative data - Not ordered - True categories: only names, labels	- Quantitative data - Ordered data - Rank order only	- Quantitative data - Ordered data - Normally distributed
Examples	Gender, school, curriculum type, hair color	1st, 2nd, 3rd place, ranked preferences	Height, good test scores, good rating scales
Frequency Distribution	Redhead - 5 Blond - 10 Brunette - 17	Best - 37 Better - 10 Good - 25	5 - 9 4 - 18 3 - 27 2 - 27 1 - 12
Frequency Polygon	No[a]	OK[b]	Yes[c]
Bar Graph/Chart	Yes	Yes	OK
Box and Whiskers Plot	No	Yes	Yes
Central Tendency			
Mean	No	No	Yes
Median	No	Yes	OK
Mode	Yes	OK	OK
Variability			
Standard Deviation	No	No	Yes
Interquartile Range	No	Yes	OK
How many categories	Yes	OK	OK

[a] No means not appropriate at this level of measurement.
[b] OK means not the best choice at this level of measurement.
[c] Yes means a good choice with this level of measurement.

The Normal Curve

Figure 3.1 is an example of a normal curve. The frequency distributions of many of the variables used in the behavioral sciences that are at the interval or ratio level and some clearly ordinal variables fit a normal curve. Examples of such variables that approximately fit a normal curve are height, weight, intelligence and many personality variables. Notice that for each of these examples, most people would fall toward the middle of the curve, with fewer people at the extremes. If the average height of men in the United States were 5'10", then this measure would be in the middle of the curve. The heights of men who are taller than 5'10" would be to the right of the middle on the curve, and those of men who are shorter than 5'10" would be to the left of the middle on the curve.

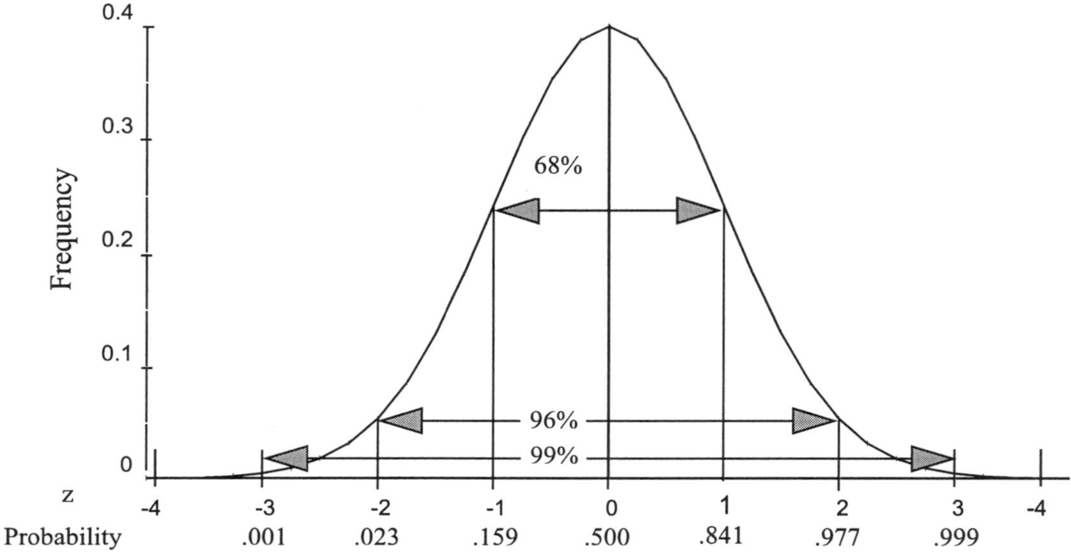

Fig. 3.1. Frequency distribution and probability distribution for the normal curve.

The normal curve can be thought of as derived from a frequency distribution. It is theoretically formed from counting an "infinite" number of occurrences of a variable. Usually when the normal curve is depicted, only the X axis (horizontal) is shown. To determine how a frequency distribution is obtained, you could take a fair coin, and flip it 10 times, and record the number of heads on this first set or trial. Then flip it another 10 times and record the number of heads. If you had nothing better to do, you could do 100 trials. (Hopefully you have something better to do with your time.) Anyway, after performing this task, you could plot the number of times, out of each trial of 10 that the coin turned up heads. What would you expect? Of course, the largest number of trials probably would show 5 heads out of 10. There would be very few, if any trials, where 0, 1, 9, or 10 heads occur. It could happen, but the probability is quite low, which brings us to a probability distribution. If we performed this experiment 100 times, or 1,000 times, or 1,000,000 times, the frequency distribution "fills in" and looks more and more like a normal curve.

The normal curve is also a probability distribution. Visualize that the area under the Normal curve is equal to 1.0. Therefore, portions of this curve could be expressed as fractions of 1.0. For example, if we assume that 5'10" is the average height of men in the United States, then the probability of a man being 5'10" *or taller* is .5. The probability of a man being over 6'5" or less than 5'5" is considerably smaller. It is important to be able to conceptualize the normal curve as a probability distribution because statistical convention sets acceptable probability levels for rejecting the null hypothesis at .05 or .01. As we shall see, when events or outcomes happen very infrequently, that is, only 5 times in 100 or 1 time in 100 (way out in the left or right tail of the curve), we wonder if they belong to that distribution or perhaps to a different distribution. We will come back to this point later in the book.

Properties of the Normal Curve

The perfectly normal curve has five properties that are always present.

1. The normal curve is unimodal. It has one "hump", and this hump is in the middle of the distribution. The most frequent value is in the middle.
2. The mean, median, and mode are equal.
3. The curve is symmetric. If you fold the normal curve in half, the right side would fit perfectly with the left side; that is, it is not *skewed.*
4. The range is infinite. This means that the extremes approach but never touch the X axis.
5. The curve is neither too peaked nor too flat and its tails are neither too short nor too long; it has no *kurtosis.* Its proportions are like those in Figure 3.1.

Skewness. If one tail of a frequency distribution is longer than the other, the curve is said to be skewed. Because most common inferential statistics (e.g., *t* test) assume that the dependent variable is normally distributed (or scale data) it is important that we know if our variables are highly skewed. We will see how to do this in chapter 6.

Figure 3.2 shows a frequency distribution that is skewed to the right. A perfectly normal

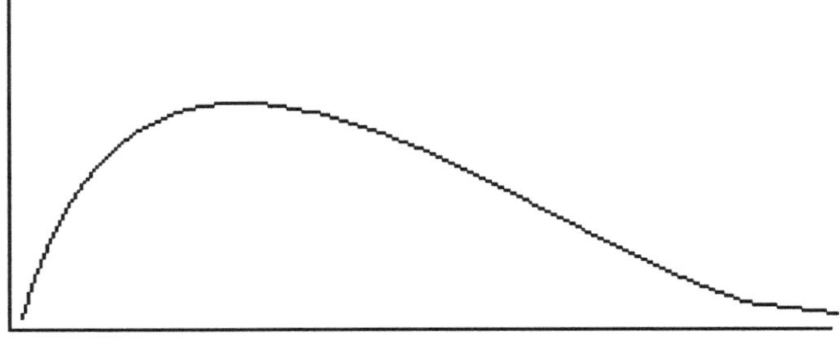

Fig. 3.2. A positively skewed frequency distribution.

curve has a skewness of zero (0.0). The curve in Fig. 3.2 should be positively skewed, and the skewness statistic will be a positive number such as + .53 or +2.74. The former would indicate

some skewness but probably not too much. The latter would indicate that the curve is very different from a normal curve. We will use a somewhat arbitrary rule of thumb that if the skewness is more than +1.0 or less than – 1.0, the distribution is markedly skewed and it would be prudent to use a nonparametric (ordinal type) statistic.

Areas Under the Normal Curve

All normal curves, regardless of whether they are narrow or spread out, can be divided into areas or units in terms of the standard deviation. Approximately 34% of the area under the normal curve is between the mean and one standard deviation above or below the mean (see Figure 3.1 again). If we include both the area to the right *and* to the left of the mean, 68% of the area under the normal curve is within one standard deviation from the mean. Another 13.5% of the area under the normal curve is accounted for by adding a second standard deviation to the first standard deviation. In other words, two standard deviations to the right of the mean accounts for an area of approximately 47.5%, and two standard deviations to the left *and* right of the mean make up an area of approximately 95% of the normal curve. If we were to subtract 95% from 100% the remaining 5% relates to that ever present probability or *p* value of 0.05 needed for statistical significance. Values not falling within two standard deviations of the mean are seen as relatively rare events.

The Standard Normal Curve

All normal curves can be converted into standard normal curves by setting the mean equal to zero and the standard deviation equal to one. Since all normal curves have the same proportion of the curve within one standard deviation, two standard deviations, etc. of the mean, this conversion allows comparisons among normal curves with different means and standard deviations. Figure 3.1, of the normal distribution, has the standard normal distribution units underneath. These units are referred to as z scores. If you examine the normal curve table in any statistics book, you can find the areas under the curve for one standard deviation (z=1), two standard deviations (z=2), etc. Any normal distribution can be converted into a standard normal distribution. We will see in chapters 5 and 6 that it is easy for SPSS to convert raw scores into *standard scores*. This is often done when one wants to aggregate or add together several scores that have quite different means and standard deviations.

Descriptive Statistics

The Importance of Type of Measurement for Descriptive Statistics

The bottom of Table 3.2 also illustrates whether and how a number of, hopefully, familiar descriptive statistics would be utilized if the data (i.e., dependent variable) were nominal, ordinal, or scale. **Frequency distributions** would be constructed in very similar ways in all three cases; the difference is that with *nominal* data the order in which the categories are listed is arbitrary. Thus, we have listed redhead, blond, and then brunette. If there are three redheads, four blonds, and two brunettes, then 33, 44, and 22% are in each category. However, redheads could be put after brunettes or between blonds and brunettes because the categories are not ordered. In *ordinal* data you can see that the order would be invariant. For *scale* (normally distributed) data the frequency distribution would look similar to the normal curve in Figure 3.1.

As mentioned above, frequency distributions indicate how many participants are in each category, whether they are ordered or unordered categories. If one wants to make a diagram of a frequency distribution there are several choices, three of them are frequency polygons, a bar chart, and box and whisker plots. As shown in Table 3.2, and Figure 3.3, a **frequency polygon** or histogram, which connects the points between the categories, is best used with *scale* data. Frequency polygons should not be used with nominal data because there is no necessary ordering of the points. Thus it is better to make a **bar graph** or chart of the frequency distribution of variables like gender, ethnic group, school curriculum, or other *nominal* variables because the points that happen to be adjacent in your frequency distribution are not by necessity adjacent (See Figure 3.4).

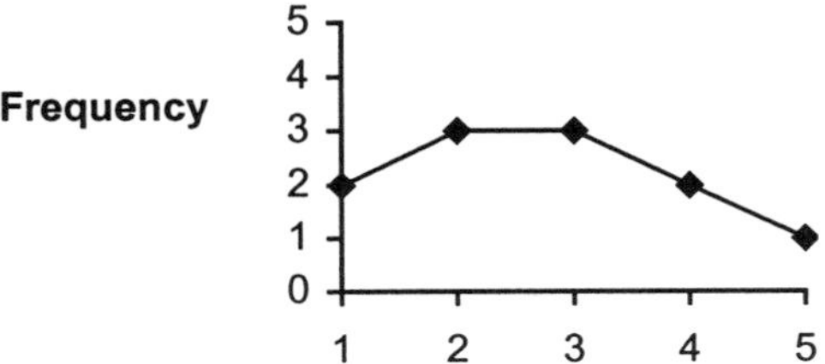

Fig. 3.3. Sample frequency polygons for scale type data.

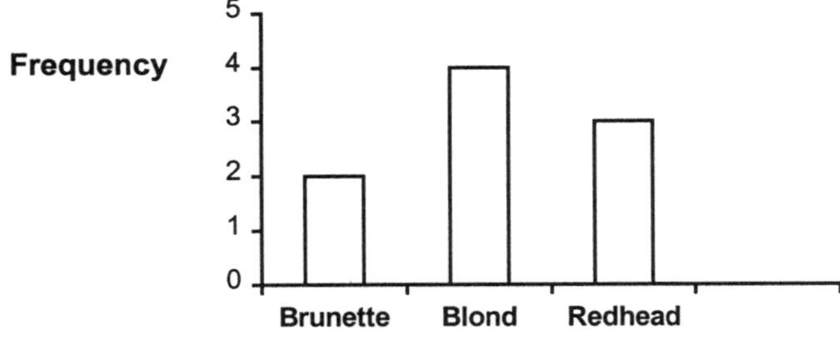

Fig. 3.4. Sample frequency distribution bar chart for the nominal scale of hair color.

For ordinal and scale data, the **box and whiskers plot** is useful (see Figure 3.5); it should not be used with nominal data because with nominal data there is no necessary ordering of the response categories. The box and whisker plot is a graphical representation of the distribution of scores and is helpful, as indicated below, in distinguishing between ordinal and normally distributed data.

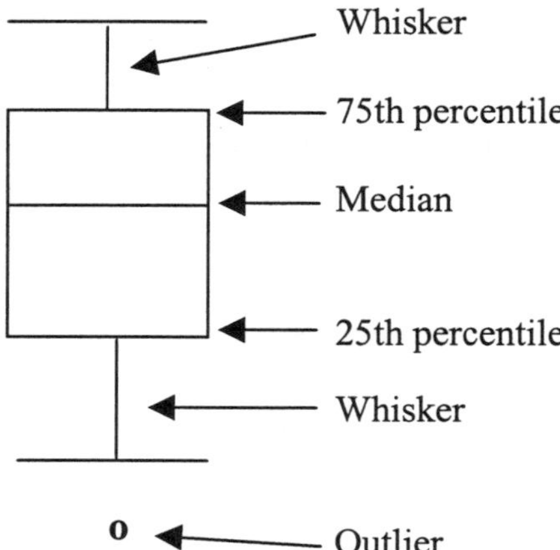

Fig. 3.5. A box and whisker plot for ordinal and scale data.

Measures of Central Tendency

Three main measures of the center of a distribution are available: mean, median, and mode. As you can see from Table 3.2 any of them can be used with scale data while with ordinal data, the mean is usually not appropriate. The **mean** or arithmetic average takes into account all of the available information in computing the central tendency of a frequency distribution. Thus, it is usually the statistic of choice assuming that one has normally distributed (i.e., scale) data. The **median** or middle score is an appropriate measure of central tendency for ordinal level data. The median may be a better measure of central tendency than the mean under certain circumstances, namely, when the frequency distribution is skewed markedly to one side. For example, the median income of 100 mid-level workers and a millionaire is substantially lower and reflects the central tendency of the group better than the average income which would be inflated in this example and for the country as a whole by a few people who make very large amounts of money. For normally distributed data the median is in the center of the box and whisker plot. Notice that in Figure 3.5 the median is not in the center of the box. Finally, the **mode**, or most common category, can be used with any kind of data but generally provides you with the least precise information about central tendency. One would use the mode as the measure of central tendency if there is only one mode, it is clearly identified, and you want a quick non-calculated measure.

Measures of Variability

Variability tells us about the spread or dispersion of the scores. In the extreme, if all of the scores in a distribution are the same, there is no variability. If they are all different and widely spaced apart, the variability will be high. You can see from Table 3.2 that the **standard deviation**, the most common measure of variability, is only appropriate when one has normally distributed scale data.

For ordinal data the **interquartile range**, seen in the box plot (Figure 3.5) by the distance between the top and bottom of the box, is the best measure of variability. Note that the whiskers indicate the expected range and scores outside that range are shown as outliers. The presence of outliers is a warning of non-normality or errors with the data. With nominal data one would need to ask how many different categories are there and what are the percentages in each.

Conclusions About Measurement and the Use of Statistics

Researchers should use the most powerful methods *consistent with the nature of their data.* Thus, statistics based on means and standard deviation are valid for normally distributed or *scale* data. Typically, these data are used in the most powerful tests called *parametric*. However, if the data are ordered but grossly non-normal, means and standard deviations may not give the right answers. Then the median and a non-parametric test would be preferred. The sacrifice in power is relatively minor. If the data were *nominal,* one would use instead the mode or counts, but then there would be a major sacrifice in power.

Interpretation Questions

1. If you have categorical, ordered data (such as low income, middle income, high income) what type of measurement would you have? Why?
2. a) What are the differences between nominal, ordinal, and scale variables? b) Why isn't it important to distinguish between interval and ratio variables?
3. What percent of the area under the normal curve is between the mean and one standard deviation above the mean?
4. a) How do z scores relate to the normal curve? b) How would you interpret a z score of –3.0?
5. Why would you not use a frequency polygon if you had nominal data? What would be better to use to display nominal data?

CHAPTER 4

Data Collection

This chapter and Appendix B are designed to provide introductory background information on developing a questionnaire, collecting data with it, and getting the data ready to enter and analyze. This chapter also explains the importance of understanding your data, how to develop a questionnaire, and how to set up data coding sheets.

There is a class assignment in this chapter that will provide an opportunity for your class to develop a short questionnaire, collect data using it, and get the data ready for entry into SPSS in chapter 5. If the class develops a set of questions, each person in the class should answer them. There will be five standard questions and then an opportunity for the class to add additional questions. However, if you are using this text as an individual learning tool or your professor wants to skip the topic of questionnaire development, there is a set of data in chapter 5 (and Appendix B) for you to enter into the SPSS data editor.

Knowing Your Data

It is important for you to have a clear understanding of the data in your data set. For example, in the class exercise one of the variables will be height. You could look around the room and intuitively know the data for that variable. You could line your class up by height to see the distribution and you could make fairly close approximations of statistics such as the average (mean), middle person (median), and tallest minus shortest (range). A few additional very tall people would skew the data positively. Conversely, several extra short people would skew the data negatively.

Students do not always have a clear understanding of the data they analyze. In your research you may receive a data set from a colleague, agency, or faculty member, where you do not really know the underlying meaning of the variables. For example, in chapter 6 you will receive a set of scores from the High School and Beyond (HSB) data, which includes a variable labeled *visualization score.* You will be told that it is a test of a person's ability to determine how a three-dimensional object would look if its spatial position were changed. But do you really know what that means? Hopefully, when abstract variables (such as visualization score, self-concept, or intrinsic motivation) are used in a research report, how they were measured (operationally defined) will be described completely enough for you to grasp the meaning.

In our first lab assignment (chapter 5), we will use data generated by your class (or the similar data provided) so you will have a sound understanding of the meaning of each variable. This kind of understanding should help you learn SPSS and the statistical tests that we will demonstrate better than data sets which may not have as much meaning to you. You will also gain experience entering data and labeling variables.

After you practice with the class data, you will move to the HSB data set. By that time, you will be more comfortable with the use of SPSS and will be able to perform SPSS tasks and understand printouts more easily.

Developing a Questionnaire

This chapter uses a questionnaire as a data collection device due to its relative simplicity. However, even a questionnaire poses issues for a researcher. Appendix B presents several topics related to questionnaire development and provides some guidance about writing good items. Appendix B also has a sample of the resulting questionnaire and a mock data set which you can use if your class does not do the exercise suggested in this chapter. If you will be developing a questionnaire in class and are not already knowledgeable about doing that, we suggest that you read Appendix B now.

Survey Questions Common to All Classes

In order to have a few variables to illustrate in the next chapter, we suggest that your class use the following five common variables: student's height, same sex parent's height, gender, marital status, and age. The questions and suggested response choices are as follows:

- *What is your height in inches?* ________
- *What is the estimated height of your same sex parent?* ________
- *Gender(circle one number)*
  1. *Male*
  2. *Female*
- *What is your marital status? (circle one number)*
  1. *Single, never married*
  2. *Married*
  3. *Divorced, separated, or widowed?*
- *What age group are you in? (circle one number)*
  1. *Less than 25*
  2. *25-34*
  3. *35 or more*

Class Exercise

As a class, develop a short questionnaire that uses the five questions above and asks other questions about your peers that are of interest to you. With guidance from your instructor, add approximately five questions to the five questions specified above. Try to include a variety of questions. Some examples of other questions the authors' classes have used include:

How many hours a week do you watch TV? __________

What type of television shows do you watch? (Check all that apply)

______Sitcoms
______Movies
______Sports
______News

I feel that the current program I am enrolled in is meeting my needs. (circle one)

1. Strongly disagree
2. Disagree
3. Neutral
4. Agree
5. Strongly agree

How many hours a week do you study? __________

Do you have children? ________Yes ________No

See Appendix B for a sample questionnaire.

Students often like to ask questions on surveys that require respondents to answer with a phrase or a word. For example: What is your favorite car? Or what state were you born in? These questions are usually answered by spelling out your response, such as Chevrolet or Ford. This type of response is called alphanumeric. Although written answers can be very useful in survey research, for this exercise, we recommend that you do not use questions that require alphanumeric responses because of the difficulty of coding and classifying these types of responses.

Once your class develops a questionnaire of approximately 10 questions (the five above plus the five your class generates), either a student or the instructor should make the questions available to the class. The instructor can write the questions on a flip chart, the board, or duplicate them. Each student should have an answer sheet numbered 1 through 10, or have some other method to record their responses.

After the class completes the questionnaire, there will be an answer sheet for each student. The instructor may provide each student with a set of raw data about the class. That is, each student may receive data for every person in the class. If you have a class of 20, you would begin this phase of the assignment with 20 sets of answers for approximately 10 questions.

Next, you will prepare to enter the data on these answer sheets into SPSS. This can be done in several ways.

Number each of your questionnaires. This will prevent confusion if you drop or mix up the stack of questionnaires. SPSS automatically labels cases from 1 through the last case or subject. Therefore, it is a good idea for you to number the questionnaires beginning with one, rather than using letters or an alternative identification system. This process will also keep the respondents' answers anonymous and thus protect against violating the privacy of the human subjects in your research.

It is common for researchers to transfer the data from the questionnaires to a coding sheet by hand before entering the data into Excel, Word, or SPSS. This is helpful if there is not a separately numbered answer sheet, if the responses are to be entered in a different order than on the questionnaire, or additional coding or recoding is required before data entry. In these cases, you could make mistakes entering the data directly from the questionnaires. On the other hand, you could make copying mistakes or take more time transferring the data from the questionnaires or answer sheets to the coding sheet. Thus, there are advantages and disadvantages of using a coding sheet as an intermediate step between the questionnaire and the SPSS data editor. The data set for your class will be small and straightforward enough that you will be able to keep track of the data fairly easily going directly from your questionnaire into the SPSS editor as explained in chapter 5.

Chapter 5 gives you a step by step approach of how to do this for the first five variables. You then can use that knowledge to add the additional five variables developed by your class. If you did not collect data as a class project, use the data set provided in chapter 5.

Interpretation Questions

1. In the first SPSS run of the class data, you noticed that the average student height was 78 inches. What does this tell you about your coding of the data?
2. Describe the advantages and disadvantages of developing and using a coding sheet.
3. Why should you number your questionnaires?

CHAPTER 5

Data Entry and Descriptive Statistics for a Class Questionnaire

In the last chapter, we developed a questionnaire based on a series of questions about the students in a college class. This questionnaire included the variables of height, parent's height, gender, marital status, age, and several other variables added by the class. The reason we started with this simple data set was that it is essential for researchers to clearly understand the variables and sample they are studying. In this case, the class was the sample and you determined the variables by writing the survey questions.

Checking Data

You should check your raw data as you collect it even *before* it is entered into the computer. Make sure that the participants marked their score sheets or questionnaires appropriately; check to see if there are double answers to a question (when only one is expected) or marking between two ratings. If this happens, you need to have a rule (e.g., "use the average") that you can apply consistently. Thus, you should "clean up" your data, making sure it is clear, consistent, and readable, before entering it into a data file.

Lab Assignment B

Logon

If you do not have SPSS open, first you need to logon. See chapter 1 if you do not remember how. You should see a blank SPSS Data Editor (see Fig. 1.4). If you see the SPSS startup screen (Fig. 1.2), then do the following:

- Click on **Type in data**[1]. (See Fig. 1.2 in chapter 1 if you need help.)
- Then click **OK**.

You should then see a blank **SPSS Data Editor**. (See Fig. 1.4 in chapter 1.)
If you already have SPSS open but do not see the **SPSS Data Editor**, click on test button at the bottom of your screen.

Define and Label the Height Variables

Chapter 1 showed each of the SPSS menus, and it presented an overview of the SPSS format and

[1] In the chapters with lab assignments, we have identified the SPSS variable names, labels and values using italics (e.g., *gender* and *male*) and have put in bold the terms used on the SPSS windows (e.g., **SPSS Data Editor**) to help you. Italics are also used for emphasis.

layout. The following section will help you name and label five variables: height, parent's height, gender, marital status, and age. Then you should be able to label your other variables and be ready to enter your data.

First, let's define and label the height variables. To do this we need to use the Variable View screen. If you are in Data View there are two ways to get to Variable View:

- Click on the **Variable View** tab at the bottom left of your screen (see Fig. 5.1). In SPSS 10, this will bring up a screen similar to Fig. 5.2. OR *double* click on **var** above the blank column to the far left side of the data matrix (see Fig. 1.3 again).

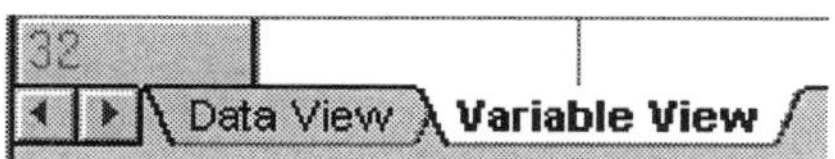

Fig. 5.1. Data view and variable view tabs.

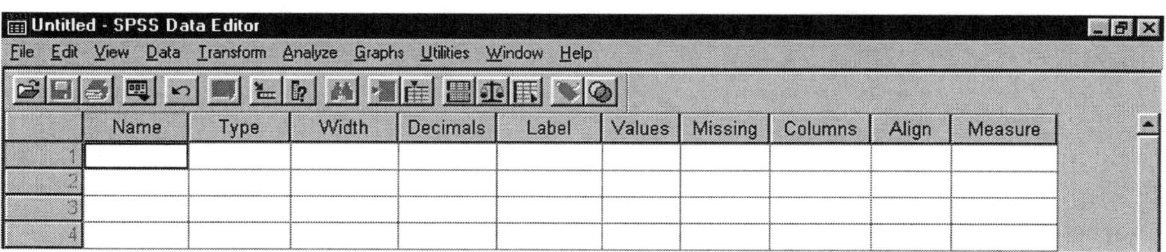

Fig. 5.2. Blank variable view screen.

In this window, you will see 10 sections that will allow you to input the variable name, type, width, decimals, label, values, missing (data), columns (width), align (data left or right), and measurement type.

Important: This is new to SPSS 10. If you have an SPSS 9 or lower version, you will not have the Variable View screen option and will have to enter the variable information differently. Please refer to your SPSS Help menu for further information in lower versions.

We will now begin to enter the variable information for Lab Assignment B.

- Click in the box directly under **Name**
- Type *height* in the box directly beneath **Name** (see Fig. 5.2). Notice the number 1 to the left of this box. This indicates that you are entering your first variable. Press enter. This will move your cursor to the next box, under **Type**, and pop up the information shown in Fig. 5.3 for **Type**, **Width**, etc.
- For now, insure the **Type** is numeric, **Width** = 8, **Decimals** = 2, **Labels** = (blank for now), **Values** = None, **Missing** = None, **Columns** = 8, **Align** = right, **Measure** = scale

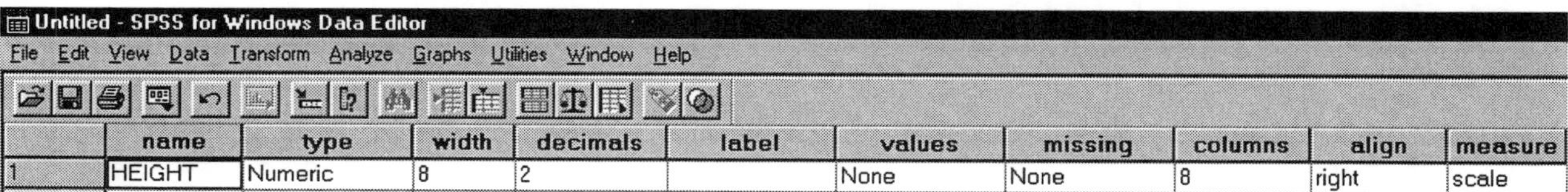

Fig. 5.3. Data editor with height variable information entered.

To change the settings from Fig. 5.3, there are several options:

- In Fig. 5.3, you will see **Width** and **Decimal Places**. We recommend keeping the width at eight. This means you *can* have an 8-digit number. For height in inches you really only need two digits, assuming no one is taller than 99 inches! However, keeping the width at eight allows our variable name, which is limited by SPSS to eight characters, to be fully included at the top of each column. You may change the number of decimal places here, but we suggest that you leave them at 2 thus allowing us to record the height of a person as 66.25, if we desired.

Now, let's label the height variables:

- Click on the blank cell under **Label**.
- Type *student's height in inches* in the **label** box. This longer label will show in appropriate SPSS windows and on your printouts. The label can be up to 40 characters but it is best to keep them about 20 or less or your outputs may wrap too much.

Leave the other cells (**values** to **measure**) as they currently appear. We will ignore the **value** cell for now, but we will use that command for *gender* and *marital status* later in this chapter.

Now let's define the next variable.

- Click on the next blank box under **Name** to enter the next variable. Note: if you are in the Data View screen (like when you begin a new SPSS session) you can double click on the next blank **var** column to begin this process as well.
- Call it *pheight* in the **Name** column and label it *same sex parent's height* in the same way that you just did for student's height.

Define and Label Gender and Marital Status

- Now, select the third cell under **Name** in the **Variable View** screen and define the variable as *gender*.
- Click on the 3rd box under **Decimals**. For this variable, there is no reason to have any decimal places since people either choose male or female (1 or 2). You will notice that when you select the box under **Decimals**, up and down arrows appear on the right side of the box. You can either click the arrows to raise or lower the number of decimals, or you can double click on the box and manually type in the desired number.
- For the purposes of this variable, select or type 0.
- Next, click the appropriate box under **Label** to type in the variable label *gender of student.*
- Under **Values**, click on the small gray box with ... (three dots) to get Fig. 5.4.
- In the **Value Labels** window, type 1 in the **Value** box, *male* in the **Value Label** box, and then click **Add**. Do the same for 2=*female*. The **Value Labels** window should resemble Fig. 5.4 just before you click **Add** for the second time.

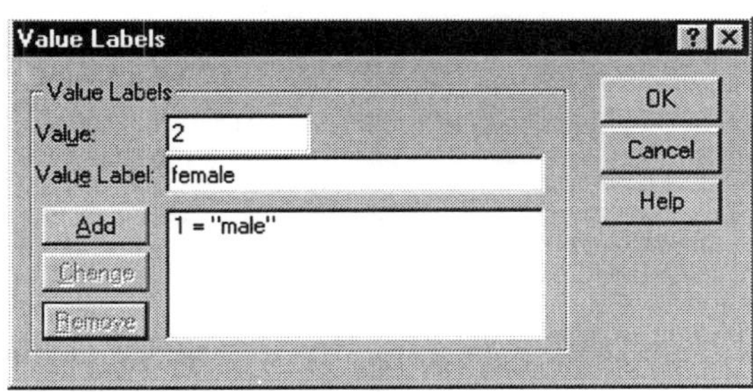

Fig. 5.4. Value labels window.

- Finally, under **Measure,** click the box that says **scale.** Click the arrow and choose **Nominal** from the list. (See Fig. 5.5.)

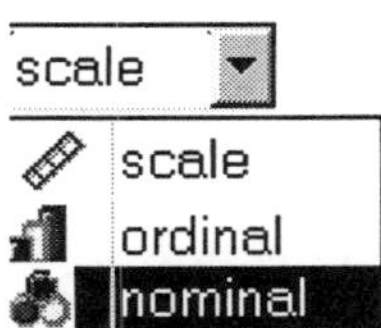

Fig. 5.5. Measurement selection.

Let's go through two more examples that require **Labels.**

- First, type the variable **Name** *marital* in the next blank row.
- Click on **Decimals** to change the decimal places to 0 (zero).
- Now click on **Labels** and label the variable *marital status.*

Now you will label the values or levels of the marital status variable. Remember that in chapter 4 we asked you to code the data as 1, 2, and 3 for marital status. You need to be sure your coding matches your labels. We arbitrarily decided to code *single* as a 1.

- Click on the **Values** cell.
- Then click on the gray three-dot box to get to Fig. 5.4 again. Remember, this is the same process you conducted when entering the labels for the values of *gender*.
- Now, type 1 to the right of **Value**.
- To the right of **Value Label** type, *single.*
- Click on **Add**. Repeat this process for 2 = *married* and 3 = *divorced.*
- Click **OK.**
- Finally, click on **scale** under **Measure** to change the level of measurement to **nominal**.

Once again, realize that the researcher is making a series of decisions that are key to the outcome of the research. For example, you could have 1 or 2 as the value for divorced or you might have had four categories under marital status. You might have included other or remarried. You, the researcher, make these decisions, and usually they are judgments. Let's continue further.

Define and Label Age Group

You should now have enough practice to define the variable *age.* Do the following:

- For **Decimals** change the decimals to zero.
- Now click on **Label** and label it *age group*.
- Click on **Values.** Remember we have divided *age group* into three sections: less than 22=1, 22-29=2, and 30 or more=3. Note that for this variable, we could have used actual age in years or more age groups. These age groups are ordered from younger to older, but the groups do not represent equal intervals and the responses of your class are probably not normally distributed. That is why we will select ordinal rather than scale. Follow the directions above to input the values for this variable.
- Select **ordinal** under **Measure**.

Define and Label the Other Variables

If you developed more questions in chapter 4, you should define and label these variables now.

Note: On the **Variable View** screen, you will notice the selection **Numeric** under **Type**. This refers to the type of variable you are entering. Usually, you will only use the **Numeric** option, which is the default. Numeric means the data are numbers. **String** would be used if you input words or letters such as "M" for males and "F" for females. However, it is best not to enter words or letters because you wouldn't be able to do many statistics without recoding them as numbers.

Problem 1: Displaying Your Codebook

Now that you have defined and labeled your variables, you can print a codebook, which is a very useful record of what you have done.

- Select **Utilities => File Info**. You will get something like Output 5.1, but if you collected additional data, your output may look different.

Output 5.1: Code book

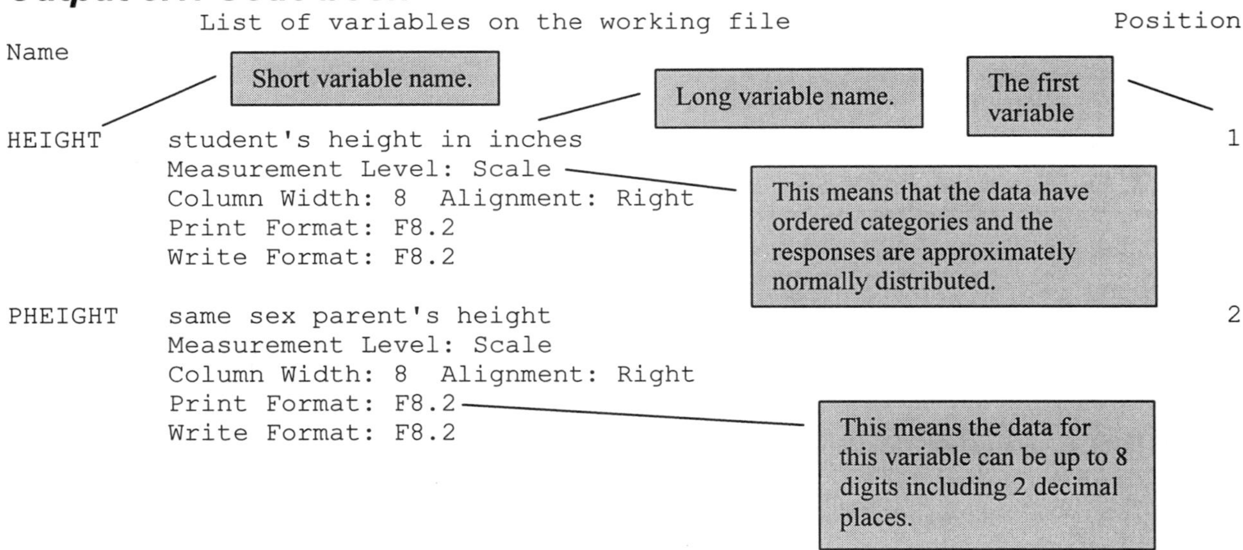

List of variables on the working file
Position
Name
Short variable name.
Long variable name.
The first variable
HEIGHT
student's height in inches
1
Measurement Level: Scale
Column Width: 8 Alignment: Right
Print Format: F8.2
Write Format: F8.2
This means that the data have ordered categories and the responses are approximately normally distributed.
PHEIGHT
same sex parent's height
2
Measurement Level: Scale
Column Width: 8 Alignment: Right
Print Format: F8.2
Write Format: F8.2
This means the data for this variable can be up to 8 digits including 2 decimal places.

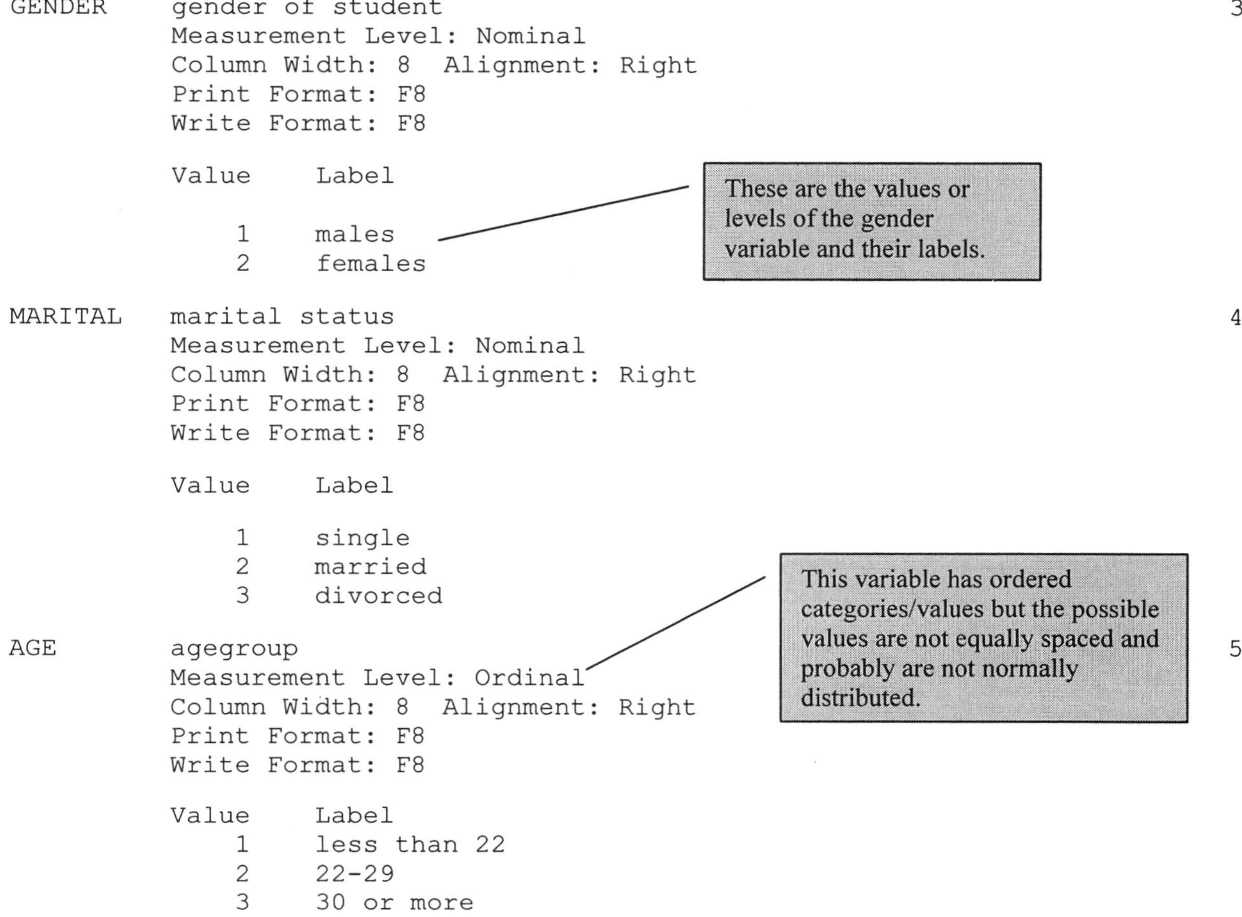

```
GENDER     gender of student                                    3
           Measurement Level: Nominal
           Column Width: 8  Alignment: Right
           Print Format: F8
           Write Format: F8

           Value    Label

               1    males
               2    females

MARITAL    marital status                                       4
           Measurement Level: Nominal
           Column Width: 8  Alignment: Right
           Print Format: F8
           Write Format: F8

           Value    Label

               1    single
               2    married
               3    divorced

AGE        agegroup                                             5
           Measurement Level: Ordinal
           Column Width: 8  Alignment: Right
           Print Format: F8
           Write Format: F8

           Value    Label
               1    less than 22
               2    22-29
               3    30 or more
```

These are the values or levels of the gender variable and their labels.
This variable has ordered categories/values but the possible values are not equally spaced and probably are not normally distributed.

Data Entry

Click on the untitled - **SPSS Data Editor** or on the **Data View** tab on the bottom of the screen to return you to the data editor. Note that the spreadsheet has numbers down the left-hand side (see Fig. 5.7). These numbers represent each subject in the study. The data for each questionnaire goes across the page with each column representing a variable from our questionnaire. Therefore, the first column will be *height*, the second will be *same sex parent's height*, the third will be *gender*, etc.

After defining and labeling the variables, your next task is to enter the data from the questionnaires or the data coding sheet; both should have all of the answers from the class questionnaire.

Imagine that the data for the first five variables for each of the first 20 students were:

	Height	Pheight	Gender	Marital	Age
1	67	66	2		1
2	72	72	1	2	3
3	61	62	2	3	3
4	71	71	1	1	2
5	65	63	2	1	1
6	67	68	1	2	2
7	69	74	1	2	2
8	75	73	1	2	3
9	62	65	2	3	3
10	61	64	2	2	3
11	64	63	2	2	2
12	64	64	1	3	2
13	70	65	1	2	2
14	63	62	2	2	3
15	64	60	2	1	2
16	63	60	2	2	3
17	65	58	2	2	3
18	71	76	1	2	3
19	72	75	1	2	3
20	68	65	2	1	2

Fig. 5.6. Mock class data.

The data from these 20 imaginary participants will be used to demonstrate what several basic outputs look like. If you developed and took the questionnaire as discussed in chapter 4, you should *enter your own class data*. If you did not do the class assignment in chapter 4, you should enter the data shown above. (Note Fig. 5.6 is the data for the first 20 participants for the first five variables in the Appendix B data set.) You do not have to enter the ID numbers in the far-left column. These are already provided in the SPSS data editor. Even though these data are included in the Appendix B data set, it is important to practice entering data.

To enter the data, ensure that your **SPSS Data Editor** is showing.

- If it is not already highlighted, click on the far left column, which should say *height.*
- To enter the data into this highlighted column simply *type* the number and press the **right arrow**. For example, first type 67 (the number will show up in the blank space above of the row of variable names) and then press the **right arrow**; the number will be entered into the highlighted box. For example, in Fig. 5.7, a 1 for gender has been typed. If you were to press the right arrow, the 1 would move into the highlighted box and the highlighted box would move to the right. Notice if a participant left the question blank or made an inappropriate answer (e.g. "6" for height in inches or other for gender), you should leave that box empty or blank; SPSS uses blanks for such **missing data**. Note, we left *marital* blank for participant 1. If you collected your own data in chapter 4, realize that the data entries in Fig. 5.7 will be different from your own, and you also will have more variables.

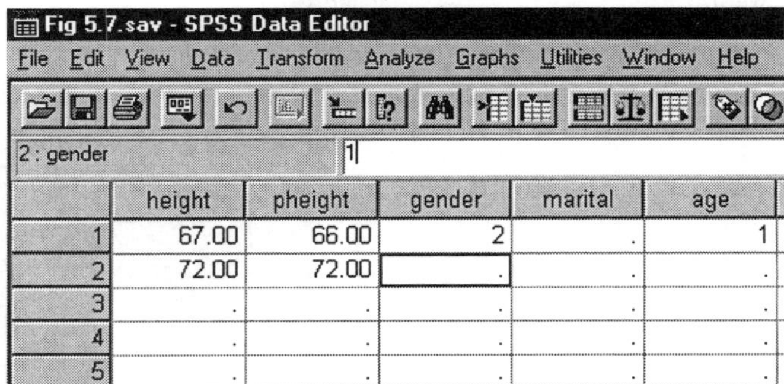

Fig. 5.7. Data entry into the SPSS data editor.

- Now enter your data or the data in Fig. 5.6. If you make a mistake when entering data, correct it by clicking on the cell (the cell will be highlighted), type the correct score, and press Enter or the Arrow key.

Problem 2: Running Descriptives

To compute the basic descriptive statistics for all your subjects you will need to do these steps:

- Select **Analyze => Descriptive Statistics => Descriptives** (see Fig. 5.8).[2]

Note: If you are using SPSS 9 or lower, you will find the statistics selections under **Statistics** on your toolbar.

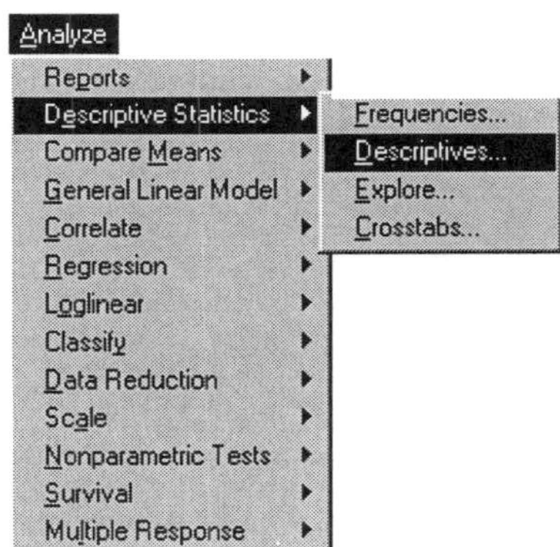

Fig. 5.8. Analyze menu.

After selecting **Descriptives**, you will be ready to compute the mean, standard deviation, minimum, and maximum for all participants/cases on all variables in order to examine the data.

- Now highlight all the variables. To highlight, begin at the top of the left box and hold the left mouse button down while you scroll downward until *all* the variables listed turn blue (see Fig. 5.9a).

[2] This is how we indicate in this and the following assignments that you first pull down the **Analyze** menu, then select **Descriptive Statistics** from the first flyout menu, and finally select **Descriptives** from the last flyout menu.

- Click on the **arrow** button pointing right. When you finish, the **Descriptives** dialog box should look like Fig. 5.9b.

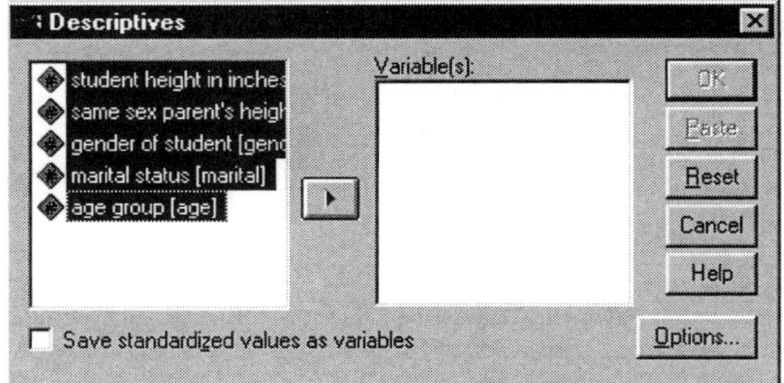

Fig. 5.9a. Descriptives-before moving variables.

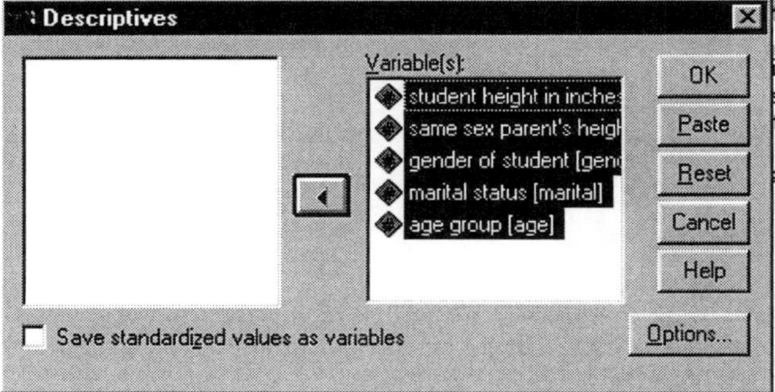

Fig. 5.9b. Descriptives-after moving variables.

- Be sure that *all* the variables have moved out of the left window. If your screen looks like Fig. 5.9b, then click on **Options**. You will get Fig. 5.10.

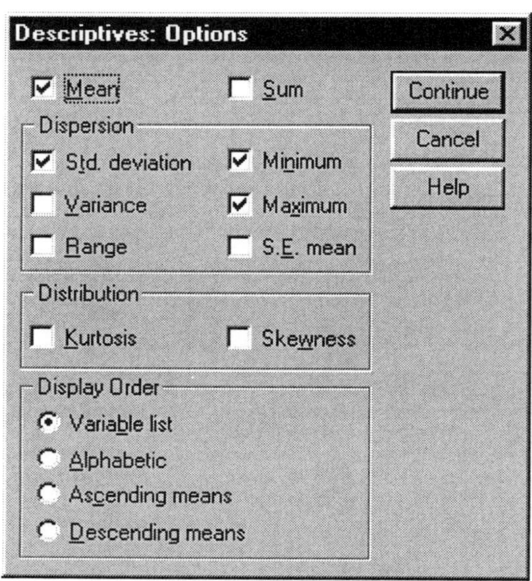

Fig. 5.10. Descriptives: Options.

Follow these steps:

- Ensure that the **Variable list** bubble is checked in the **Display Order** section. *Note*: You can also click on **Ascending or Descending means** if you want your variables listed in order of the means. If you wanted the variables listed alphabetically, you would check **Alphabetic**.
- Notice that the **mean, standard deviation, minimum,** and **maximum** were already checked. At this time, we will not request more descriptive statistics because we will do them in Assignment C, and with only these checked, we will get a compact, easy-to-read output.
- Now, click on **Continue**, which will bring you back to the main **Descriptives** dialog box (Fig. 5.9b).
- Then click on **OK** to run the program.

You should get an output like Fig. 5.11 if you used data similar to ours. Compare your output to Fig. 5.11 and Output 5.2. If it looks similar, you have done the steps correctly. If you chose to collect your own data, your output may differ. Note that near most outputs we have provided a brief interpretation in a gray box. On the output itself, we have pointed out some of the key things by circling them and making some comments in gray boxes, which are known as callout boxes. Of course, these circles and information boxes will not show up on your printout.

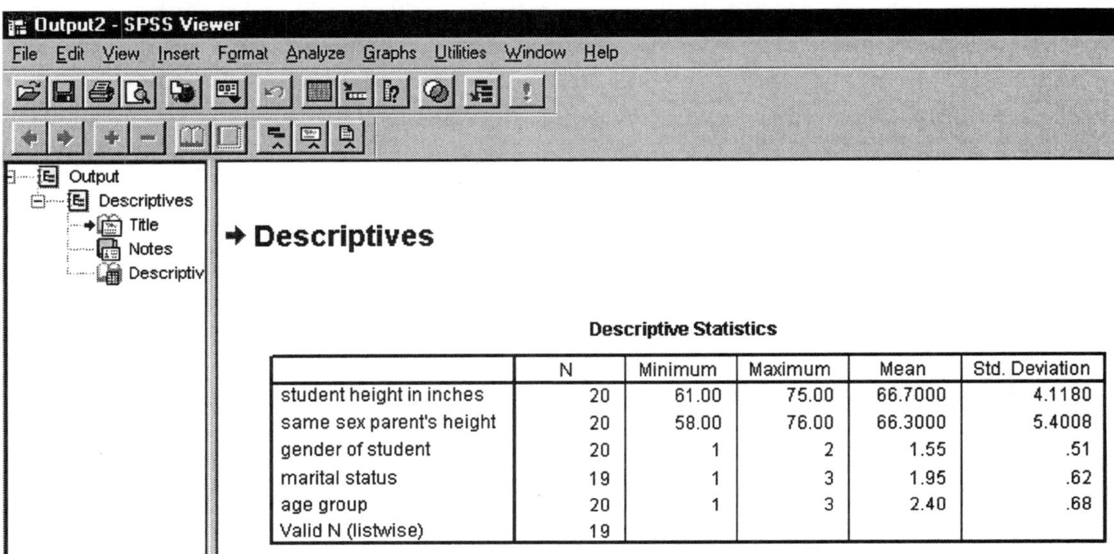

Descriptive Statistics

	N	Minimum	Maximum	Mean	Std. Deviation
student height in inches	20	61.00	75.00	66.7000	4.1180
same sex parent's height	20	58.00	76.00	66.3000	5.4008
gender of student	20	1	2	1.55	.51
marital status	19	1	3	1.95	.62
age group	20	1	3	2.40	.68
Valid N (listwise)	19				

Fig. 5.11. Output navigator window.

The left side of Fig. 5.11 indicates the various parts of your output. You can click on any item on the left (e.g., **Title, Notes,** or **Descriptive Statistics**) to activate the output for that item, and then you can edit it. For example you can click on **Title** and then expand the title or add information as we have in Output 5.2. (See also chapter 1 for more on editing outputs.)

- Double click on **Descriptives**. Type your name so it will appear on your output when you print it later. This step is an alternative for **Insert New Text** procedure (Fig. 1.11) that you learned to insert in chapter 1.

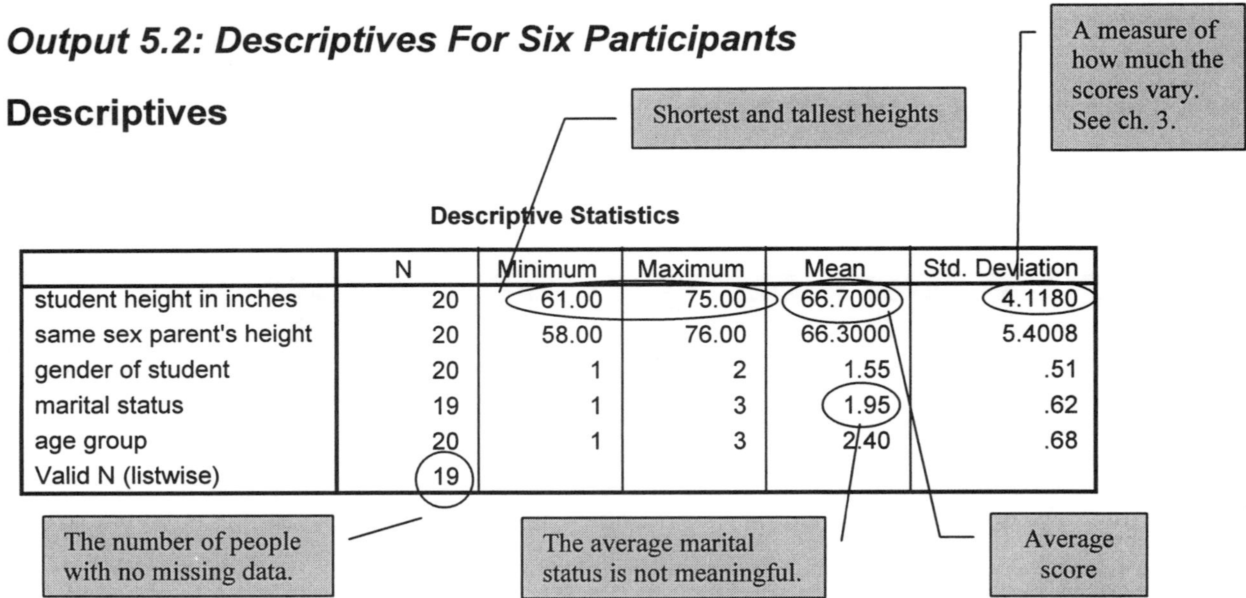

Output 5.2: Descriptives For Six Participants

Descriptives

Descriptive Statistics

	N	Minimum	Maximum	Mean	Std. Deviation
student height in inches	20	61.00	75.00	66.7000	4.1180
same sex parent's height	20	58.00	76.00	66.3000	5.4008
gender of student	20	1	2	1.55	.51
marital status	19	1	3	1.95	.62
age group	20	1	3	2.40	.68
Valid N (listwise)	19				

Problem 3: Box Plots of Student's Height for Males and Females

Return to the **SPSS Data Editor** by clicking on it at the bottom left side of your screen. Now let's make a box plot comparing males and females on height. Do the following commands:

- Select **Analyze => Descriptive Statistics => Explore**. See Fig. 5.12.

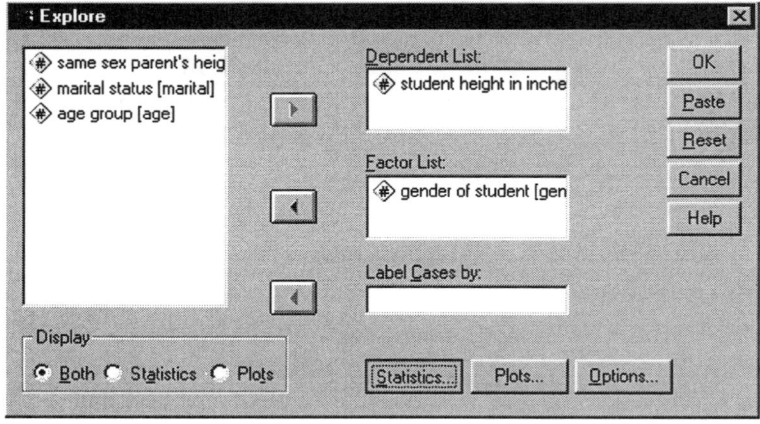

Fig. 5.12. Explore.

- Click on *student's height in inches* and move it to the **Dependent List**.
- Next, click on *gender of student* and move it to the **Factor** (or independent variable) **List.**
- Click on the **Statistics** button (*not the **Statistics** under **Display***) to get Fig. 5.13.

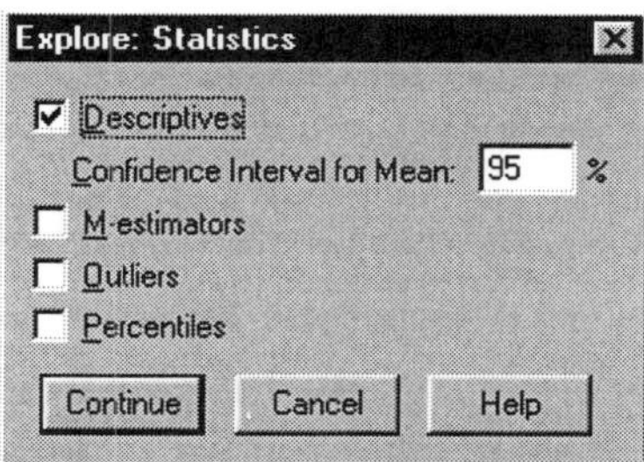

Fig. 5.13. Explore: Statistics.

Verify that **Descriptives** is checked (see Fig. 5.13).

- Click on **Continue** and you will be back to Fig. 5.12.
- Click on **OK**.

You will get an output file with stem-and-leaf plots and box plots. See Output 5.3 and compare it to your own output and syntax. As with most SPSS subprograms, we could have requested a wide variety of other statistics, but we chose not to.

Output 5.3: Descriptive Statistics. Stem and Leaf, and Box Plots by Gender

Explore

Case Processing Summary

		Cases					
		Valid		Missing		Total	
	gender of student	N	Percent	N	Percent	N	Percent
student height in inches	males	9	100.0%	0	.0%	9	100.0%
	females	11	100.0%	0	.0%	11	100.0%

Descriptives

	gender of student			Statistic	Std. Error
student height in inches	males	Mean		70.1111	1.0599
		95% Confidence Interval for Mean	Lower Bound	67.6669	
			Upper Bound	72.5553	
		5% Trimmed Mean		70.1790	
		Median		71.0000	
		Variance		10.111	
		Std. Deviation		3.1798	
		Minimum		64.00	
		Maximum		75.00	
		Range		11.00	
		Interquartile Range		4.0000	
		Skewness		-.640	.717
		Kurtosis		.899	1.400
	females	Mean		63.9091	.6803
		95% Confidence Interval for Mean	Lower Bound	62.3933	
			Upper Bound	65.4249	
		5% Trimmed Mean		63.8434	
		Median		64.0000	
		Variance		5.091	
		Std. Deviation		2.2563	
		Minimum		61.00	
		Maximum		68.00	
		Range		7.00	
		Interquartile Range		3.0000	
		Skewness		.456	.661
		Kurtosis		-.403	1.279

These two descriptive statistics tell you about the average height of the 9 males and distribution of their responses. See the interpretation of Output 5.3.

Stem-and-Leaf Plots

```
student height in inches Stem-and-Leaf Plot for
GENDER= males
 Frequency    Stem &  Leaf

     1.00 Extremes    (=<64)
     2.00        6 .  79
     5.00        7 .  01122
     1.00        7 .  5

 Stem width:      10.00
 Each leaf:        1 case(s)
student height in inches Stem-and-Leaf Plot for
GENDER= females

 Frequency    Stem &  Leaf

     2.00        6 .  11
     3.00        6 .  233
     4.00        6 .  4455
     1.00        6 .  7
     1.00        6 .  8

 Stem width:      10.00
 Each leaf:        1 case(s)
```

Box Plot of Students Height for Each Gender

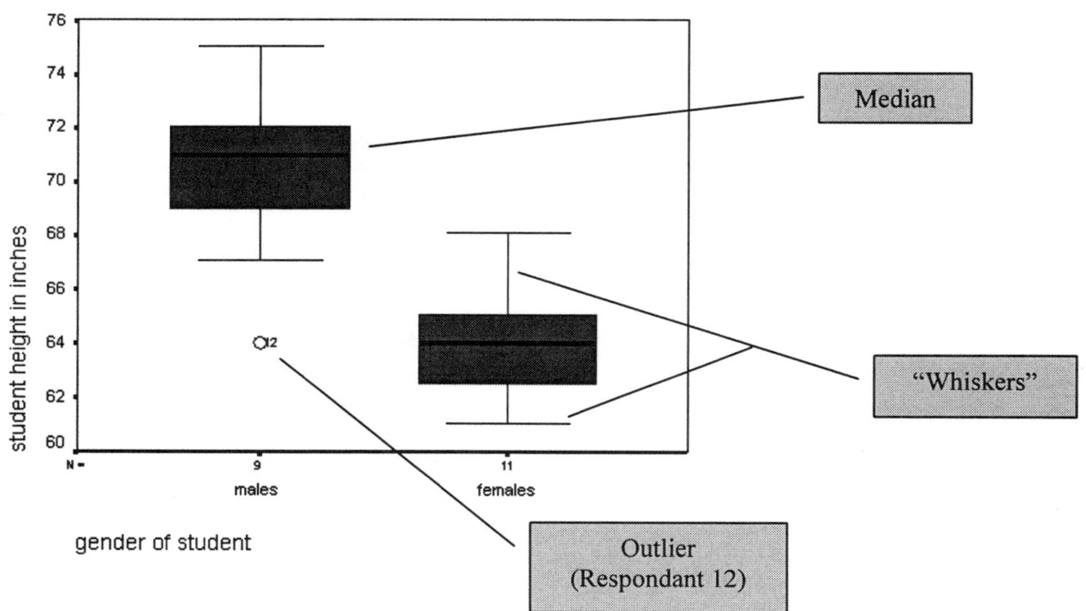

Interpretation of Output 5.3

The first table under **Explore** provides descriptive statistics about the number of males and females. Note that we only have 9 males and 11 females for the data in Fig. 5.6. If you used your class data the numbers will be different. The **Descriptives** table contains many different statistics for males and females separately. Several of them are beyond what we will cover in this book. Note that the average height 70.11 inches (5'10"+) for the males and 63.91 (5'4") for females. The skewness of both male and female heights is less than + or –1.0 so the heights of both genders are approximately normal.

The next table is a **stem-and-leaf plot** for each gender. These plots are sort of like a histogram or frequency distributions turned on the side. They give a visual impression of the distribution, and they show each person's score on the dependent variable (student height). Each number in the "leaf" column represents the last digit of a person's height, so it might have been helpful to have commas between numbers. The number in the "stem" column tells you the first digit of the heights of participants in that row. The numbers in the "frequency" column indicate how many participants are in that stem. So for males, there is one extreme score (64), two in the high 60s (67 and 69), and five in the low 70s (70, 71, 71, 72, 72).

Box plots are a graphical representation of the distribution of scores on a variable, with the whole group divided on the basis of another variable, in this case gender. The line in the box is the median (middle score) for each group. Each "box" represents the middle 50% of the cases and the "whiskers" at the top and bottom of the box indicates the "expected" top and bottom 25%. However, there may be outliers (shown with Os) and really extreme scores (shown with *), above and below the ends of the whiskers. Thus, box plots can be useful for identifying variables with extreme scores. Check your raw data or score sheet to be sure there is not a coding error. Notice that there is one **Outlier** but no *s in the box plot.

By inspecting the plots we can see that the median height for males is quite a bit taller than that for females, although there is some overlap. However, we need to be careful in concluding that males are taller than females, especially based on such a small number of students. Later, we will show how an inferential statistic (the *t* test) can help us know how likely it is that this apparent difference could have occurred by chance.

We have shown in Outputs 5.2 and 5.3, four methods of producing somewhat overlapping descriptive statistics. In chapter 6, we will show two more displays of descriptive statistics, again somewhat overlapping with those in this chapter. Ordinarily, you would not do all these descriptive outputs for your data. Be selective by choosing the ones you need to answer your questions.

Printing

It is probably not necessary to print the output for this assignment because you have seen and compared your outputs to those shown in this chapter. However, if you wanted to print the whole output for this assignment, do it as shown below. Remember to put your name on it. To print your output, ensure the desired file is fully showing by clicking on the **Output1 - SPSS Output Viewer** at the very bottom of your screen (see Fig. 5.14).

- Then go to **File => Print**. You will get a window like Fig. 5.15.
- Choose **All visible output** if you want to print everything in your output.
- Choose **Selection** if you want to print only selected tables and charts. To do that you must first highlight only those area on the left side of your output file that you want to print (see Fig. 5.16).
- Click on **OK**.

Fig. 5.14. SPSS output viewer.

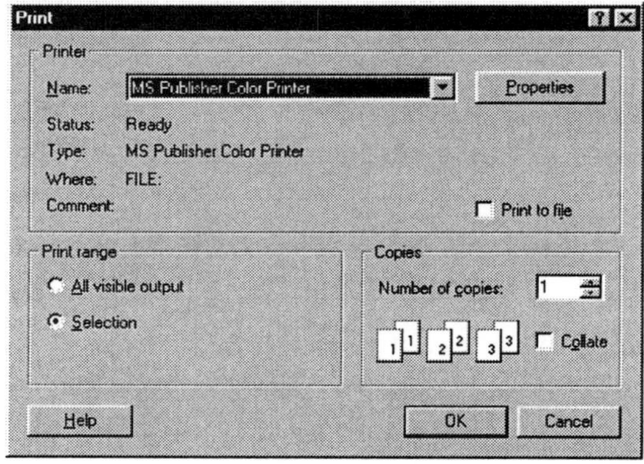

Fig. 5.15. Print.

Fig. 5.16. Window bars.

You have two types of files: **Data** (see Fig. 5.7) and **Output** (see Fig. 5.11). You must save the data file if you made any additions, changes, or corrections.

Saving the Output File

Because the whole **output file** may take a lot of space, it may not be possible to save many of them on a floppy disk. Thus, if you save them, you may want to save them to your hard drive or a network drive, assuming you have access to one. Outputs are quite easy to reproduce so, especially if you print one, it may not be worthwhile to also save it.

Saving the Data file

You should *always* save your **data file** if you entered new data or made any changes to it. It is probably a good idea to be safe and save the data at the end of each session so you do not forget to do it when you make new variables. To do this, follow these steps:

- Click on the **SPSS Data Editor** button at the bottom of your screen.
- Then click **File => Save As**.
- Go ahead and name your data file as **Classdata.**
- Make sure you select **Drive A:** (or use C: or a network drive if you have the capability).
- Complete the saving procedure by clicking on **OK**.

Interpretation Questions

1. a) How are the nominal, ordinal, and scale types of levels of measurement different?
   b) Why is it important to know what level of variable you are labeling?

2. a) Why is it important to check your raw data before entering it into SPSS?
   b) What are ways to check it?

3. a) When would it be helpful to use a box plot?
   b) What does the line in the box tell you?

Extra Problems Using Class Data

Using your class data or the Appendix B data, do the following problems. Print your outputs after typing your explanatory descriptions on them. Circle the key parts of the output that you discuss.

1. Does it look like there is a difference between male and female students in regard to the heights of their same sex parent? Explain, including any cautions.

2. Does it look like there are differences between the three marital statuses in regard to the ages of the research class? In other words, are married people more likely to be older or younger? What about single people ... or divorced? Explain, including cautions.

CHAPTER 6

Overview of the High School and Beyond (HSB) Data Set, Checking Data, and Descriptive Statistics

The Modified HsbData File

The file name of the main data set used with this manual is HsbData; it stands for high school and beyond data. It is based on a national sample of data from more than 28,000 high school students. The current data set is a sample of 75 students drawn randomly from the larger population. The data that we have from this sample includes school data such as grades and whether or not the students took specific mathematics courses such as algebra and calculus in high school. Also there are several kinds of standardized test data and demographic data about gender and mother's and father's education.

In Assignment B, you entered some data as well as labeled the variables and their values so that your printouts would include the variable labels and the value labels. For the rest of the assignments in this book, you will work with the high school and beyond data for each of the 75 participants on 14 HSB variables. The HsbData file is shown in Table 6.1.

The Raw HSB Data and Data Editor

Notice the short variable names at the top of the HsbData file. (Actually, we have transferred the HSB file from the SPSS data editor to Excel and reduced it so that it would fit on two pages, but in SPSS it will look very similar to Table 6.1.) Be aware that the subjects/participants are listed down the page from ID 1 to ID 75 (on the second page), and the variables are listed across the top. You will always enter data this way. If a variable is measured more than once, such as a pretest and posttest, it will be entered as two variables perhaps called Pre and Post. This method of entering data follows that suggested in chapter 7. Note that most of the values are single digits but that *visual, mosaic,* and *mathach* include some decimals and even minus numbers. Notice also that some cells like gender for participant ID1 are blank because a datum is missing. Perhaps participant 1 did not answer the question about gender and participant 2 did not know her father's education. Recall from the earlier discussion that blank is the "system missing" value that can be used for any missing data in an SPSS data file. For your purposes we suggest that you always leave missing data blank; however, you may run across “user defined” missing data codes like -1 or 9 in other researchers' data. Note that in the original HSB data set there were no missing data, which does not happen very often in social science research, especially when using questionnaires.

Table 6.1. *Hsbdata With Errors Data Set in the SPSS Data Editor*

id	visual	Mosaic	grades	mathgr	alg1	alg2	geo	trig	calc	mathach	faed	maed	gender
1	8.75	31	4	0	0	0	0	0	0	9	10	10	
2	4.75	56	5	0	0	0	0	0	0	10.33	7		2
3	4.75	25	6	1	0	0	0	0	0	7.667	2	2	2
4	1	22	3	0	100	0	0	0	0	5		3	1
5	2.25	17.5	3	0	0	0	0	0	0	-1.667	3	3	2
6	1	23.5	5	1	0	0	0	0	0	1	3	2	2
7	2.5	28.5	6	0	1	1	10	0	0	12	9	6	1
8	3.5	29.5	4	0	1	0	0	0	0	8	5	3	2
9	3.5	28	7	1	1	0	0	0	0	13	3	3	2
10	3.75	27.5	5	0	0	0	0	0	0	3.667	8	2	1
11	11	27	6	0	1	1	1	1	1	21	3	4	1
12	4.75	26.5	8	1	1	1	1	1	1	23.667	8	9	1
13	1	13	5	0	1	0	0	0	0	4	2	2	2
14	1	18	2	0	1	0	0	0	0	9	6	3	1
15	4.75	25	3	0	1	1	0	0	0	5.333	2	3	2
16	13.5	33	7	1	1	1	1	0	0	19.667		3	1
17	-0.25	33	7	0	1	0	1	0	0	7.667	3	3	1
18	6	27	5	0	1	0	1	0	0	14.333	9	7	1
19	9.75	26	6	1	1	1	1	0	0	14.333	3	3	1
20	8.75	25	8	1	1	1	1	1	0	19.667	8	3	2
21	-0.25	41	5	0	1	0	1	0	0	17	5	5	1
22	7.25	27	3	0	0	0	0	0	0	7.667	2	3	2
23	4.75	22	5	0	1	1	1	1	0	19.667	9	7	1
24	1	53	4	0	0	0	0	0	0	6.667	2	2	2
25	9.75	27	7	1	1	1	1	1	0	14.333	6	6	2
26	7.25	31	5	0	1	0	0	0	0	10.667	5	3	2
27	2.25	29	6	0	1	0	1	0	0	14.333	3	6	2
28	2.25	26	5	1	1	1	0	0	0	14.333	3	2	1
29	1	22	6	1	1	0	0	0	0	14.333	5	3	2
30	13.5	31	3	0	0	0	0	0	0	9	2	3	1
31	9.75	27	7	1	1	1	1	1	0	17	2	3	2
32	9.5	34	6	0	1	1	1	0	0	23.667	9	5	1
33	9.75	24.5	4	0	1	1	1	1	0	18.333	5	7	1
34	6	23	7	1	1	1	1	1	0	15.667	8	8	1
35	2.25	32.5	8	1	1	0	0	0	0	17	4	2	2
36	9.75	29.5	6	0	1	1	1	1	0	15.667	8	6	1
37	-0.25	33	7	0	1	0	1	0	0	7.667	3	3	1
38	3.75	24	7	1	1	1	1	1	1	22.667	2	2	2
39	6	11	7	1	1	1	0	0	0	14.333	4	2	2
40	6.5	23	5	0	1	1	1	0	0	21	2	2	1
41	1	26	6	1	0	0	0	0	0	6.333	2	2	2
42	6	22.5	6	1	1	0	1	0	0	3.667	3	6	2
43	3.5	20.5	7	0	1	1	0	0	0	10.333	10	10	1
44	3.5	28	8	1	1	1	1	1	1	23.667	8	8	2
45	1	16	7	1	1	0	0	0	0	4	2	3	2
46	-0.25	30	6	0	1	1	0	0	0	17	4	6	2
47	-0.25	23.5	6	0	1	1	1	0	0	6.333	10	9	2
48	-0.25	20.5	5	0	1	0	0	0	0	3.667	2	3	2
49	4.75	22.5	5	0	1	0	0	0	0	9	3	5	

Table 6.1. *Hsbdata With Errors Data Set in the SPSS Data Editor (continued)*

id	visual	mosaic	grades	mathgr	alg1	alg2	geo	trig	calc	mathach	faed	maed	gender
50	5	24	6	0	1	1	1	1	0	20.333	8	7	2
51	4.75	37	6	0	1	0	0	0	0	13	2	2	2
52	4.75	31	5	1	1	0	0	0	0	12	2	3	2
53	5	56	6	1	0	0	0	0	0	17	6	2	2
54	11	35.5	8	1	1	1	1	1	1	23.667	5	7	2
55	11	28	8	1	1	1	1	1	0	21	2	2	1
56	7.25	36	7	1	1	1	1	1	1	22.333	10	9	1
57	3.5	35	3	0	0	0	0	0	0	2.333	2	3	2
58	7.25	44	8	1	1	1	1	1	0	22.333	10	5	2
59	3.5	-4	7	1	1	0	0	0	0	5	2	2	2
60	6	24.5	5	1	0	0	0	0	0	5	2	3	2
61	9.75	25	8	1	1	1	1	0	0	10.333	2	3	2
62	2.25	51.5	3	0	0	0	0	0	0	5	3	3	1
63	1	25	7	0	1	0	0	0	0	1	10	3	2
64	3.5	30.5	4	0	1	0	1	0	0	13	2	3	1
65	4.75	29	4	0	0	0	0	0	0	9.333	3	2	2
66	-0.25	20	7	0	1	1	0	0	0	10.333	2	3	2
67	4.75	22	7	1	1	1	1	1	1	23.667	9	3	1
68	6	7.5	3	0	0	0	0	0	0	5	5	5	1
69	7.25	32	8	1	1	1	1	1	1	23.667	9	8	1
70	1	23	5	0	1	1	0	0	0	14.667	3	3	1
71	11	24.5	4	0	1	1	1	1	0	18.667	7	3	1
72	8.5	23	7	0	1	1	1	0	0	11.667	5	4	1
73	8.5	30.5	4	0	1	0	0	0	0	14.333	3	6	1
74	14.75	13.5	5	0	1	0	1	0	0	11.667	3	3	1
75	14.75	30	7	1	1	1	1	1	0	14.333	6	3	1

The HSB Variables

The following 14 variables (with the range of their values in parentheses) are found in the HsbData file. A complete codebook and how to generate it in SPSS are found in Appendix C. Note, minus scores result from a penalty for guessing.

1. Identification number (1 to 75). We will not actually use this as a variable.
2. Visualization score (-4 to 16). This is a 16-item test that assesses visualization in three dimensions (i.e., how a three-dimensional object would look if its spatial position were changed).
3. Mosaic, pattern test score (-4 to 56). This is a test of pattern recognition ability involving the detection of relationships in patterns of tiles.
4. Grades in h.s. (1=less than a D average to 8=mostly an A average)
5. Math grades (0=low, 1=high)
6. Algebra 1 in h.s. (1=taken, 0=not taken)
7. Algebra 2 in h.s. (1=taken, 0=not taken)
8. Geometry in h.s. (1=taken, 0=not taken)
9. Trigonometry in h.s. (1=taken, 0=not taken)
10. Calculus in h.s. (1=taken, 0=not taken)
11. Math achievement score (-8.33 to 25) This is a test like the SAT or ACT math.

12. Father's education (2=less than h.s. grad to10=PhD/MD).
13. Mother's education (2=less than h.s. grad to 10=PhD/MD).
14. Gender (1=male, 2=female).

Lab Assignment C

Logon and Get Data

- Logon and open SPSS as you did in Lab Assignment A in chapter 1.
- Open the **HsbDataWithErrors.sav** data file. With the data disk in the floppy drive, you should get a window looking like Figure 6.1.
- Go to the **Look in** box.
- Select **3 ½ Floppy (A:)**. The file **HsbDataWithErrors** should appear in the window below **Look in**. (Note: Your data may be in your C: or network drive if you downloaded or copied it to your hard drive).
- Then click on **Open** (see Fig. 6.1).

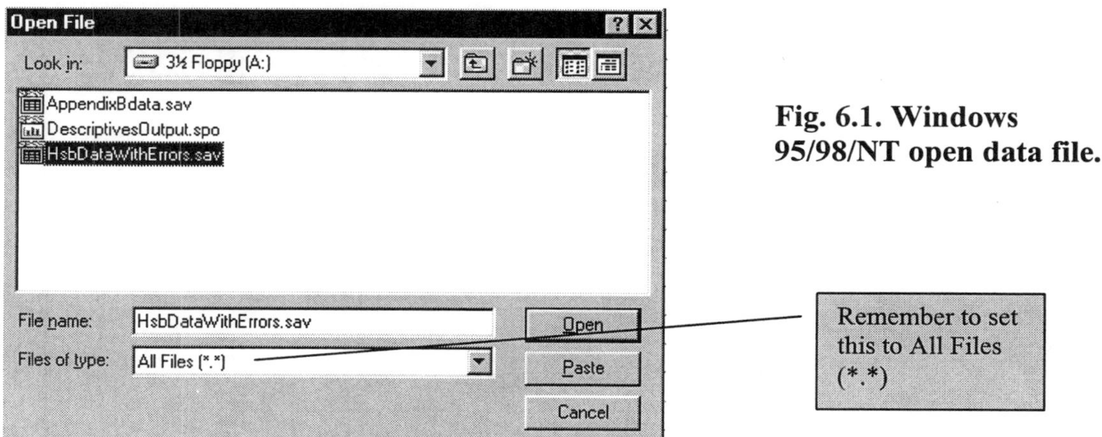

Fig. 6.1. Windows 95/98/NT open data file.

- After a few moments, you should get a data file looking like Fig. 6.2. The full data file is shown in Table 6.1.

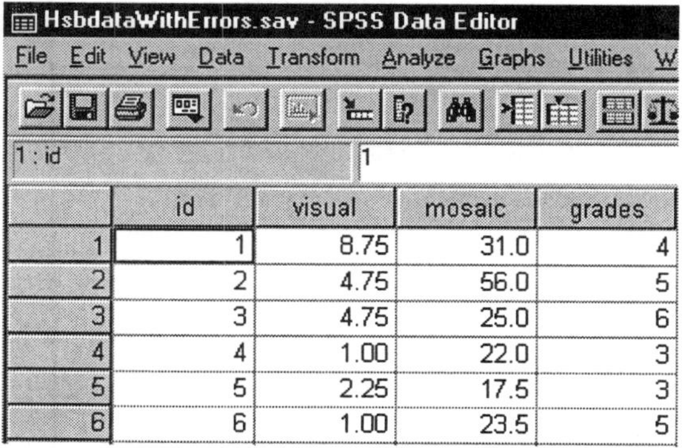

	id	visual	mosaic	grades
1	1	8.75	31.0	4
2	2	4.75	56.0	5
3	3	4.75	25.0	6
4	4	1.00	22.0	3
5	5	2.25	17.5	3
6	6	1.00	23.5	5

Fig. 6.2. SPSS data editor.

Problem 1: Descriptives for All Subjects

Checking Data

Before using statistics to help answer your research questions, you should get a good feel for the data and check carefully for errors. Assignment C will help you do this for the HSB data. After the data have been entered into the **SPSS Data Editor**, you should compute some basic descriptive statistics, as demonstrated in Assignments B. Certain kinds of errors should be noticeable from the data (Table 6.1) or Output 6.1, Problem 1 of this assignment. To spot these errors, you will need to examine the data in conjunction with the possible ranges of values for each variable, which are found in the list of variables (above) and in Appendix C.

Problem/Research Question

What are the mean, standard deviation, minimum, and maximum scores for all 75 participants or cases on all variables? Are there any errors in the data that can be spotted by comparing the above output with the codebook?

To compute the basic descriptive statistics for all subjects you will need to do these steps:

- Select **Analyze**, then **Descriptive Statistics**, and finally **Descriptives** (see Fig. 6.3).[1]

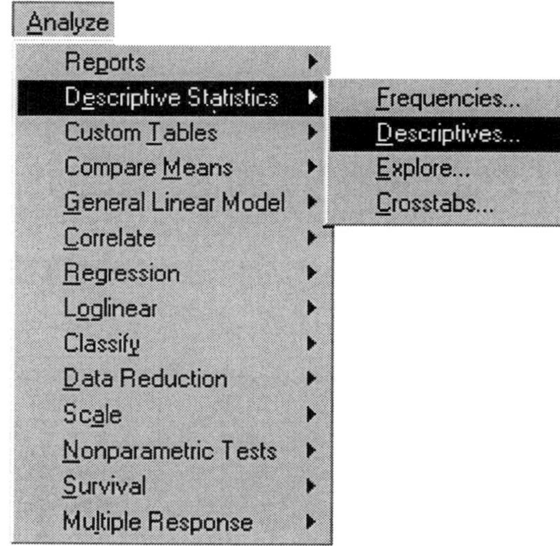

Fig. 6.3. Analyze menu.

After selecting **Descriptives**, you will be ready to compute the mean, standard deviation, minimum, and maximum for all participants or cases on all variables in order to examine the data.

- Now *highlight all* the variables in the left box. Recall that to highlight, begin at the top of the box and hold the left mouse button down while you scroll downward until *all* the variables listed turn blue.

---

[1] In most assignments, this progression through several screens is indicated as follows: Analyze => Descriptive Statistics => Descriptives.

- Click on the **arrow** button pointing right. When you finish, the **Descriptives** dialog box should look like Fig. 6.4.
- Be sure that all the variables have moved out of the left window and your screen looks like Fig. 6.4. If not, you will not get descriptives for all the variables.
- Click on **OK**.

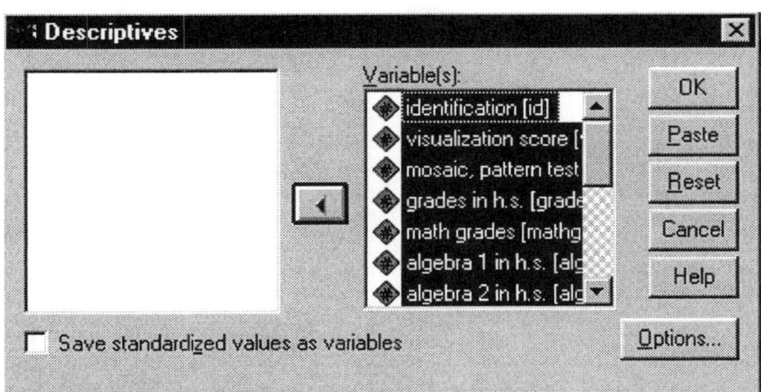

Fig. 6.4. Descriptives.

Standardized Scores

Note that if you intended to combine variables with markedly different means and standard deviations, you should standardize (make *z* scores) those variables by checking that box (bottom left) in Fig. 6.4. If variables to be combined in a given study did not use the same metric, some scores would have more weight unless you standardized the variables before combining them. With the HSB data, we will not combine scores, so we will not make and **save standardized values as variables**.

Compare your output to Output 6.1. If it looks the same you have done the steps correctly. Note that after the output we have provided a brief interpretation in a gray box. Also, on the output itself, we have pointed out some of the key things by circling them and making some comments in gray callout boxes. Of course, these circles and information boxes will not show up on your printout.

Output 6.1: Descriptives With Errors

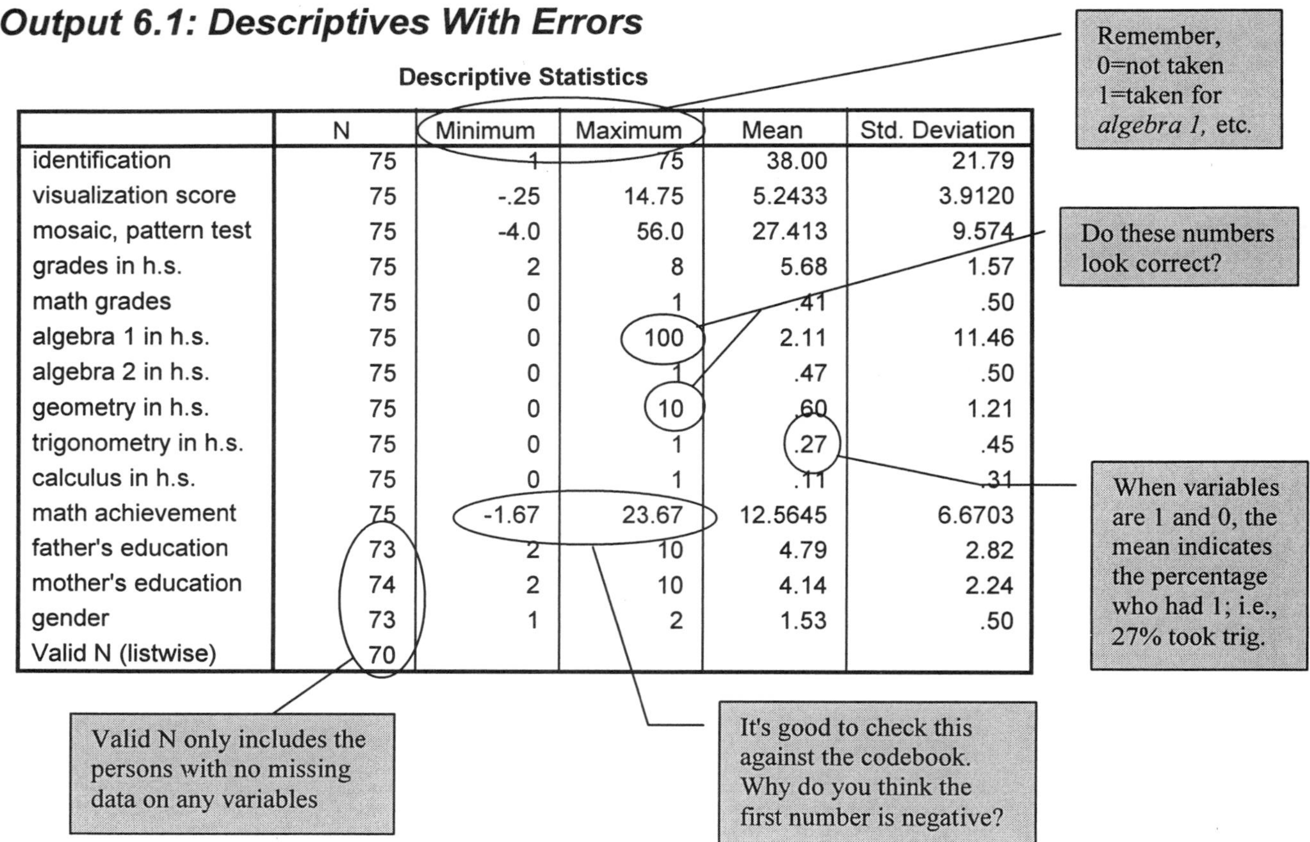

Descriptive Statistics

	N	Minimum	Maximum	Mean	Std. Deviation
identification	75	1	75	38.00	21.79
visualization score	75	-.25	14.75	5.2433	3.9120
mosaic, pattern test	75	-4.0	56.0	27.413	9.574
grades in h.s.	75	2	8	5.68	1.57
math grades	75	0	1	.41	.50
algebra 1 in h.s.	75	0	100	2.11	11.46
algebra 2 in h.s.	75	0	1	.47	.50
geometry in h.s.	75	0	10	.60	1.21
trigonometry in h.s.	75	0	1	.27	.45
calculus in h.s.	75	0	1	.11	.31
math achievement	75	-1.67	23.67	12.5645	6.6703
father's education	73	2	10	4.79	2.82
mother's education	74	2	10	4.14	2.24
gender	73	1	2	1.53	.50
Valid N (listwise)	70				

Remember,
0=not taken
1=taken for
algebra 1, etc.
Do these numbers
look correct?
When variables
are 1 and 0, the
mean indicates
the percentage
who had 1; i.e.,
27% took trig.
Valid N only includes the
persons with no missing
data on any variables
It's good to check this
against the codebook.
Why do you think the
first number is negative?

Interpretation of Output 6.1

This Output provides the number of subjects (*N*), the lowest and highest score, mean or average, and standard deviation for each variable. At the beginning of your data analysis, check to make sure that all means seem reasonable (given the information in your codebook), and check to see that the minimum and maximum are within the appropriate range for each variable. For example, note in the codebook that *alg1, alg2, geo,* and *trig* have to be **0 = not taken** or **1 = taken** so the minimum should be 0 and maximum 1. Likewise, *Mathgr* has to be 0 or 1. If not, you have an error to correct before proceeding. Did you find the two errors in the data? You will correct them in **Problem 2**. Note, from the bottom of Output 6.1 that the valid number (*N*) of observations/subjects (listwise) is 70, rather than 75, which is the number of participants in the data file. This is because the listwise *N* only includes the persons with *no* missing data on any variable. Notice that several variables (e.g., *father's education*) each have a few participants missing.

Problem 2: Correct Errors and Rerun Descriptives

Problem/Research Question

Correct any errors in the data set, rerun descriptives.

Now click on **hsbdata-SPSS Data Editor,** at the bottom of your screen, to get back to the **SPSS Data Editor** so that you can correct the errors before proceeding. To make the corrections, you must find the participants whose data are in error. Look at the data file (Table 6.1*)*. In this example, Participant 4 had a 100 for *algebra 1* and Participant 7 had a 10 for *geometry*. Neither of those can be correct because *algebra* and *geometry* are to be scored either 0 or 1. In your study, you would check the questionnaires to see what these participants had answered.

It is, of course, wise to check *all* the data against the original answer sheets because the method of checking shown here will only pick up errors when the recorded number is outside the acceptable range. This type of error can, however, distort the means and standard deviation quite seriously, as in this example. Let's assume that the true score in these two cases was 1 instead of 100 and 10. To correct the errors, *highlight* the box/cell (in the data editor) with the error by clicking on it. Then correct it. That is, highlight *algebra 1* for Subject 4, delete the 0 0, and press enter. Do a similar correction for Subject 7 in the *geometry* column. Delete the 0 and press enter.

Rerun the basic descriptive statistics by repeating the steps in Problem 1. This should be easy since the variables will already be in the correct (right) box, unless you pressed **Reset.**

Output 6.2: Descriptives Corrected

Descriptives

Descriptive Statistics

	N	Minimum	Maximum	Mean	Std. Deviation
identification	75	1	75	38.00	21.79
visualization score	75	-.25	14.75	5.2433	3.9120
mosaic, pattern test	75	-4.0	56.0	27.413	9.574
grades in h.s.	75	2	8	5.68	1.57
math grades	75	0	1	.41	.50
algebra 1 in h.s.	75	0	1	.79	.41
algebra 2 in h.s.	75	0	1	.47	.50
geometry in h.s.	75	0	1	.48	.50
trigonometry in h.s.	75	0	1	.27	.45
calculus in h.s.	75	0	1	.11	.31
math achievement	75	-1.67	23.67	12.5645	6.6703
father's education	73	2	10	4.79	2.82
mother's education	74	2	10	4.14	2.24
gender	73	1	2	1.53	.50
Valid N (listwise)	70				

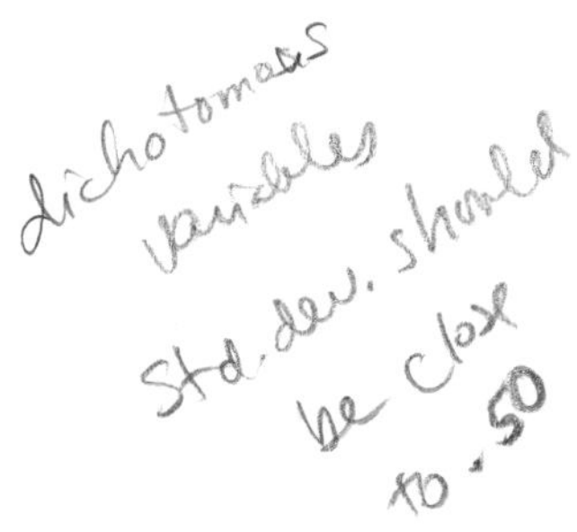

dichotomous
variables
Std. dev. should
be close
to .50

Problem 3: Frequency Distributions

Problem/Research Question

What are the percentages of males and females?

Let's determine frequencies for gender, a nominal, categorical variable.

- Click on **Analyze => Descriptive Statistics => Frequencies**.
- Click on the variable *gender.*
- Now click on the **arrow** button to move it over. Does it look like Fig. 6.5?
- Click on **OK** to see your output file. Does it look like Output 6.3?

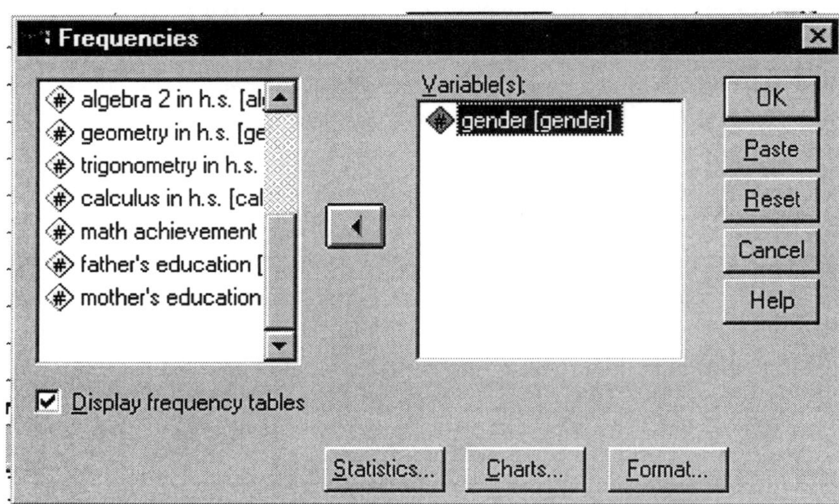

Fig. 6.5. Frequencies.

Output 6.3: Frequencies

Frequencies

Statistics

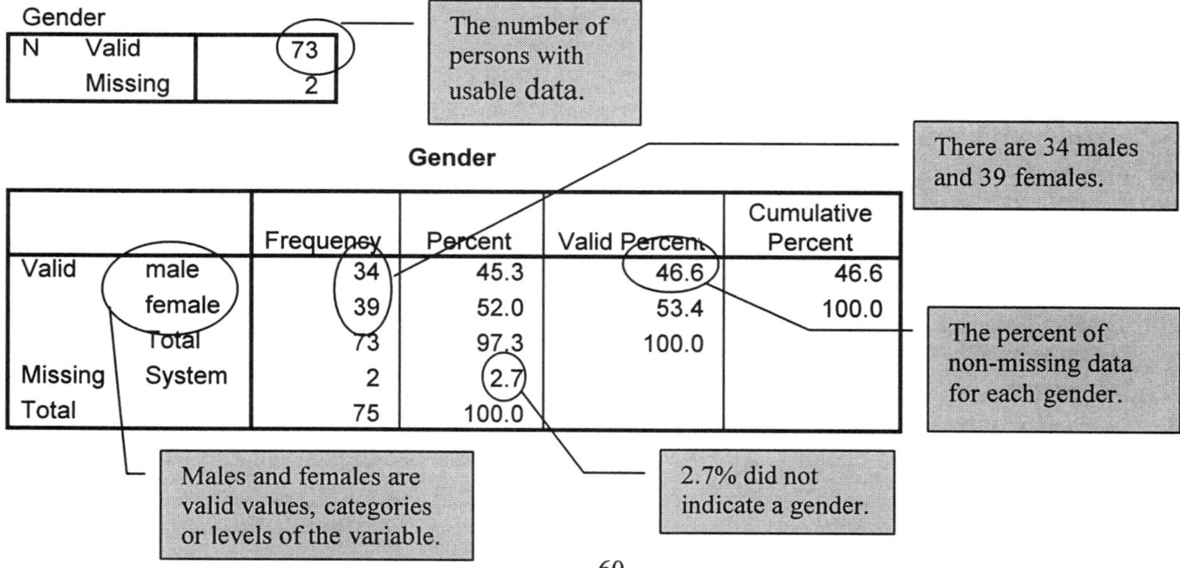

Gender

N	Valid	73
	Missing	2

Gender

		Frequency	Percent	Valid Percent	Cumulative Percent
Valid	male	34	45.3	46.6	46.6
	female	39	52.0	53.4	100.0
	Total	73	97.3	100.0	
Missing	System	2	2.7		
Total		75	100.0		

The number of persons with usable data.
There are 34 males and 39 females.
The percent of non-missing data for each gender.
Males and females are valid values, categories or levels of the variable.
2.7% did not indicate a gender.

Interpretation of Output 6.3

The first table, titled statistics, provides only the number of participants for whom we have valid gender data and the number with missing data. We did not request any other statistics because almost all of them (e.g., median, range, standard deviation) are not appropriate to use with nominal data. (See Table 3.2). The other table is a frequency distribution for gender. The left-hand column shows the **valid** categories or levels or values, **missing** values, and **totals**. The frequency column gives the number of participants who had each value. The **percent** column is the percent who had each value, including missing values. For example, 52 % were female, 97.3% had a valid gender and 2.7% were missing. The **valid percent** shows the percent of those with *nonmissing* data at each value; e.g., 53.4% of the 73 who gave a gender were females. Finally, **cumulative** percent is the percent of subjects in a category *plus* the categories listed above it. This last column is not very useful with nominal data, but can be quite informative in frequency distributions with many ordered categories, as we will see in Output 6.4.

Problem 4: Frequencies, Statistics, and Histograms

More Descriptive Statistics and Skewness

This problem includes more descriptive statistics and ways to examine your data to see if the variables are approximately normally distributed, an assumption of most of the parametric inferential statistics that we will use. A key statistic is skewness, an index that helps determine how much a variable's distribution deviates from the distribution of the normal curve. Review chapter 3 if you do not remember these concepts. **Skewness** refers to the lack of symmetry in a frequency distribution. Distributions with a long "tail" to the right have a positive skew and vice versa. If a frequency distribution of a variable has a large (plus or minus) skewness, that variable is said to deviate from normality. In this assignment, we examine this assumption for several key variables. However, the parametric inferential statistics that we will use are robust or quite insensitive to violations of normality. Thus, we will assume that it is okay to use parametric statistics to answer most of our research questions.

Problem/Research Question

What are the frequency distributions and other descriptive statistics for these four **scale** variables: *visualization score, mosaic pattern test, grades, math achievement*? Are these variables approximately normally distributed?

Now let's take a look at some histograms along with the frequency distributions for four scale variables. Follow these commands:

- **Analyze => Descriptive Statistics => Frequencies**.
- It is important to click on **Reset.**
- Let's then use the variables *grades, math achievement*, *visualization, and mosaic*. Highlight each and then click on the **arrow** button. It should look like Fig. 6.6.

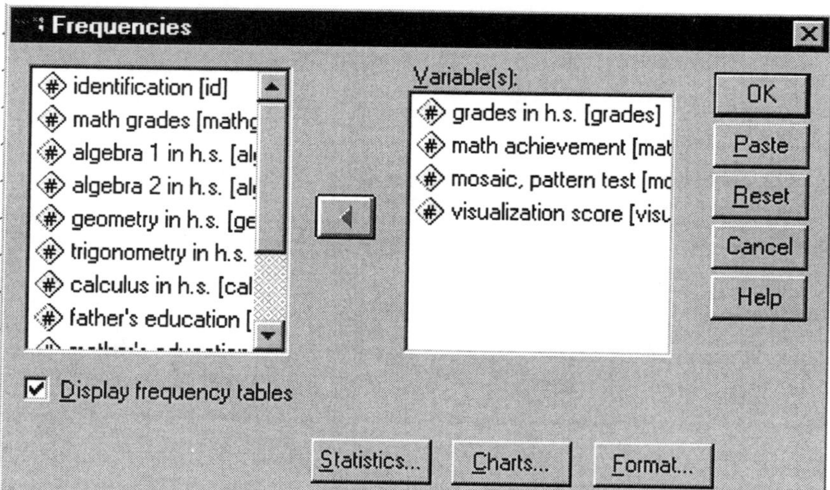

Fig. 6.6. Frequencies.

Follow these steps to get more statistics:

- Now, click on **Statistics** and select **Mean, Median, Mode, Skewness, Standard Deviation, Variance,** and **Range** (see Fig. 6.7).
- Click on **Continue**.

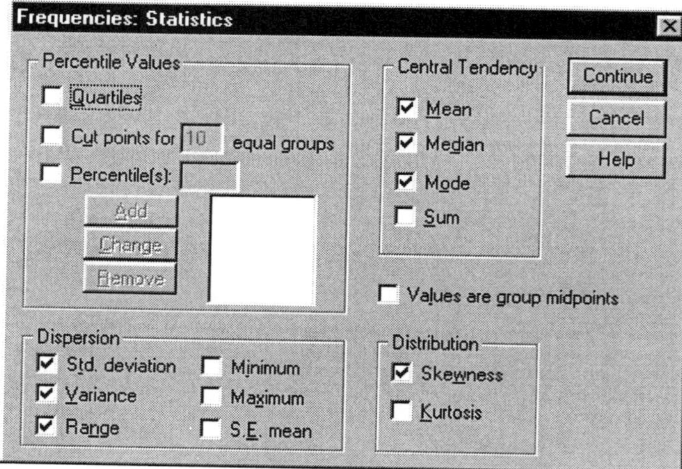

Fig. 6.7. Frequencies: Statistics.

Continue with these steps:

- Next, click on **Charts** (see Fig. 6.6).
- Select **Histogram[s]** and **With normal curve**. Does it look like Fig. 6.8?

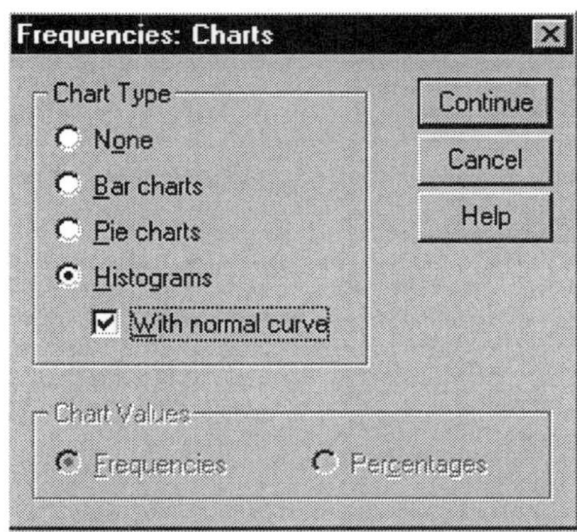

Fig. 6.8. Frequencies: Charts.

- Click on **Continue**.
- Finally, click on **OK** to get an output file. Does it look like Output 6.4? You may need to edit the output like we did in chapter 1 so it will fit your page.

Output 6.4: Frequencies, Statistics, and Histograms

Frequencies

Statistics

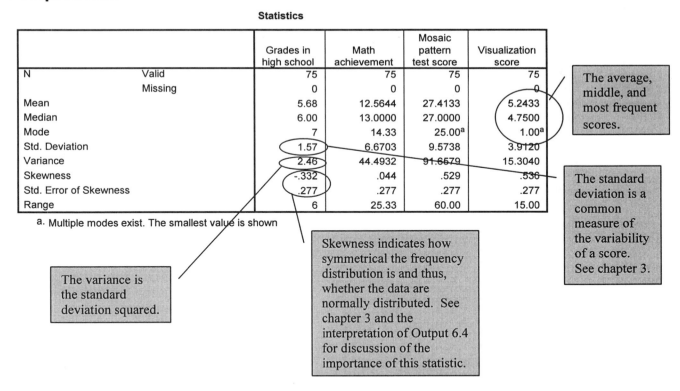

		Grades in high school	Math achievement	Mosaic pattern test score	Visualization score
N	Valid	75	75	75	75
	Missing	0	0	0	0
Mean		5.68	12.5644	27.4133	5.2433
Median		6.00	13.0000	27.0000	4.7500
Mode		7	14.33	25.00[a]	1.00[a]
Std. Deviation		1.57	6.6703	9.5738	3.9120
Variance		2.46	44.4932	91.6579	15.3040
Skewness		-.332	.044	.529	.536
Std. Error of Skewness		.277	.277	.277	.277
Range		6	25.33	60.00	15.00

a. Multiple modes exist. The smallest value is shown

The average, middle, and most frequent scores.

The standard deviation is a common measure of the variability of a score. See chapter 3.

The variance is the standard deviation squared.

Skewness indicates how symmetrical the frequency distribution is and thus, whether the data are normally distributed. See chapter 3 and the interpretation of Output 6.4 for discussion of the importance of this statistic.

Frequency Table

grades in h.s.

		Frequency	Percent	Valid Percent	Cumulative Percent
Valid	mostly D	1	1.3	1.3	1.3
	half CD	8	10.7	10.7	12.0
	mostly C	8	10.7	10.7	22.7
	half BC	16	21.3	21.3	44.0
	mostly B	15	20.0	20.0	64.0
	half AB	18	24.0	24.0	88.0
	mostly A	9	12.0	12.0	100.0
	Total	75	100.0	100.0	

23% have a mostly C average *or less*.

Cumulative percentage will end with 100.

Math achievement

		Frequency	Percent	Valid Percent	Cumulative Percent
Valid	-1.67	1	1.3	1.3	1.3
	1.00	2	2.7	2.7	4.0
	2.33	1	1.3	1.3	5.3
	3.67	3	4.0	4.0	9.3
	4.00	2	2.7	2.7	12.0
	5.00	5	6.7	6.7	18.7
	5.33	1	1.3	1.3	20.0
	6.33	2	2.7	2.7	22.7
	6.67	1	1.3	1.3	24.0
	7.67	4	5.3	5.3	29.3
	8.00	1	1.3	1.3	30.7
	9.00	4	5.3	5.3	36.0
	9.33	1	1.3	1.3	37.3
	10.33	1	1.3	1.3	38.7
	10.33	3	4.0	4.0	42.7
	10.67	1	1.3	1.3	44.0
	11.67	2	2.7	2.7	46.7
	12.00	2	2.7	2.7	49.3
	13.00	3	4.0	4.0	53.3
	14.33	9	12.0	12.0	65.3
	14.67	1	1.3	1.3	66.7
	15.67	2	2.7	2.7	69.3
	17.00	5	6.7	6.7	76.0
	18.33	1	1.3	1.3	77.3
	18.67	1	1.3	1.3	78.7
	19.67	3	4.0	4.0	82.7
	20.33	1	1.3	1.3	84.0
	21.00	3	4.0	4.0	88.0
	22.33	2	2.7	2.7	90.7
	22.67	1	1.3	1.3	92.0
	23.67	6	8.0	8.0	100.0
	Total	75	100.0	100.0	

Mosaic pattern test score

		Frequency	Percent	Valid Percent	Cumulative Percent
Valid	-4.00	1	1.3	1.3	1.3
	7.50	1	1.3	1.3	2.7
	11.00	1	1.3	1.3	4.0
	13.00	1	1.3	1.3	5.3
	13.50	1	1.3	1.3	6.7
	16.00	1	1.3	1.3	8.0
	17.50	1	1.3	1.3	9.3
	18.00	1	1.3	1.3	10.7
	20.00	1	1.3	1.3	12.0
	20.50	2	2.7	2.7	14.7
	22.00	4	5.3	5.3	20.0
	22.50	2	2.7	2.7	22.7
	23.00	4	5.3	5.3	28.0
	23.50	2	2.7	2.7	30.7
	24.00	2	2.7	2.7	33.3
	24.50	3	4.0	4.0	37.3
	25.00	5	6.7	6.7	44.0
	26.00	3	4.0	4.0	48.0
	26.50	1	1.3	1.3	49.3
	27.00	5	6.7	6.7	56.0
	27.50	1	1.3	1.3	57.3
	28.00	3	4.0	4.0	61.3
	28.50	1	1.3	1.3	62.7
	29.00	2	2.7	2.7	65.3
	29.50	2	2.7	2.7	68.0
	30.00	2	2.7	2.7	70.7
	30.50	2	2.7	2.7	73.3
	31.00	4	5.3	5.3	78.7
	32.00	1	1.3	1.3	80.0
	32.50	1	1.3	1.3	81.3
	33.00	3	4.0	4.0	85.3
	34.00	1	1.3	1.3	86.7
	35.00	1	1.3	1.3	88.0
	35.50	1	1.3	1.3	89.3
	36.00	1	1.3	1.3	90.7
	37.00	1	1.3	1.3	92.0
	41.00	1	1.3	1.3	93.3
	44.00	1	1.3	1.3	94.7
	51.50	1	1.3	1.3	96.0
	53.00	1	1.3	1.3	97.3
	56.00	2	2.7	2.7	100.0
	Total	75	100.0	100.0	

Visualization score

		Frequency	Percent	Valid Percent	Cumulative Percent
Valid	-.25	7	9.3	9.3	9.3
	1.00	10	13.3	13.3	22.7
	2.25	5	6.7	6.7	29.3
	2.50	1	1.3	1.3	30.7
	3.50	7	9.3	9.3	40.0
	3.75	2	2.7	2.7	42.7
	4.75	10	13.3	13.3	56.0
	5.00	2	2.7	2.7	58.7
	6.00	6	8.0	8.0	66.7
	6.50	1	1.3	1.3	68.0
	7.25	5	6.7	6.7	74.7
	8.50	2	2.7	2.7	77.3
	8.75	2	2.7	2.7	80.0
	9.50	1	1.3	1.3	81.3
	9.75	6	8.0	8.0	89.3
	11.00	4	5.3	5.3	94.7
	13.50	2	2.7	2.7	97.3
	14.75	2	2.7	2.7	100.0
	Total	75	100.0	100.0	

Histograms

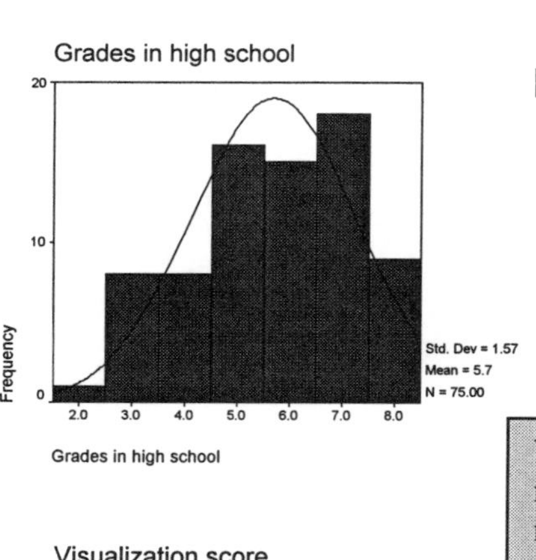

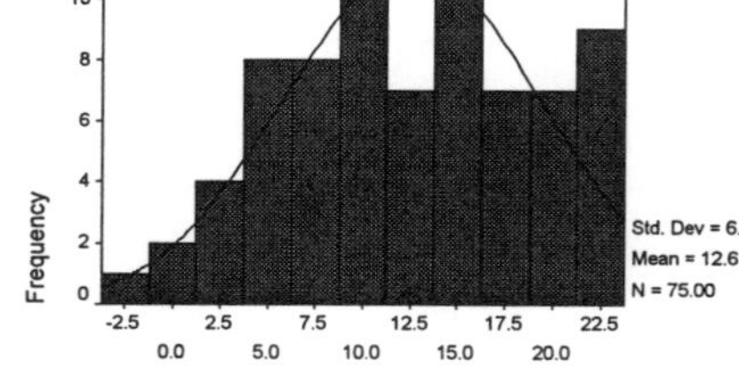

Note these look roughly like the normal curve.

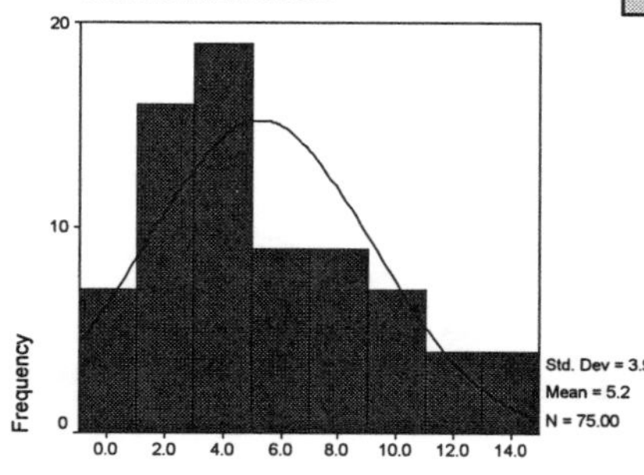

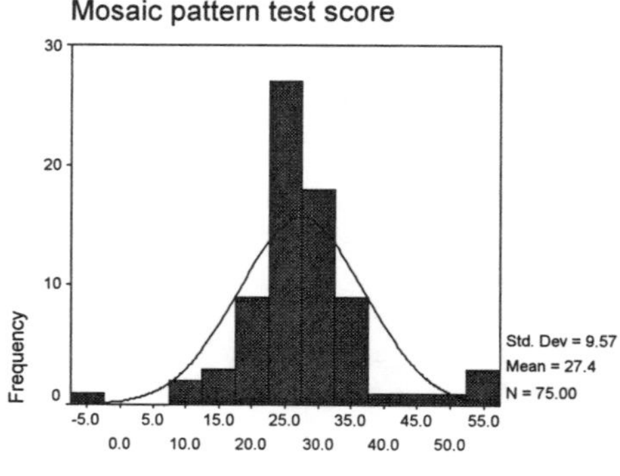

Interpretation of Output 6.4

The output file provides all the requested statistics for the four variables as a group. Then the four frequency distributions and histograms with the normal curve superimposed over them are given individually so you can visualize whether the frequency distribution (histogram) looks normal. However, visual inspection can be deceiving because distributions need only be approximately normal. In the Statistics table at the beginning of Output 6.4, note the rows for the skewness of the variables. Most statistics books do not provide advice about how to decide whether a variable is at least approximately normal. SPSS recommends that you divide the skewness by its standard error. If the result is less than 2.5 (which is approximately the $p = .01$ level) then skewness is *not* significantly different from normal. A problem with this method, aside from having to use a calculator, is that the standard error depends on the sample size so with large samples many variables would be found to be nonnormal. A simpler rule of thumb is that if the skewness is less than plus or minus one (< +/- 1.0) the variable is at least approximately normal. Note that, using either index, none of the four variables is markedly skewed. Thus, they can be considered *scale* level variable, which is important as you will see in chapter 7.

Remember, that in Output 6.3 the **cumulative percent** in the frequency table had little value because the data were dichotomous (or nominal). Note, however, in Output 6.4 in the **Frequency Table** for *grades in high school* that 22.7% of the students had mostly C grades *or less*.

Problem 5: Recode, Relabel, and Check

Data Transformations (Recode)

In this assignment, you also will do a data transformation to get the father's and mother's education data in the form needed to answer the research questions. This aspect of data analysis is sometimes called file management and can be quite time consuming. That is especially true if you have a lot of questions/items that need to be reversed (because they were negatively worded) and/or combined to compute the summated or composite variables that you want to use in later analyses. (See Appendix G for how to do these and other useful data transformations.) This is a somewhat mundane and tedious aspect of research, but it is important to do it carefully so you do not introduce errors into your data. The SPSS tutorial has additional information on transformations so we suggest you review it.

Problem/Research Question

Recode *mother's and father's* education so that those with no postsecondary education have a value of 1, those with some postsecondary have a value of 2, and those with a bachelor's degree or more have a value of 3. **Label** the new variables and values.

We will **Recode** *mother's and father's education* so that those with no postsecondary education (originally 2s and 3s) have a value of **1**, those with some postsecondary will have **2** and those with a bachelor's degree or more will have a value of **3**.

Explanation

It is usually *not* desirable to dichotomize or trichotomize a good *scale* type of variable. However, *father's* and *mother's education* have a flaw in the categories/values (and we needed another independent variable with a few levels or categories to demonstrate certain analyses later). The flaw can be seen in the codebook. A value of 5 is given for students who had a parent with 2 years of vocational college (presumable an A.S. degree), but a 6 is given to a parent with less than 2 years of (a 4-year) college. Thus, a parent who went 1 week (or 1 credit) to a 4-year college would be rated as having more education than a parent with an associate's degree. This makes the variable not fully ordered so we have recoded it. Recodes also are used to combine two or more small groups/categories of a variable so that group size will be large enough to perform statistical analyses. For example, one might have only a few "widowed" parents that might be combined with "divorced" parents and called "not married" to compare to a larger group of "married" parents.

Follow these steps:

- Click **Data View** in bottom left hand corner to display your data.
- Click on **Transform => Recode => Into Different Variables** and you should get Fig. 6.9.
- Now click on *mother's education* and then the **arrow** button.
- Click on *father's education* and the **arrow** (These steps will move both variables the **Numeric Variable -> Output Variable** box.)
- Now highlight *faed* in the **Numeric Variable** box so that it turns blue. (Leave *mother's education* where it is for now).
- Click on the **Output Variable Name** box and type *faedr*.
- Click on the **Label** box and type *father's educ rev.*
- Click on **Change**. Did you get *faed =>faedr* in the **Numeric Variable** box as in Fig. 6.9?

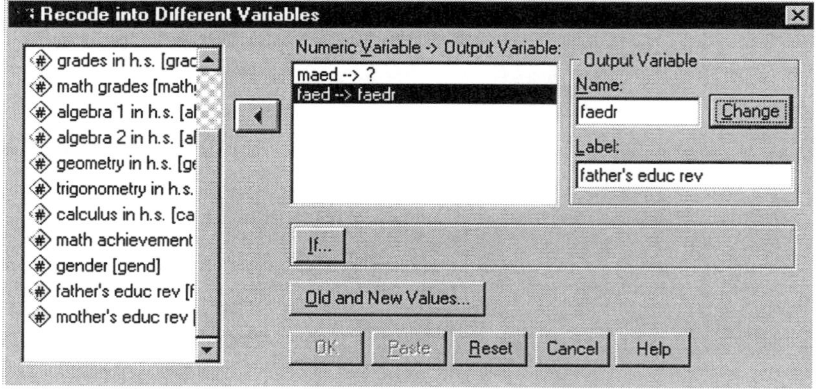

Fig. 6.9. Recode into different variables.

Now repeat these procedures with *mother's education.*

- Highlight *mother's education.*
- Click on **Output Variable Name,** type *maedr.*

- Click **Label**, type *Mother's educ rev,* and click **Change**.
- Then click on **Old and New Values** to get Fig. 6.10.
- Click on **Range** (on the left) and type **2** in the first box and **3** in the second box.
- Click on **Value** (part of **New Value** at the upper right) and type **1**.
- Then click on **Add**.
- Repeat these steps to change old values **4** through **7** to a new **Value** of **2.** Then **Range: 8** through **10** to **Value: 3**. Does your window look like Fig. 6.10?
- If it does, click on **Add**.
- Click on **Continue** to get Fig. 6.9 again.
- Finally, click on **OK**.

Check your **Data Editor**, by clicking on **Data View** on the bottom corner of your screen. See if *faedr* and *maedr* with numbers ranging from 1 to 3 have been added on the far right side. (Note: the 1 to 3 may look like 1.00 to 3.00.) Also, to be *extra* careful, check the data file for a few participants to be sure the recodes were done correctly. For example, the first participant had 10 for *father's education* which should be 3 for *father's education revised.* Is it? Check a few more to be sure.

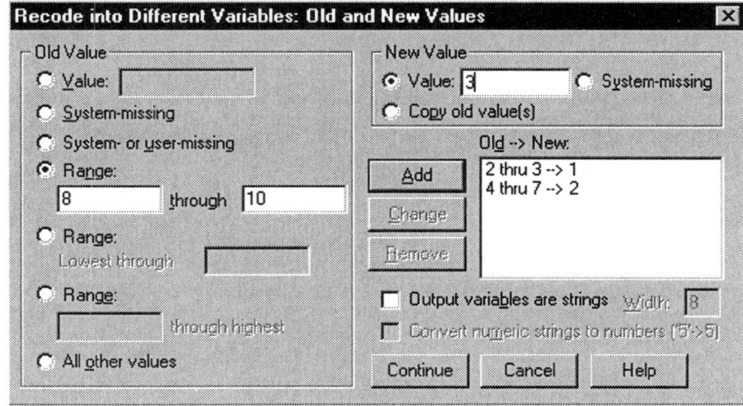

Fig. 6.10. Recode: old and new values.

Here are some changes to make to your new variables *faedr* (after you change *faedr* start here again to change *maedr*):

- Click on the **Variable View** tab at the bottom left of your screen (see Fig. 5.1).
- Scroll down your list of variables to *faedr*.
- Click on the **decimals** cell and change decimal places to "**0**"; Click on **Continue**.
- Change **measure** to **Ordinal**.
- Click on **Continue** then **OK**.

Now, we will **label** the new values.

- Click on the **value** cell and then the gray three-dot box to get Fig. 6.11.
- Type **1** where it says "**Value**" and type **HS grad or less** where it says "**Value Label**."
- Click on **Add**.
- Then click on the **Value** box again and type **2**.
- Click on the **Value Label** box and type **Some College**.
- Click on **Add**.

- Click once more on the **Value** box and type **3**.
- Click on the **Value Label** box and type **BS or More.** Does your window look like Fig. 6.11?
- Now click on **Add**.
- Click on **OK.**

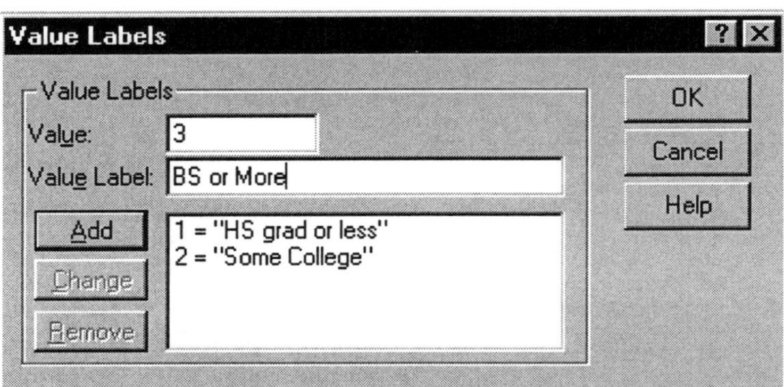

Fig. 6.11. Value labels.

- Now go back and repeat these steps for *mother's education revised,* and make **Value Labels,** on your own.

You have two types of files: **Data (HsbDataWithErrors**, see Fig. 6.1) and **Output** (see Outputs 6.1-6.4).

Saving the Data File

You should *always* save your data file if you made *any* changes to it. In this case, we corrected two errors and recoded *father's and mother's education,* making two new variables. To save your revised and corrected file do the following:

- Click on the **HsbDataWithErrors - SPSS Data** button at the bottom of your screen.
- Then click **File => Save As**.
- Go ahead and rename your data file as **HsbData**. (Note, the new file will not be called **HsbDataWithErrors**).
- Make sure you select **Drive A:** (or use C: or a network drive if you have the capability).
- Complete the saving procedure by clicking on **OK**.
- In this case, we corrected two errors so it would be wise to delete **HsbDataWithErrors,** after saving the corrected file.

Exit

Follow these steps:

- Click on **File => Exit**. Note: If you get asked to save anything, return to the saving steps listed previously because it was not done.

Interpretation Questions

1. Using Output 6.1, look for any obvious errors or problems in the data. What will you look for?

2. Using Output 6.2: a) Name the dichotomous variables. Can you interpret their means? Explain. b) How many participants are there all together? c) How many have complete data (nothing missing)? d) What percentage took algebra 1 in high school? e) What is the range of *father's education* scores? Does this agree with the codebook?

3. Using Output 6.3: a) Did any participants have missing data? If so, how many? b) What percent of students have a valid (non-missing) *gender*? c) How *many* participants were male? d) What percent and valid percent were male? Why are these different?

4. Using Output 6.4, note that you have many statistics including skewness, frequency distributions, and histograms for each of the four variables: a) Is the skewness statistic more than 1.00? b) Why is the answer to a) important? c) Do the distributions of *mosaic*, *grades*, *math achievement* and *visualization* scores seem to be approximately normal from looking at the histograms? d) Does this agree with what you found from examining the skewness scores? e) What is the mean *visualization* score? f) What percentage of students have *grades* of mostly B or less? g) What percentage of students have mostly A grades?

5. Using your initial HSB data file (or the file at the beginning of this chapter) compare the original data to your new variables: Why did you recode *father's* and *mother's education*? What should *father's education revised* be for participants 2, 5, and 8?

Extra Problems Using Class Data

Using your class data or the data from Appendix B if your class had less than 25 students, do the following problems. Print your outputs after typing your answers on them. Please circle the key parts of the output that you use discuss.

1. Compute the mean, median, standard deviation, range, and skewness for *height of student*, *height of same sex parent,* and any other scale variables in the data set. Describe the results briefly. Include comments about whether the variable is approximately normally distributed.

2. Run frequencies for *gender*, *marital status, age* and any other nominal or ordinal data. Comment on the results.

3. Print *a* graphic display that is interesting to you (bar chart, box plot, or histogram). Describe the results.

CHAPTER 7

Selecting and Interpreting Inferential Statistics

General Design Classifications for Difference Questions

Many research questions focus on whether there is a significant difference between two or more groups or conditions. When a group comparison or difference question is asked, the design can be classified as between groups or within subjects. Understanding this distinction is essential in order to determine the proper statistical analysis for this type of question.

Between Groups Designs

Between groups designs are defined as designs where each participant in the research is in *one and only one* condition or group. For example, in a study investigating the effects of teaching style on student satisfaction, there may be three groups (or conditions or values) of the independent variable, teaching style. These conditions could be authoritarian, participatory, and a combination of the two. In a between groups design, each participant receives only one of the three conditions or levels. If the investigator wished to have 20 participants in each group, then 60 participants would be needed to carry out the research.

Within Subjects or Repeated Measures Designs

Within subjects designs are conceptually the opposite of between groups designs. In these designs, each participant in the research *receives or experiences all of the conditions* or levels of the independent variable in order to complete the study. Using the above example of the investigation of the effects of the independent variable, teaching style, on the dependent variable, student satisfaction, there still would be three conditions or levels to the independent variable, teaching style. These conditions are authoritarian teaching style, participatory teaching style, and a combination of the two. In a within subjects design, each participant would experience and be measured for student satisfaction on all three conditions or levels of the independent variable. If the researcher wished to have 20 participants for each condition, only 20 participants would be needed to carry out the research because each participant undergoes all three conditions of the independent variable in the research. Because each participant is assessed more than once (i.e., for each condition), these designs are also referred to as *repeated measures* designs. Within subjects designs have appeal due to the smaller number of participants needed and reduction in error variance. However, they may be less appropriate than between groups designs in applied settings because of the possibility of *carryover* or *practice effects*. If the purpose of the study is to investigate conditions that may result in a long-term or permanent change, such as learning, it is not possible for a participant to be in one condition, and then "unlearn" that condition to be in the same previous state to start the next condition. Within subjects designs may be appropriate, if the effects of order of presentation are negligible, when participants are asked, for example, to evaluate several topics. Order effects can be controlled by presenting the conditions to participants in different orders (e.g., in random orders or counterbalanced so that, for example, half receive Condition A first and half receive Condition B first). Within subjects designs also are used when there is a pretest and a posttest. In this introductory book, we will demonstrate only one within subjects statistic, the paired samples *t* test, because the statistics used for three or more repeated measures are quite complex. We also use within subject designs when we have paired or related or matched samples.

Data Formats

The data format for between groups and within subjects designs can be illustrated to help visualize what is happening in the research. This method *depicts how the data are entered into the computer* for statistical analyses. All the data for *each participant* are placed in a single horizontal row.

Between group designs. Suppose that we have a between groups design with two independent variables, teaching style and gender. Each independent variable has two levels (teaching style, traditional or participatory; and gender, male or female). The data would be entered as follows, assuming 12 participants were assigned (3 each) to the four groups. Of course, most studies would have many more participants.

Participant Number	**Teaching Style**	**Gender**	**Math Achievement**
1	1	1	DV
2	1	1	DV
3	1	1	DV
4	1	2	DV
5	1	2	DV
6	1	2	DV
7	2	1	DV
8	2	1	DV
9	2	1	DV
10	2	2	DV
11	2	2	DV
12	2	2	DV

Key to Values

Teaching Style
1 Traditional
2 Participatory

Gender
1 Male
2 Female

Math Achievement
DV = a score, or value on the dependent variable, math achievement

In this example, each participant in each group is observed/measured once on the dependent variable, a measure of math achievement. Four columns are seen in this example. The first column is a participant identification number. The next two columns represent the two independent variables. The last column is for the dependent variable. The order of the columns is usually not important when using SPSS.

Within subjects or repeated measures designs. In contrast to between groups designs, no one column is used to identify the *independent variable* in within subjects designs. SPSS will compute and you will name the independent variable based on the dependent variable, which is measured two or more times. Each measurement is placed in a separate column with a somewhat different SPSS name. Suppose that we have a study which uses a within subjects design, with one within subjects independent variable. Let's call the independent variable "education"; it has two levels, one for each parent. Because the independent variable is a within subject independent variable, each participant has two scores, one for his/her father and one for mother.

Note that the dependent variable (math achievement) scores are what go in each column. The data are entered as follows:

Participant Number	**Mother's Education**	**Father's Education**
1	DV	DV
2	DV	DV
3	DV	DV
4	DV	DV
5	DV	DV
6	DV	DV

Note that each dependent variable must have a different SPSS variable name such as *MoEduc* and *FaEduc*.

Designs with more than one within subject/repeated measures variable are possible but less common.

Labeling Difference Question Designs

It is helpful to have a brief descriptive label for a research design that identifies the design for other researchers. The labels we use, based on the **design classification,** also guide us toward the proper statistics to use. We do not have classifications for the descriptive or associational approaches so this section applies to difference questions and the randomized experimental, quasi-experimental, and comparative approaches. Designs are usually labeled in terms of the *overall type of design* (between groups or within subjects), the *number of independent variables*, and the *number of levels within each* independent variable.

Single factor designs. If the design has only one independent variable (either a between groups design or a within subjects design), then it should be described as a basic or *single factor design*. (Factor is another name for independent variable). For example, a between groups design with one independent variable and four levels would be described as a single factor design with four levels. If the same design was a within subjects design with four levels, then it would be described as a single factor repeated measures design with four levels. Note that "between groups" is not stated directly in the first example but is implied because there is no mention of repeated measures.

Between groups factorial designs. When there is more than one independent variable, the design is called a factorial or complex design. In these cases the number of levels of *each* independent variable becomes important in the description of the design. For example, suppose that a design has two between groups independent variables; the first independent variable has two levels and the second independent variable has three levels. The design is written as a 2 x 3 factorial design (factorial means two or more independent variables or factors). Notice again that between groups is not explicitly mentioned but is implied because there is no mention of repeated measures, as in a within subjects design description. Since the design is a between groups design, the number of groups needed to carry out the study is 2 multiplied by 3 or 6 groups.

Mixed factorial designs. If the design has a between groups variable and a within subjects variable, it is called a mixed design. For example, if the design has two independent variables, each with two levels, it is described as a 2 x 2 factorial design with repeated measures on the second factor. This design is common in experimental studies with a pretest and posttest, but the analysis can be complex. In this book we will not analyze mixed factorial designs as such, however, the independent samples *t* test can be used to compare experimental and control groups on *change scores* based on the difference between pretest and posttest scores.

Remember, when describing a design, that *each* independent variable is given one number, which is the number of *levels* for that variable. Thus a design description with three numbers (e.g., 2 x 3 x 4) has *three* independent variables or factors, which have 2, 3, and 4 levels. A single factor design is described in words, as above, and not with numerals and multiplication signs. The *dependent* variable is *not* part of the design description, so is not considered in this section.

Selection of Inferential Statistics

Now that we have introduced the basic design concepts, it is time to begin thinking about which of the many possible inferential statistics to use. This section may seem overwhelming at first because many statistical tests are introduced. It is probably wise to come back to this chapter later, from time to time, when you have to make a decision about which statistic to use.
We will present three steps that will help in the selection of the proper statistical test for data analysis. In order to utilize these steps, you must review a number of things from chapter 1 and the first part of this chapter. Remember that difference questions compare groups and utilize the statistics, which we called difference inferential statistics (see Fig. 2.1). These statistics (e.g., *t* test and analysis of variance) will be computed in chapter 10 and 11 and are shown here in Table 7.1.

Associational questions utilize what we called associational inferential statistics and will be computed in chapters 9 and 11. The statistics in this group examine the association or relationship between two or more variables and are shown in Table 7.2.

It is worth noting that there may be more than one appropriate statistical analysis. One might assume, since the statistical formulas are precise mathematically, that this precision generalizes to the choice of a statistical test. As we shall see, that is not always true.

Using Tables 7.1 and 7.2 to Select Statistics

As with research questions and hypotheses (discussed in chapter 1), we divide inferential statistics into two levels of complexity: basic and complex. For *basic* statistics there is *one* independent and *one* dependent variable. For complex statistics there are more than two variables. We call them *complex* rather than multivariate because there is not unanimity about the definition of multivariate, and several such complex statistics (e.g., factoral ANOVA) are not usually classified as multivariate.

The statistics shown in Tables 7.1 and 7.2 are each discussed in the remaining chapters in this book, and assignments and outputs are given demonstrating how to compute them using SPSS 10.0. There are many other statistics, but these tables include the most common inferential statistics that you will encounter in reading research articles. Fig. 7.1 is a decision tree to help you use Tables 7.1 and 7.2.

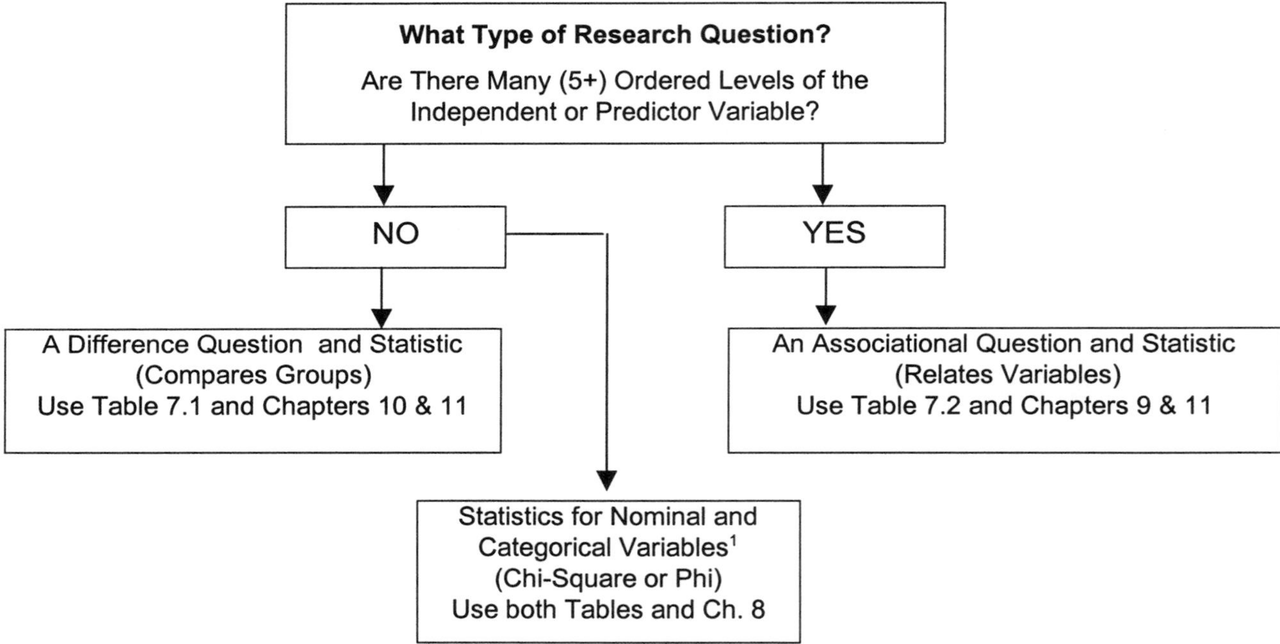

Fig. 7.1. A decision tree to decide how to select the appropriate statistic from Tables 7.1 to 7.2.

[1] If the dependent or both variables are nominal (including dichotomous) or have a few ordered categories, it is best to use the inferential statistics displayed in chapter 8: chi-square or phi/Cramer's V. Use phi or Cramer's V (Table 7.2) if you want to assess the *strength* of the association between two nominal variables.

First, decide whether your research question or hypothesis is a *difference* one (i.e., compares groups) or an *associational* one (relates variables). Our rule of thumb is that if the independent or predictor variable has five or more *ordered* levels or values, the question should be considered an associational one. The former leads you to Table 7.1 and the latter to Table 7.2.

Table 7.1. ***Selection of an Appropriate Inferential Statistic for Basic, Two Variable, Difference Questions or Hypotheses (for Comparing Groups)*** [♦]

Scale of measure of **dependent variable** ↓	Independent samples or groups (between)			Repeated measures or related samples (within)
	One independent variable with only 2 values or levels or groups	One independent variable 2 or more values or levels or groups	Two independent variables	One independent variable with 2 categories or levels or groups
Dependent variable is scale data; i.e., is normally distributed	**Independent Samples *t* Test Ch. 10**	**One-Way ANOVA (*F*) ch. 10**	**Two-Way Factorial ANOVA (3*F*s) ch.11**	**Paired Samples *t* Test ch.10**
Dependent variable is categorical, especially if nominal data	**Chi-Square (χ^2) ch. 8**	**Chi-Square(χ^2) ch. 8**		

Second, if your question is a *difference question*, you must determine: (a) the measurement of the *dependent* variable (b) whether the design is between groups or within subjects, (c) whether there is one or more than one (i.e., two) independent variables, and (d) how many (values or levels or groups or samples) there are in your independent variable. The answers to these questions lead to a specific box and statistic in Table 7.1.

Table 7.2. ***Selection of an Appropriate Inferential Statistic for Associational Questions or Hypotheses (for the Associational Approach)***

Two variables or scores for the same or related subjects 1 independent/predictor variable & 1 dependent variable			3 or more variables; 2 or more independent or predictor variables & 1 dependent variable
One or both variables nominal	Both variables at least ordinal data (one can be scale)	Both Variables scale, approximately normal	Independent variables are scale and/or dichotomous, dependent variable is scale
Phi or Cramer's *V* Ch. 8	**Spearman (rho) Ch. 9**	**Pearson (*r*) Ch.9**	**Multiple Regression (*R*) Ch.11**

[♦] It is acceptable to use statistics which are in the box(es) **below** the appropriate statistic, but there is usually some loss of information and power. **It is not acceptable to use statistics above the appropriate box.**

Third, if instead you ask an *associational question*, use Table 7.2. Which column you use depends on (a) whether you have two or more than two independent/predictor variables and (b) the measurement of the variables.

A Qualification

Something that is not obvious from Tables 7.1 and 7.2 or the decision tree is that the broad question *of whether there is a relationship between variables X and Y can be answered two ways.*[2] If both the independent variable and dependent variable provide approximately interval level data with five or more levels, the statistic to use, based on Figure 7.1, is the Pearson correlation, and that would be our recommendation. However, some researchers choose to divide the independent variable into two or several categories or groups such as low, medium, and high and then do a one-way ANOVA. Conversely, others who start with an independent variable that has only a few (say two through four *ordered* categories) may choose to do a correlation instead of a one-way ANOVA. While these choices are not necessarily wrong, they are less common, and we do not think they are the best practices.

Interpreting the Results of a Statistical Test

The rationale, SPSS commands, and interpretation of each of the above specific statistics are presented in the following chapters in some detail. For each statistic (i.e., t, F, χ^2, r, etc.) the calculations produce a number or *calculated value* based on the specific data in your study. See the left side of Fig. 7.2 for *approximate* values when the study has about 50 participants or is a 2 x 2 chi-square.

Statistical Significance

To interpret the calculated value, it is compared to *critical values* found in a statistics table or stored in the computer's memory, taking into account the degrees of freedom, which are usually based on the number of participants. Remember that the critical values in Fig. 7.2 are only correct for studies with about 50 participants. The middle column of Fig. 7.2 shows how to interpret any inferential test once you know the probability level (p) from the computer or whether the calculated value is greater than the critical value. In general, if the calculated value of the statistics (t, F, etc.) is relatively large, the probability or p is small, e.g., .05, .01, .001. If the probability is *less than* the preset alpha level (usually .05), we can say that the results are *statistically significant* or that they are significant at the .05 level or that $p < .05$. We can also reject the null hypothesis of no difference or no relationship. We do not usually state it, but we could think about the degree of certainty ($1-p$) in the results as shown on the right side of Fig. 7.2. Note that computer printouts such as those from SPSS make determination of statistical significance of the various statistics quite easy by printing the actual significance or probability

[2] As discussed in chapter 1, difference and associational questions are subcategories of the general relationship question. This is consistent with the statement by statisticians that all common parametric inferential statistics are relational. However we think it is helpful to students to make the distinction between difference questions (and statistics) and associational questions (and statistics.)

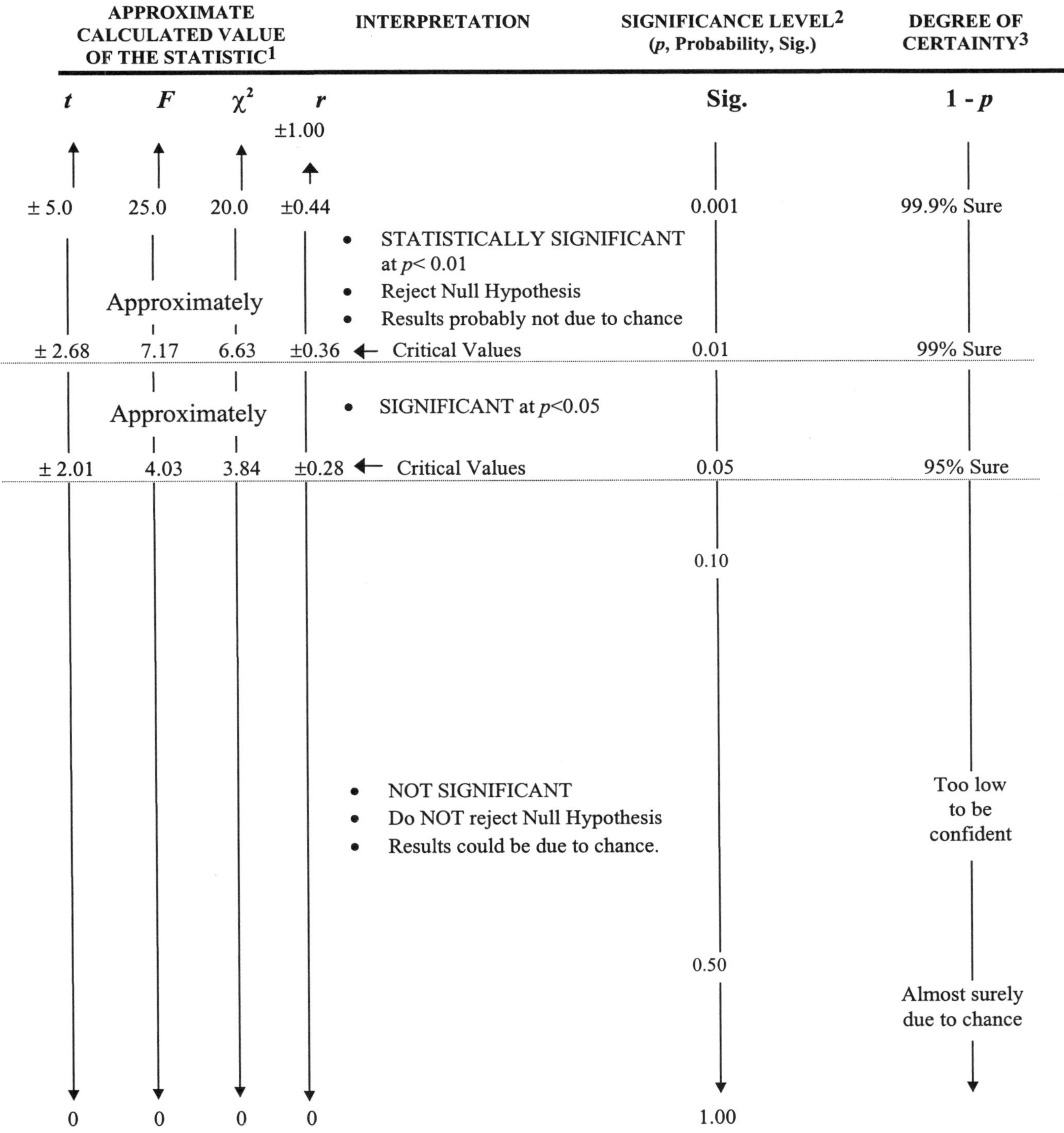

APPROXIMATE CALCULATED VALUE OF THE STATISTIC[1]
INTERPRETATION
SIGNIFICANCE LEVEL[2] (p, Probability, Sig.)
DEGREE OF CERTAINTY[3]
t
F
χ²
r
Sig.
1 - p
±1.00
± 5.0
25.0
20.0
±0.44
0.001
99.9% Sure
STATISTICALLY SIGNIFICANT at p< 0.01
Reject Null Hypothesis
Results probably not due to chance
Approximately
± 2.68
7.17
6.63
±0.36
Critical Values
0.01
99% Sure
Approximately
SIGNIFICANT at p<0.05
± 2.01
4.03
3.84
±0.28
Critical Values
0.05
95% Sure
0.10
NOT SIGNIFICANT
Do NOT reject Null Hypothesis
Results could be due to chance.
Too low to be confident
0.50
Almost surely due to chance
0
0
0
0
1.00

[1] For these examples, $df = 50$ for t test; $df = 1, 50$ for F (ANOVA); $df = 1$ for χ^2 ; $df = 50$ for r (Pearson Correlation). **Note, if your sample is more or less than 50, the critical values will not be exactly the same.**

[2] This is the probability that the results are due to chance; i.e., probability of a *Type I Error.*

[3] This is the probability or level of confidence that the results are not due to chance.

Note: When the output indicates that the probability or significance = 0.000, you should state that $p<0.001$.

Fig. 7.2. Interpreting inferential statistics.

level (*p*) so you do not have to look up a critical value in a table. This translates all of the common inferential statistics into a common metric, the significance level or **sig**. This level is also the probability of a Type I error or the probability of rejecting the null hypothesis when it is actually true. Thus, regardless of what specific statistic you use, if the sig. or *p* is small (usually less than .05) the finding is *statistically* significant and you reject the null hypothesis.

Practical Significance and Effect Size

However, statistical significance is not the same as *practical* significance or importance. With large samples we can find statistical significance even when the differences or associations are quite small/low. Thus, in addition to statistical significance, we will, in the assignments, examine measures of the *confidence interval* and *effect size* (or how much variance in the dependent variable can be predicted from the independent variable). We will see that it is quite possible to have a statistically significant result that is quite weak (i.e., has a low effect size.) Remember that the null hypothesis is that there is *no* difference or *no* association. A significant result with a low effect size means that we can be very confident that there is *some* difference or association, but it is small and maybe not of practical importance.

Further Steps in Interpreting Inferential Statistics

When you interpret inferential statistics, you first *decide whether to reject the null hypothesis.* However, that is not enough for a full interpretation. If you find that the outcome is statistically significant, you need to answer two *more* questions.

Second, *what is the direction of the effect?* Difference inferential statistics compare groups so it is necessary to state which group performed better. We discuss how to do this in chapters 10 and 11. For associational inferential statistics (e.g., correlation), the sign is very important, so you must indicate whether the association or relationship is positive or negative. We discuss how to interpret correlations in chapters 8, 9, and 11.

Third, *what is the size of the effect?* We, and the American Psychological Association Publications Manual (1994), recommend that you include confidence intervals or effect size measures or both in the description of your results. We will discuss confidence intervals and effect sizes in the next section.

Problems with Null Hypothesis Significance Testing (NHST)

There has been an increase in resistance to null hypothesis significance testing (NHST) in the social sciences during recent years. Although researchers have periodically objected to the use of NHST throughout the past three decades, the intensity of objection has increased recently, especially within the disciplines of psychology and education.

The first problem with NHST involves the interpretation of statistically significant difference in the form of an all-or-none decision. There is a tendency to accept something as significant or not significant, rather than acknowledge that statistical significance implies a probability of uncertainty. In addition when we dichotomize statistical significance in this way, we become removed from the actual data of our study. One alternative approach to NHST is to create *confidence intervals.*

Confidence Intervals

These provide more practical information than does NHST. For example, suppose one knew that an increase in reading scores of 15 points obtained on a particular instrument would lead to a functional increase in reading performance. Two different methods of instruction are compared. One method results in a statistically significant gain compared to the other method. According to NHST, we would reject the null hypothesis of no difference between methods and conclude that our new method is better. If we apply confidence intervals to this same study, we can determine an interval that contains our population mean difference 95% of the time. We can also see that, if the lower bound of that interval is greater than 15 points, we can conclude that using this method of instruction would increase functional reading levels.

Effect Size

A second major problem with NHST also concerns the interpretation of statistical significance. This second misinterpretation of statistical significance occurs when one assumes that a statistically significant outcome gives information about the size of the outcome. Therefore, it is important to state, in addition to information on statistical significance, the size of the effect. An effect size is defined as the strength of the relationship between the independent variable and the dependent variable.

Effect size for difference statistics. If one compares two groups, perhaps an intervention group to a control group, the effect size (*d*) could be computed by subtracting the mean of the control group from the mean of the intervention group and dividing by the pooled standard deviation of both groups as follows:

$$d = \frac{M_I - M_e}{SD_{pooled}}$$

Note that *d* is expressed in standard deviation units so a *d* of .5 means that the groups differ by one half a pooled standard deviation.

Effect size for associational statistics. Another method of expressing effect sizes is as a correlation coefficient, *r,* (Rosenthal, 1994). Chapter 9 provides a discussion of correlation and how to interpret it. Using this method, effect sizes are always less than 1.0, varying between –1.0 and +1.0.

Issues about effect size measures. Unfortunately, there are many different effect size measures and little agreement about which to use. Although *d* is the most commonly discussed effect size measure, it is not usually available from the popular computer packages such as SPSS. The correlation coefficient, *r,* or similar measures of the strength of association such as eta^2 are more commonly available in statistical outputs.

There is disagreement among researchers about whether it is best to express effect size as r or r^2 (eta or eta^2). It has been common to use the squared versions because they indicate the percentage of variance in the dependent variable that can be predicted from the independent variable(s). However, Rosenthal (1994) argues that these usually small percentages give you an underestimated impression of the strength or importance of the effect. Thus, he and we argue that it is better to use *r*, eta, or *R* (multiple correlation).

Although the *Publication Manual of the American Psychological Association* (APA, 1994) recommends that researchers report effect sizes, relatively few researchers did so before 1999 when The APA Task Force on Statistical Inference stated that effect sizes should *always* be reported for your primary results (Wilkinson & The Task Force, 1999). In the future, it is likely that most articles will discuss the size of the effect as well as whether or not the result was statistically significant and the direction of the effect.

Interpreting Effect Sizes

Assuming that you have computed either *d* or *r*, how should it be interpreted? Cohen (1988) provides a rule of thumb for interpreting the practical importance in the behavioral sciences of both *d* and *r* as follows:

small effect	$d = .2$	$r = .1 = r^2$ or eta^2 of .01
medium effect	$d = .5$	$r = .3 = r^2$ or eta^2 of .09
large effect	$d = .8$	$r = .5 = r^2$ or eta^2 of .25

Note that these guidelines are based on the effect sizes *usually found* in studies in the behavioral sciences and education. Thus, they have no absolute meaning; large, medium, and small are only relative to typical findings in these areas. This rule of thumb will not apply to all subfields in the behavioral sciences, and it definitely will not apply to disciplines where the usually expected effects are either larger or smaller. For example, the effects of taking a daily aspirin on heart attacks is much smaller than shown here but is important because it is a life or death matter.

Cohen provides research examples of small, medium, and large effects to support the suggested *d* and *r* values. Most researchers would not consider a correlation (*r*) of .5 to be very strong because only 25% of the variance in the dependent variable is predicted. However, Cohen argues that a *d* of .8 (and an *r* of .5, which he shows are mathematically similar) are "grossly perceptible and therefore large differences, as (for example is) the mean difference in height between 13- and 18-year-old girls" (p.27). Cohen states that a small effect may be difficult to detect, perhaps because it is in a less well controlled area of research. Cohen's medium size effect is "...visible to the naked eye. That is, in the course of normal experiences, one would become aware of an average difference in IQ between clerical and semi-skilled workers..." (p. 26).

Figure 7.3 summarizes the three steps discussed above about how to fully interpret the results of an inferential statistic.

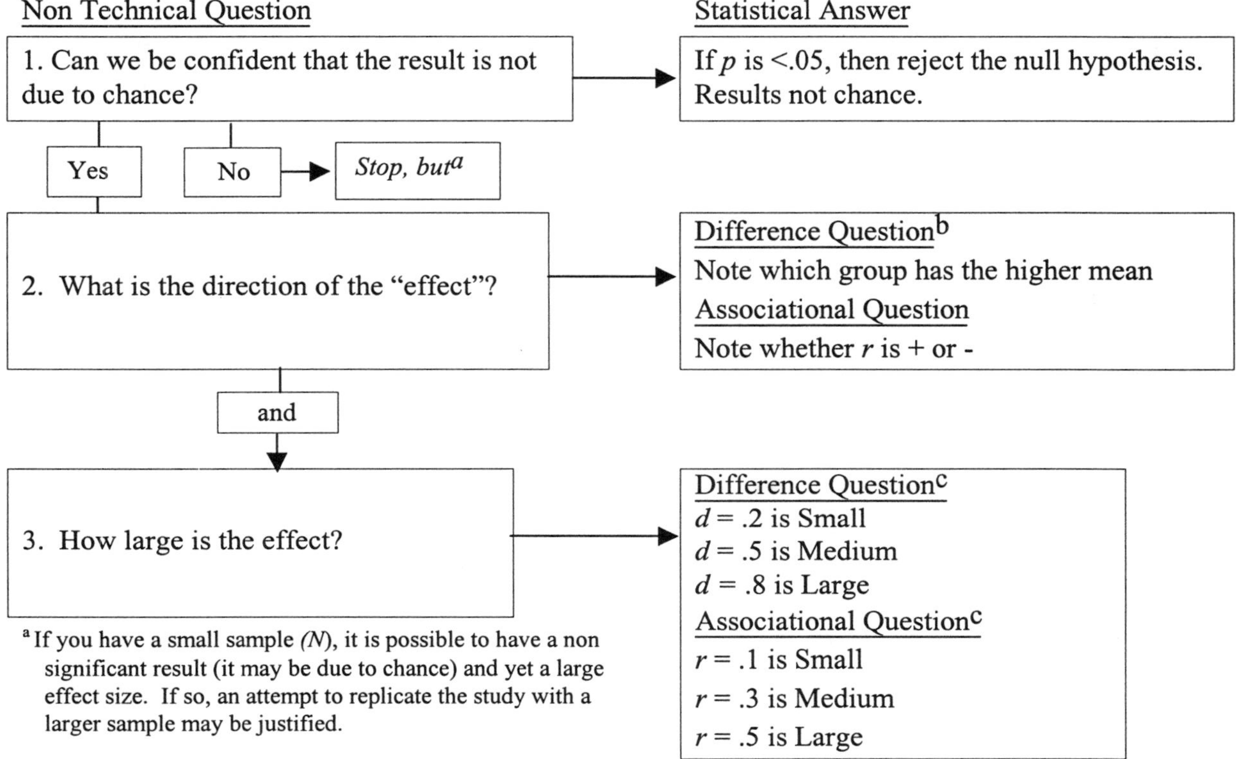
Non Technical Question
Statistical Answer
1. Can we be confident that the result is not due to chance?
If p is <.05, then reject the null hypothesis. Results not chance.
Yes
No
Stop, but[a]
2. What is the direction of the "effect"?
Difference Question[b]
Note which group has the higher mean
Associational Question
Note whether r is + or -
and
3. How large is the effect?
Difference Question[c]
d = .2 is Small
d = .5 is Medium
d = .8 is Large
Associational Question[c]
r = .1 is Small
r = .3 is Medium
r = .5 is Large
[a] If you have a small sample (N), it is possible to have a non significant result (it may be due to chance) and yet a large effect size. If so, an attempt to replicate the study with a larger sample may be justified.

[b] If there are three or more means or a significant interaction a post hoc test (e.g., Tukey) will be necessary for complete interpretation.

[c] Interpretation of effect size is based on Cohen (1988). A "large" effect is one that Cohen states is "grossly perceptible." It is larger than typically found but does not necessarily explain a large amount of variance. You might use confidence intervals in addition or instead of d with difference questions.

Fig. 7.3. Steps in the interpretation of an inferential statistic.

An Example of How to Select and Interpret Inferential Statistics

As a review of what you have read in chapters 2, 3, and 7 and computed with SPSS in chapters 5 and 6, we will provide an extended example. We will walk you through the process of identifying the variables, research questions, and approach, and then we will show how we selected appropriate statistics and interpreted the results.

Research problem. Suppose your research problem was *to investigate the relationships of gender and test anxiety to math achievement.*

Identification of the variables and their measurement. The research problem specifies three variables: gender, test anxiety, and math achievement. The latter appears to be the outcome or dependent variable, and gender and test anxiety are the independent or predictor variables. As such, they are *presumed* to have an effect on math achievement scores.

What is the level of measurement for these three variables? *Gender* is clearly dichotomous (male or female), which would be labeled "nominal" in SPSS. *Test anxiety* is probably measured with some sort of inventory and has many ordered values, from very low to very high anxiety. Assume that this is scale data because it is very likely that most students have anxiety scores in the middle of the range with fewer that have very high or very low scores. Likewise, *math achievement* test scores would have many levels, with more scores (the mode) somewhere in the middle than at the high and low ends. It would be wise to check whether test anxiety and math achievement are at least approximately normally distributed by requesting that SPSS compute the skewness of each as you did in chapter 6.

Research questions. There are a number of possible research questions and statistics that could be used with these three variables, including all the types of questions in Appendix A, the descriptive statistics discussed in chapter 3, and the inferential statistics in this chapter. However, we will focus on three research questions and three inferential statistics because they deal well with the research problem and fit our earlier recommendations for good choices. First, we will discuss two basic research questions, given the above specification of the variables and their measurement. Later, we will discuss a complex research question that could actually be used instead of question 1 and 2, which are:

1. *Is there a difference between male and female genders in regard to their average math achievement scores?*

2. *Is there an association between test anxiety and math achievement?*

Type of research question. Using Fig. 7.1 and Table 7.2, you should see that the first question is phrased as a *basic difference question* because there are only two variables and two (nominal) levels of the independent variable. The second question is phrased as *a basic associational question* because there are many ordered levels of test anxiety, the predictor (or independent variable).

Selection of an appropriate statistic. If you examine Table 7.1, we hope you will see that the first question should be answered with an *independent samples t test* because a) the dependent variable (math achievement) is scale data, b) the design is between groups (males and females form two independent groups), c) there is only one independent variable, and d) it has two values (male and female). As you can see from Table 7.2, the second research question should be answered with a *Pearson correlation* because both anxiety and math achievement are normally distributed, scale data.

Interpretation of the results for question 1. The interpretation of the t for question 1 depends, of course, on the data. Lets assume that about 50 students participated in the study and that $t =$

2.05. SPSS will give you the exact **Sig.**, but you can also tell from Fig. 7.2 that $p < .05$ and, thus, t is *statistically significant*. **(However, if you had 25 participants this *t* would not have been significant.** Remember that the t, F, χ^2 and r values in Table 7.2 necessary for statistical significance are only *approximate* and depend on the sample size!)

Deciding whether the statistic is significant only means the result is unlikely to be due to chance. You still have to state the direction of the result and the effect size and/or the confidence interval (See Fig. 7.3). *To determine the direction*, we need to know the mean (average) math achievement scores for males and females. Let's assume that males have the higher mean. If so, you can be quite certain that males in the population are at least a little better at math achievement than females.

The *effect size* can be determined by computing d as shown earlier. First, figure the pooled (weighted average) standard deviation for male and female math achievement scores. Let's say that the difference between the means was 2.0 and the pooled standard deviation was 4.0, then d would be .50, a medium size effect according to Cohen (1988). This means that the difference is typical of the statistically significant findings in the behavioral sciences, but $d = .5$ may or may not be a large enough difference to use for recommending programmatic changes.

Confidence intervals might help you decide if the difference in math achievement scores was large enough to have practical significance. For example, say you found (from the lower bound of the confidence interval as discussed in chapter 10) that you could only be confident that there was a 2 point difference between males and females. Then you could decide whether that was a big enough difference to justify, for example, a programmatic change.

Interpretation of the results for research question 2. The interpretation of r is based on similar decisions. If $r = -.30$ (with 50 subjects), it would be *statistically significant* at the $p < .05$ level. Figure 7.3 shows that, if the r is statistically significant, you still need to discuss the *direction* of the correlation. Because the correlation is negative, we would say that students with *high* test anxiety tend to perform at the *low* end on math achievement and those with low anxiety tend to perform well on math achievement. The *effect size* of $r = -.30$ is the same as +.30; i.e., medium according to Cohen (1988).

Note that if N were 25, the r would not be significant. On the other hand, if N were 1000 and $r = .30$, p would be $< .0001$. With $N = 1000$, even $r = .10$ would be statistically significant, indicating that you could be quite sure the association was not zero, but the effect size would be small.

Complex research question and statistics. As you will see in chapter 11, there are advantages of considering the two independent variables (gender and test anxiety) together rather than separately as in questions 1 and 2. There are two statistics, that you will compute, that could be used to consider gender and test anxiety together. The first is *multiple regression*. If you examine Table 7.2 again, you will see that with two (or more) independent variables that are scale and/or dichotomous and one dependent variable that is scale data, the appropriate associational statistic would be multiple regression. The interpretation of the results would be similar to that for *r*. The research question, which subsumes both 1 and 2, would be:

3. *Is there a combination of gender and test anxiety that predicts math achievement better than either one alone?*

We will wait to discuss the interpretation until chapter 11. Finally, a two way *factorial ANOVA* would be another statistic that could be used to consider both gender and test anxiety simultaneously. However, to use ANOVA the many levels of test anxiety would have to be recoded into two or three (perhaps high, medium, and low). Because information is lost when you do such a recode, we would not recommend factorial ANOVA for this example. Chapter 11 and Appendix A provide more information about the research questions and interpretation of this complex difference statistic.

Conclusion. Now you should be ready to study each of the statistics in Tables 7.1 and 7.2 and learn more about their computation and interpretation. It may be tough going at times, but hopefully this overview has given you a good foundation. It would be wise for you to review this chapter, especially the tables and figures from time to time. If you do, you will have a good grasp of how the various statistics fit together, when to use them, and how to interpret the results. You will need this information to understand the chapters that follow.

Interpretation Questions

1. Compare and contrast a between groups design and a within groups design.

2. What things about variables, levels, and design should you keep in mind in order to choose an appropriate statistic?

3. a) A design description of 2 x 4 x 4 has how many independent variables or factors? How many levels of each?
   b) What part does the dependent variable play in labeling a design?

4. a) Is there always only one appropriate statistic to use for each research design?
   b) Explain your answer.

5. When $p < .05$, what does this signify?

6. Given a study with two variables, each of which has 10 ordered levels and the responses for both variables are normally distributed, which statistic would you recommend?

7. If you computed a correlation of $r = -.31$ ($p < .035$) between anxiety and test performance, how would you interpret the results? (Use Fig. 7.3)

8. What statistic would you use if you had two independent variables, income group (<$10,000, $10,000-$30,000, >$30,000) and ethnic group (Hispanic, Caucasian, African-American), and one normally distributed dependent variable (self-efficacy at work).

9. What statistic would you use if you had one independent variable, geographic location (North, South, East, West), and one dependent variable (satisfaction with living environment, Yes or No)?

10. What statistic would you use if you had three normally distributed (scale) and one dichotomous independent variable (weight of participants, age of participants, height of participants and gender)? The dependent variable was positive self-image, which is normally distributed.

11. A teacher *ranked* the students in her Algebra I class from 1=highest to 25=lowest in terms of their grades on several tests. After the next semester, she checked the school records to see what the students received from their Algebra II teacher. The research question is 'Is there a relationship between rank in Algebra I and grades in Algebra II?' What statistic should she use?

CHAPTER 8

Cross-Tabulation, Chi-Square, and Phi (or Cramer's V)

In this chapter you will learn how to make cross-tabulation tables from two variables, both of which have a few categories or values. You will also learn how to decide if there is a statistically significant relationship between the two variables.

Lab Assignment D

Logon and Get Data

- First logon and get **HsbData** (you saved it after correcting errors in chapter 6).

Problem 1: Cross-Tabulate Math Grades and Gender

When you have two variables both of which have nominal categories or have a few ordered categories, you can do a cross-tabulation to see how many participants of each category on one variable have scores that fall into each category on the other variable. The first problem involves producing a cross-tabulation table, using the SPSS command **Crosstabs**. This table, shown in Output 8.1, is a descriptive statistic. In problem 2, you will start by cross-tabulating two variables, as in problem 1, but go on to request two inferential statistics: chi-square and phi (or Cramer's V). These inferential statistics tell you how likely it is that the relationship between the two variables is due to chance.

Problem/Research Question

What does the cross-tabulation of *math grades* and *gender* tell us?

To do **Crosstabs** follow these steps:

- Click on **Analyze => Descriptive Statistics => Crosstabs**.
- Put *math grades* in the **Rows** box using the arrow key and put *gender* (gender of student) in the **Columns** box (see Fig. 8.1). It is arbitrary which variable is put in rows and which in columns, but it is logical to put the independent variable in the columns.
- Click on **Cells**.
- Now, click on **Expected** and **Total**; ensure that **Observed** is also checked (see Fig. 8.2).
- Click on **Continue** then **OK** in Fig. 8.1. Compare your syntax and output to Output 8.1.

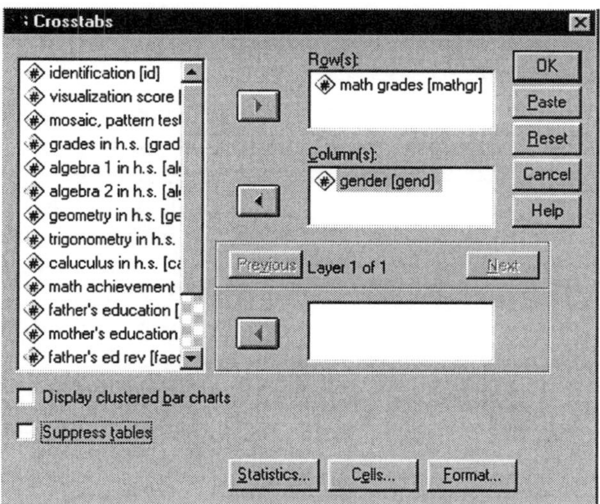

Fig. 8.1. Crosstabs.

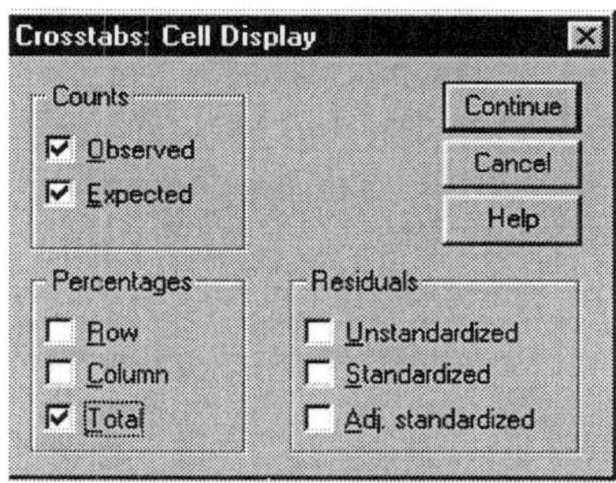

Fig. 8.2. Crosstabs: Cell display.

Output 8.1: Crosstabs

Case Processing Summary

	Cases					
	Valid		Missing		Total	
	N	Percent	N	Percent	N	Percent
math grades * gender	73	97.3%	2	2.7%	75	100.0%

math grades * gender Crosstabulation

			gender		Total
			male	female	
math grades	less A-B	Count	24	18	42
		Expected Count	19.6	22.4	42.0
		% of Total	32.9%	24.7%	57.5%
	most A-B	Count	10	21	31
		Expected Count	14.4	16.6	31.0
		% of Total	13.7%	28.8%	42.5%
Total		Count	34	39	73
		Expected Count	34.0	39.0	73.0
		% of Total	46.6%	53.4%	100.0%

Note that there is a moderate size discrepancy between the observed **Count** and the **Expected Count.** If these discrepancies are large the relationship would be statistically significant.

Interpretation of Output 8.1

The first table indicates that 2 of the 75 cases or participants are missing information about either *math grades* or *gender* or both. The crosstabulation table shows the **Count** or number of persons of each gender that have a high or low math grade. It also shows the **Expected Count** based on what one would expect by chance. In addition to the counts and expected counts, each cell also has a **% of Total.** For example, there are 24 males with low math grades, which is 32.9% of the 73 students. The bottom row and the right hand column provide total percentages for the two levels of each variable. For example, 34 or 46.6% of the 73 students were males, and 42 or 57.5% of both genders had low math grades.

By examining the discrepancy between the Count and the Expected Count, we can get clues about the difference between male and female students with regard to whether their math grades are high or low. However, we need to be cautious about this interpretation. In problem 2 we will use an inferential statistic (chi-square) to inform us about how likely it is that differences such as these could occur by chance.

Problem 2: Chi-Square and Phi or Cramer's V

These statistics are used when you have data that can be easily cross-tabulated. You can use ordered data with a few categories (e.g., low, medium, and high) but chi-square and Cramer's V will treat the data as if they were nominal. Both chi-square and phi (or Cramer's V) tell you whether there is a significant relationship between the two variables. Chi-square tells you whether the relationship is statistically significant, but the size of the chi-square does not indicate the strength of the relationship. Another way to interpret chi-square is as a test of whether there are differences between the groups formed from one variable, (gender in this problem) on the incidence (counts) of each category of the other variable.

Phi and Cramer's V also provide a test of statistical significance, but in addition indicate the *strength* of the relationship. These are measures of association as are the correlations you will compute in the next chapter. Like correlation, a strong phi or Cramer's V would be close to 1.0 while one close to zero would indicate no relationship.

Problem/Research Question

Do boys and girls differ on whether they take geometry or not?

Let's see if boys and girls differ in terms of whether they took geometry. Remember, this variable has two values: less A-B = 0 (low) and most A-B = 1 (high). If we assumed that *math grades* is a nominal variable, then chi-square is the appropriate statistic.

- Click on **Analyze => Descriptive Statistics => Crosstabs**.
- Click on **Reset.**
- Put *geometry* in the **Rows** box using the arrow key and put *gender* in the **Columns** box (see Fig. 8.3).

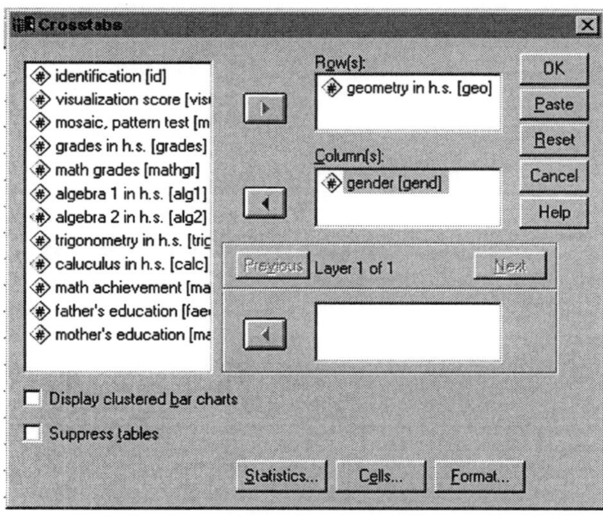

Fig. 8.3. Crosstabs.

- Next, click on **Statistics** to see Fig. 8.4.
- Check **Chi-square** and **Phi and Cramer's V**.
- Click on **Continue**.
- Once you return to the **Crosstabs** menu, click on **Cells**.

- Now, click on **Expected** and **Total**; ensure that **Observed** is also checked (see Fig. 8.5).

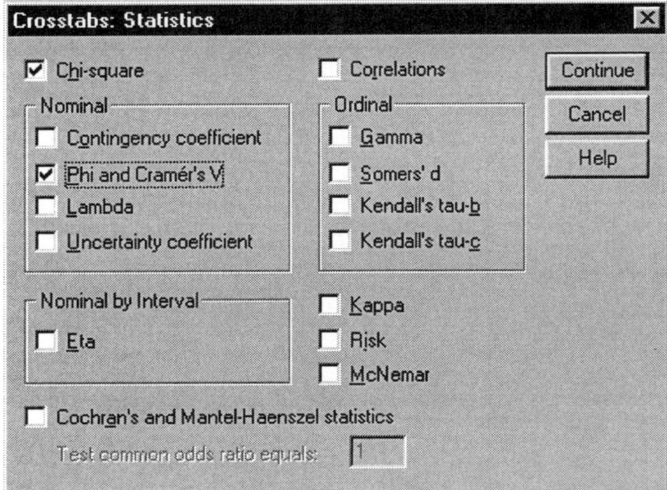

Fig. 8.4. Crosstabs statistics.

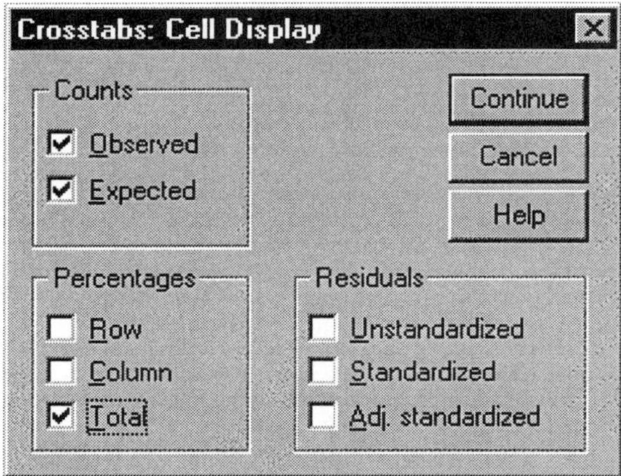

Fig. 8.5. Crosstabs: Cell display.

- Click on **Continue** then **OK**. Compare your output to Output 8.2.

Output 8.2: Crosstabs Plus Chi-Square and Phi

Case Processing Summary

	Cases					
	Valid		Missing		Total	
	N	Percent	N	Percent	N	Percent
geometry in h.s. * gender	73	97.3%	2	2.7%	75	100.0%

geometry in h.s. * gender Crosstabulation

			gender		Total
			male	female	
geometry in h.s.	not taken	Count	10	27	37
		Expected Count	17.2	19.8	37.0
		% of Total	13.7%	37.0%	50.7%
	taken	Count	24	12	36
		Expected Count	16.8	19.2	36.0
		% of Total	32.9%	16.4%	49.3%
Total		Count	34	39	73
		Expected Count	34.0	39.0	73.0
		% of Total	46.6%	53.4%	100.0%

Compare the expected and observed counts.

Chi-Square Tests

	Value	df	Asymp. Sig. (2-sided)	Exact Sig. (2-sided)	Exact Sig. (1-sided)
Pearson Chi-Square	11.522[b]	1	.001		
Continuity Correction[a]	9.984	1	.002		
Likelihood Ratio	11.847	1	.001		
Fisher's Exact Test				.001	.001
Linear-by-Linear Association	11.365	1	.001		
N of Valid Cases	73				

a. Computed only for a 2x2 table

b. 0 cells (.0%) have expected count less than 5. The minimum expected count is 16.77.

This is good!

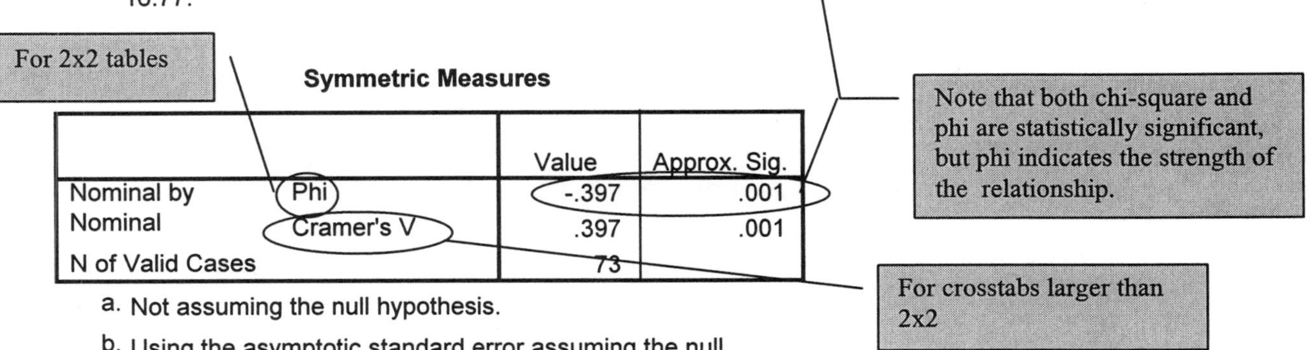

For 2x2 tables
Note that both chi-square and phi are statistically significant, but phi indicates the strength of the relationship.
For crosstabs larger than 2x2

Symmetric Measures

		Value	Approx. Sig.
Nominal by Nominal	Phi	-.397	.001
	Cramer's V	.397	.001
N of Valid Cases		73	

a. Not assuming the null hypothesis.

b. Using the asymptotic standard error assuming the null hypothesis.

Interpretation of Output 8.2

The case processing summary table indicates that there are two participants with missing data. Note, in the second table (Crosstabulation), that the **expected count** of the number of male students who didn't take geometry is 17.2 and the observed or actual **count** is 10. Thus, there are somewhat (7.2) fewer males who didn't take geometry than would be expected by chance, given the **totals** shown in the table. There are also discrepancies between observed and expected counts in the other three cells of the table. A question answered by the chi-square test is whether these discrepancies between observed and expected counts are bigger than one might expect by chance.

The **chi-square** statistic is used to determine if there is a statistically significant relationship between two categorical variables. It tells you whether the relationship is statistically significant but does *not* indicate the *strength* of the relationship, like phi or a correlation does. In Output 8.2, we use the **Pearson chi-square** with (p= .001) or the **Fisher's exact test** (p = .001, two tailed) to interpret the results of the chi-square test. These results indicate that we can be quite certain that males and females are different on whether they take geometry. Note that footnote b states that no cells have expected counts less than 5. That is good because otherwise assumptions of chi-square would be violated. A good rule of thumb is that no more than 20% of the cells should have expected frequencies less than 5. For chi-square with 1 *df* (i.e., 2 x 2 cross-tabulation as in this case) *none* of the cells should have expected frequencies less than 5, some say 10. In a paper you would summarize this result as χ^2=9.98, df=1, p=.001.

In addition to phi and Cramer's V, there are several other nonparametric measures of association that we could have chosen in Fig. 8.4. They attempt, in different ways, to measure the *strength* of the association between two variables. If both variables are nominal and you have a 2x2 crosstabulation, like the one in Output 8.2, **phi** is the appropriate statistic to use in the symmetric measures table. For larger crosstabulations with nominal data (like a 3x3 crosstab), **Cramer's V** is the appropriate statistic. If the association between variables is weak, the value of the statistic will be close to zero (usually <.20) and the significance level **(sig. or *p*)** will be greater than .05, which is the usual cutoff to say that an association is statistically significant. In Output 8.2, phi is . -.397, which is statistically significant. You would report the phi in as phi = -.397, p = .001. Note that this is a measure of effect size for an associational statistic. According to Cohen (1988) this is a medium to large size effect (see chapter 7).

- ***Exit SPSS***

Interpretation Questions

1. a) In Output 8.1, what do the terms "count" and "expected count" mean? b) What does the difference between them tell you?

2. In Output 8.2: a) Is the (Pearson) chi-square statistically significant? Explain what it means. b) Are the expected values in at least 80% of the cells ≥ 5? How do you know?

Extra Problems Using Class Data

Using your class data or the data from Appendix B, do the following problems. Print your outputs after typing your interpretations on them. Please circle the key parts of the output that you discuss.

1. Run crosstabs and interpret the results (as discussed in chapter 7 and in the interpretation of Output 8.2) of chi-square, and phi (or Cramer's V) for: a) gender and marital status and b) age group and marital status.

2. Select two other appropriate variables, run and interpret the output as we did in Output 8.2.

CHAPTER 9

Associating Variables: Pearson and Spearman Correlations

In this chapter you will learn how to compute two basic associational statistics: the Pearson product moment correlation and Spearman rho. These associational inferential statistics are used when you have two ordinal or scale variables. You will also compute a correlation matrix given three or more such variables. Finally, you will learn how to make a scatterplot and learn how to interpret it. It would be wise to review chapter 7. It will help you understand when to compute/choose these associational inferential statistics, and it will remind you about what the significance test means and how to interpret it.

Although we do not show you how to compute measures of reliability and validity in this book, it is important to point out that correlations are often used for these purposes.

Lab Assignment E

Logon and Get Data

- Retrieve **HsbData** from your diskette.

Problem 1: Correlate Mother's Education and Math Achievement

Pearson and Spearman Correlations

The **Pearson** product moment is a parametric statistic used when both variables are at least approximately normally distributed (i.e., scale data). When you have ranked data or when other assumptions are markedly violated, one should use a nonparametric equivalent of the Pearson correlation coefficient. One such nonparametric, ordinal statistic is **Spearman's rho**. Here we ask you to compute both parametric and nonparametric correlations and compare them.

Both types of correlations can vary from –1.0 (a perfect negative relationship or association) through 0.0 (no correlation) to +1.0 (a perfect positive correlation). Note that +1 and –1 are equally high or strong, but they lead to different interpretations. A high *positive correlation* between anxiety and grades would mean that students with high anxiety tended to have high grades, those with medium anxiety had medium grades and those with low anxiety had low grades. That is, high was associated with high and low with low. A high *negative correlation* would mean that students with high anxiety tended to have low grades and vice versa. Also, low grades are associated with high anxiety. With a *zero correlation* there are no consistent associations. A student with high anxiety might have low, medium, or high grades.

Problem/Research Question

What is the association between mother's education and math achievement? You will compute two similar bivariate (2 variable) **correlations** (Pearson and Spearman) with the variables *mother's education* and *math achievement.*

To do Pearson and Spearman correlations follow these commands:

- **Analyze => Correlate => Bivariate**.
- Move *math achievement* and *mother's education* to the **Variables** box.
- Next, ensure that the **Spearman** and **Pearson** boxes are checked
- Make sure that the **Two-tailed** (under **Test of Significance**) and **Flag significant correlations** are checked (see Fig. 9.1).

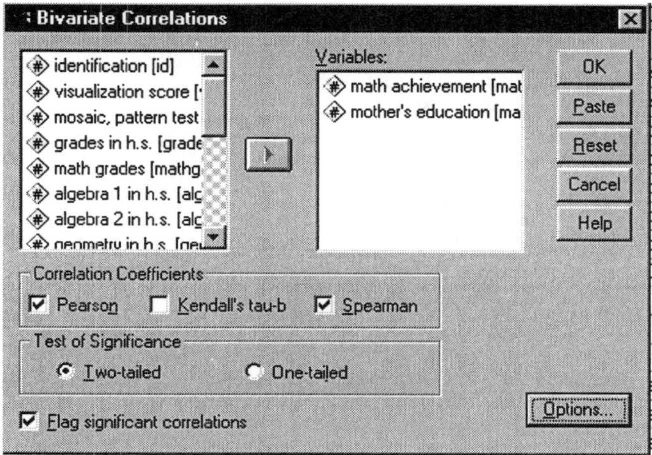

Fig. 9.1. Bivariate correlations.

- Now click on **Options** to get the dialog box.
- Click on **Means and standard deviations** and click on Exclude **cases listwise**. Does your screen look like Fig. 9.2?

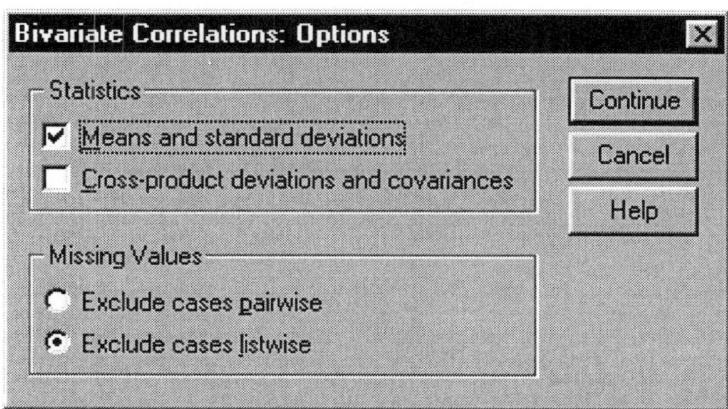

Fig. 9.2. Bivariate correlations: Options.

- Click on **Continue** then on **OK**. What does your output file look like? Compare Output 9.1 to your output and syntax.

Output 9.1: Pearson and Spearman Correlations

Correlations

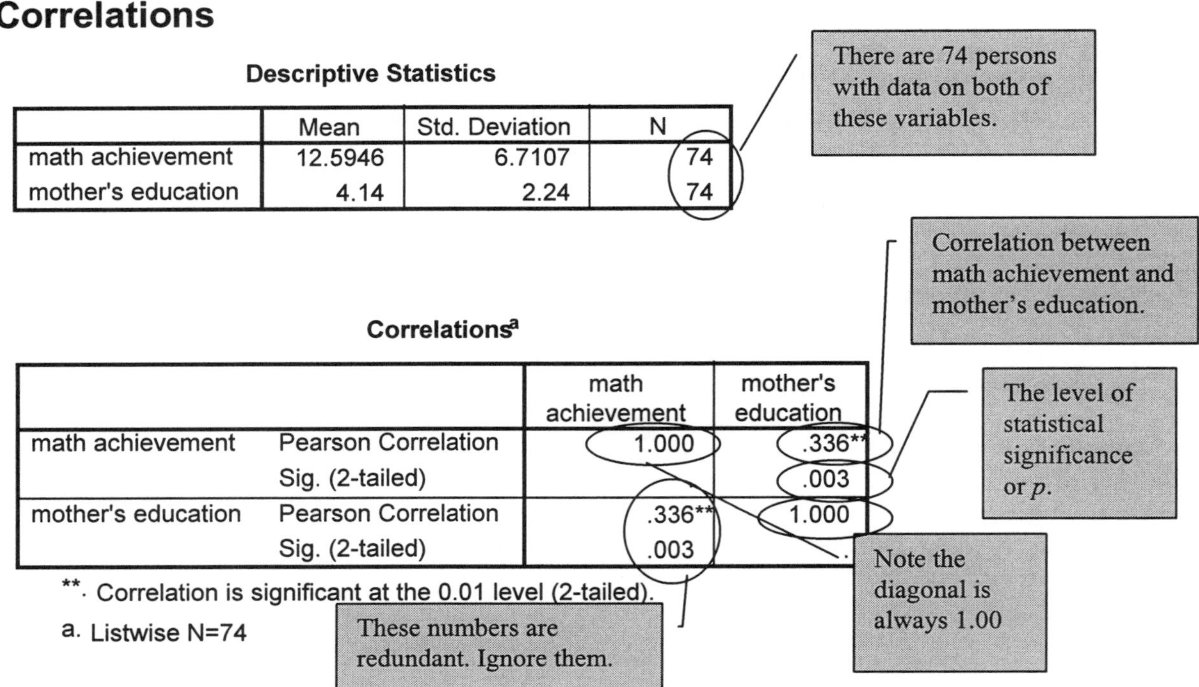

Descriptive Statistics

	Mean	Std. Deviation	N
math achievement	12.5946	6.7107	74
mother's education	4.14	2.24	74

Correlations[a]

		math achievement	mother's education
math achievement	Pearson Correlation	1.000	.336**
	Sig. (2-tailed)	.	.003
mother's education	Pearson Correlation	.336**	1.000
	Sig. (2-tailed)	.003	.

**. Correlation is significant at the 0.01 level (2-tailed).

a. Listwise N=74

There are 74 persons with data on both of these variables.
Correlation between math achievement and mother's education.
The level of statistical significance or *p*.
Note the diagonal is always 1.00
These numbers are redundant. Ignore them.

Nonparametric Correlations

Correlations[a]

			math achievement	mother's education
Spearman's rho	math achievement	Correlation Coefficient	1.000	.315**
		Sig. (2-tailed)	.	.006
	mother's education	Correlation Coefficient	.315**	1.000
		Sig. (2-tailed)	.006	.

**. Correlation is significant at the .01 level (2-tailed).

a. Listwise N = 74

Interpretation of Output 9.1

The first table provides **descriptive statistics** for the variables to be correlated, in this case math achievement and mother's education. The two tables labeled **correlations** are our primary focus.

The information is displayed in matrix form which, unfortunately, means that every number is presented twice. We have provided callout boxes to help you.

The **Pearson** correlation coefficient is .34; the significance level or *p* is .003 and the number of participants with both variables (*math achievement* and *mother's education*) is 74. In a report, this would usually be written as: r (72) =. 34, $p < .01$. Note that the degrees of freedom (N-2 for correlations) is put in parentheses after the statistic (r for **Pearson** correlation) which is usually rounded to two decimal places. The significance or *p* value follows and is stated as .003, or as less than .01.

The correlation value for **Spearman's rho** is somewhat different from r, but usually, as in this case, it has a similar significance level (p=.006 or p<.01). The nonparametric Spearman correlation is based on ranking the scores (1st, 2nd, etc.) rather than using the actual raw scores. It should be used when the scores are already ranks (ordinal data) or when assumptions of the Pearson correlation (such as normality of the scores) are markedly violated. Note, you should *not* report both the Pearson and Spearman correlations; they provide similar information. Pick the one whose assumptions best fit the data.

It is usually best to choose two-tailed tests as we did in Fig. 9.1. We also chose (in Fig. 9.1) to flag (put an asterisk beside) the correlation coefficients that are statistically significant so that they can be identified quickly. The output also prints the exact significance level (*p*), which is redundant with the asterisk, so in a thesis or paper table you usually either report the exact *p* or you use asterisks with a footnote, as in Output 9.1.

This correlation is significant, because the "sig" is less than .05, ($p < .05$) so we can reject the null hypothesis of no association and state that there *is an association* between grades and math achievement. Because the correlation is positive, students who have mothers with high (a lot of) education generally have high math achievement scores and vice versa. In nontechnical language this means that high mother's education is generally *associated* with high achievement, medium education with medium achievement, and low with low. If the correlation were significant and *negative* (e.g., -.50), high mother's education would be associated with low achievement and vice versa. If the correlation were not significant, there would be *no* systematic association between a mother's education and her child's achievement. In that case you could not predict anything about math achievement from knowing someone's mother's education. In addition to statistical significance and the sign of the correlation, you should comment on the effect size for a full interpretation of the correlation. In this case, the correlation is .34, so, using Cohen's (1988) rule of thumb, the effect size is medium (see chapter 7).

Problem 2: Correlation Matrix for Several Scale Variables

If you have more than two variables that you want to correlate, SPSS will produce a correlation matrix showing the correlation of each selected variable with all the others.

Problems/Research Question

What are the associations among the four variables: *visualization, mosaic, grades,* and *math achievement?*

Now, on your own, compute **Pearson** correlations among all the following variables: *visualization, mosaic, grades,* and *math achievement.* Follow procedures outlined previously except:

- Do not use Spearman (under **Correlation Coefficients**) but do use **Pearson.**
- For **Options,** obtain **Means and standard deviations**, and **Exclude cases listwise**.

This will produce Output 9.2. To see if you are doing the work right, compare your output to Output 9.2.

Output 9.2: Pearson Correlation Matrix

Correlations

Descriptive Statistics

	Mean	Std. Deviation	N
visualization score	5.2433	3.9120	75
mosaic, pattern test	27.413	9.574	75
grades in h.s.	5.68	1.57	75
math achievement	12.5645	6.6703	75

Circled are the correlations of *visualization, mosaic,* and *grades* with math achievement.

This is the correlation of *mosaic* and visualization; *r* is on the top line and *p* is on the bottom line.

Correlations[a]

		visualization score	mosaic, pattern test	grades in h.s.	math achievement
visualization score	Pearson Correlation	1.000	.030	.127	.423**
	Sig. (2-tailed)	.	.798	.279	.000
mosaic, pattern test	Pearson Correlation	.030	1.000	-.012	.213
	Sig. (2-tailed)	.798	.	.920	.067
grades in h.s.	Pearson Correlation	.127	-.012	1.000	.504**
	Sig. (2-tailed)	.279	.920	.	.000
math achievement	Pearson Correlation	.423**	.213	.504**	1.000
	Sig. (2-tailed)	.000	.067	.000	.

**. Correlation is significant at the 0.01 level (2-tailed).

a. Listwise N=75

75 persons have data for all four variables.

The diagonal

Examine correlations above *or* below the diagonal. The same correlations are in both places.

Interpretation of Output 9.2

Notice that after the descriptive statistics table, there is a larger **correlations** table that shows the Pearson correlation coefficients, and significance levels. These numbers are, as in Output 9.1, each given twice so you have to be careful in reading them. It is a good idea to look only at the numbers above or below the diagonal (the 1.00s). There are 6 different correlations in the table. In the last column, there is the correlation of each of the other variables with math achievement. In the second to last column, each of the other three variables is correlated with grades, but note that the .504 for *grades* and *math achievement* is the same as the correlation of *math achievement* and *grades* in the last column, so ignore it. The Pearson correlations on this table are interpreted similarly to the one in Output 9.1. However, because there are 6 correlations, the odds are increased that one could be statistically significant by chance. Thus, it would be prudent to use a smaller value of *p*. The Bonferroni correction is a conservative approach designed to keep the significance level at .05 for the whole study. Using it, you would divide the usual significance level (.05) by the number of tests. In this case a $p<.008$ (.05/6) would be required for statistical significance. Another approach is simply to set alpha (the *p* value required for statistical significance) at a more conservative .01 instead of .05.

Problem 3: Scatterplots

A scatterplot is a plot or graph of two variables that shows how the score for individuals on one variable associates with their scores on the other variable. If the correlation is *high positive* the plot will be close to a straight line from the lower left corner of the plot to the upper right. This regression line will slope downward from the upper left if the correlation is *high negative*. For correlations *near zero* the regression line will be flat with many points far from the line.

Doing a scatterplot with SPSS is somewhat cumbersome, as you will see, but it provides a visual picture of the correlation. The plot also allows you to see if there are extreme outliers (far from the regression line), and it may show that the best fitting line would be a curve rather than a straight line.

Problem/Research Question

What are the **Scatterplots,** linear regression line, and r^2 for *grades* and *math achievement* and for *mosaic* and *math achievement?*

Let's now work on developing a scatterplot of the correlations of *math achievement* with *grades*. Follow these commands:

- **Graphs** => **Scatter**. This will give you Fig. 9.3.
- Click on **Simple** then **Define** which will bring you to Fig. 9.4.

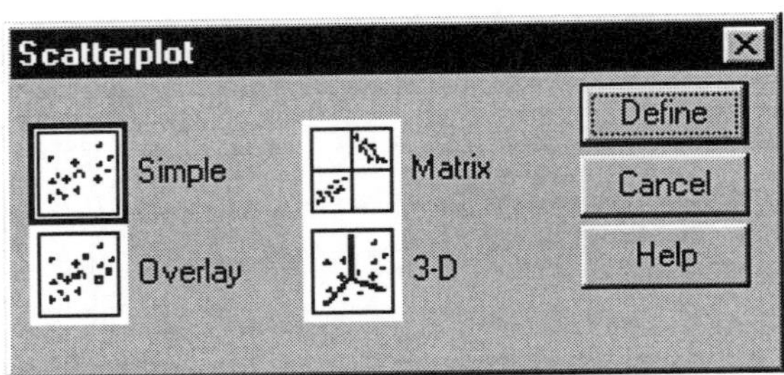

Fig. 9.3. Scatterplot.

- Now, move *math achievement* to the **Y** axis and *grades* to the **X** axis. *Note: the dependent variable goes on the Y axis.*

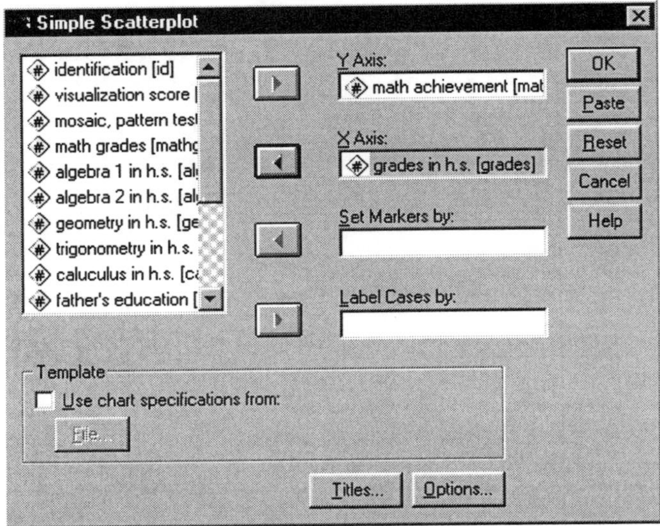

Fig. 9.4. Simple scatterplot.

- Click on **Options**. Then check that **Exclude cases listwise** is selected (see Fig. 9.5).
- Click on **Continue**.

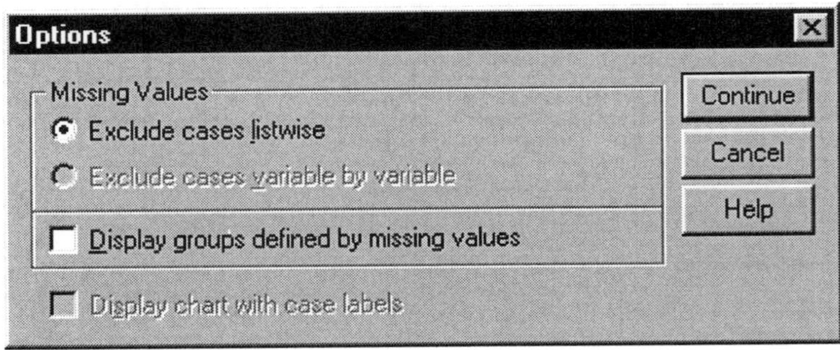

Fig. 9.5. Options.

- Next, click on **Titles** (in Fig. 9.4) and type "**Correlation of math achievement with high school grades**" (see Fig. 9.6). Note that we put it on two lines purely for aesthetic reasons.
- Click on **Continue** then on **OK**. You will get an output chart, which looks like Fig. 9.7. You will not print this because we want to add the regression line first.

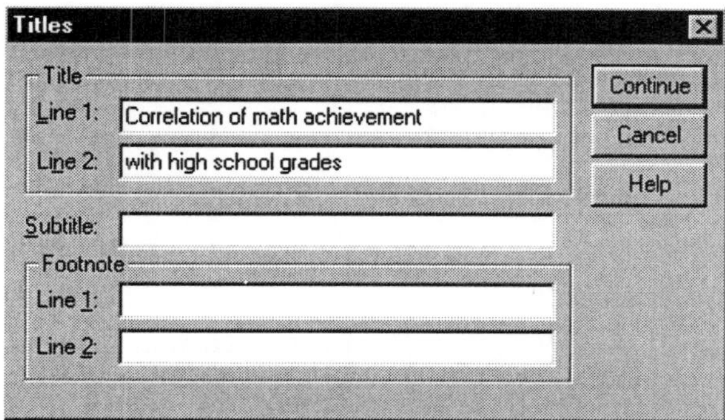

Fig. 9.6. Titles.

Graph

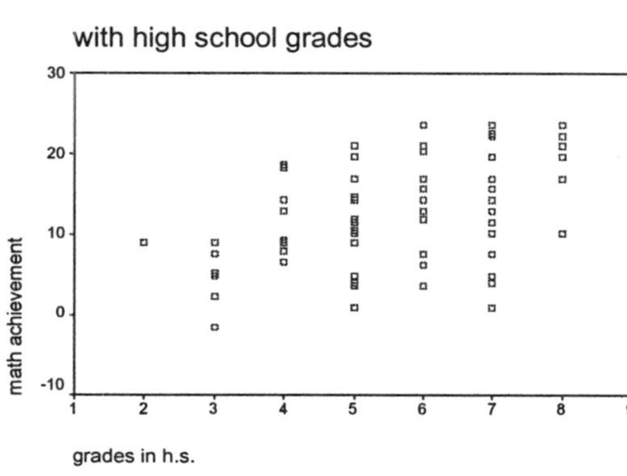

Fig. 9.7. Scatterplot output.

Now let's put the regression lines on the scatterplot so we can get a better sense of the correlation and how much scatter or deviation from the line there is.

- *Double* click on the **scatterplot** in Fig. 9.7. A dialog box like Fig. 9.8 will appear.

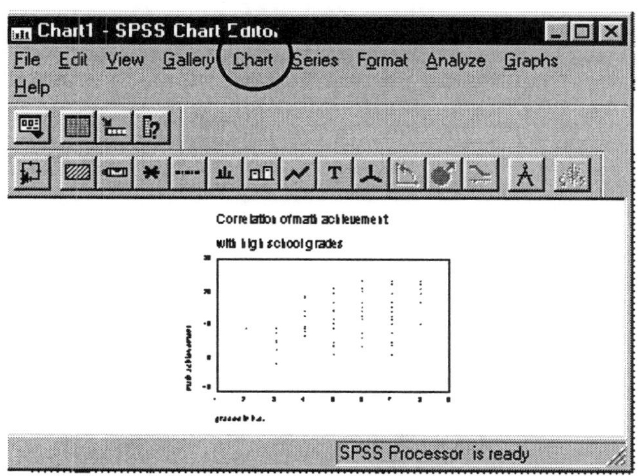

Fig. 9.8. SPSS chart editor.

- Select **Chart => Options** from the dialog box (circled in Fig. 9.8), and you will get Fig. 9.9.

- Click on **Total** in the **Fit Line** box and **Show sunflowers** in the **Sunflowers** box; there is no need to change the **Sunflower Options**. The sunflowers indicate, by the number of petals, how many participants had essentially the same point on the scatterplot.

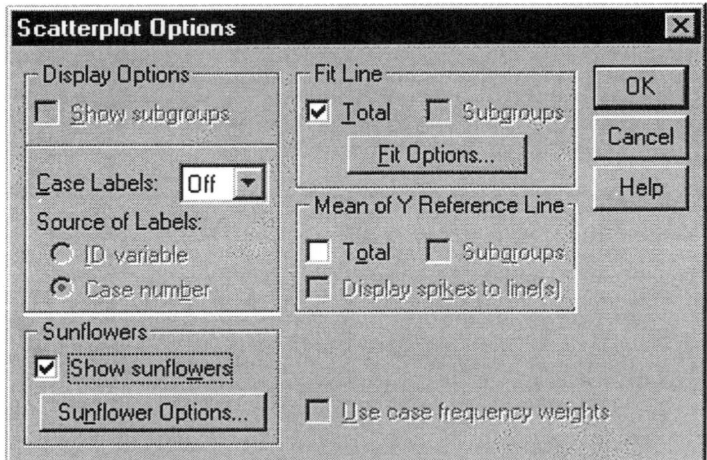

Fig. 9.9. Scatterplot options.

- Next, click on the **Fit Options** button, which will give you Fig. 9.10.
- Ensure that the **Linear Regression** box is highlighted.
- Then check the **Display R-Square in legend** box. Check to be sure your window is like Fig. 9.10, with **Include constant in equation** checked.
- Click on **Continue** then **OK** to get the first part of Output 9.3.
- Select **File => Close** to return to the normal Output file.

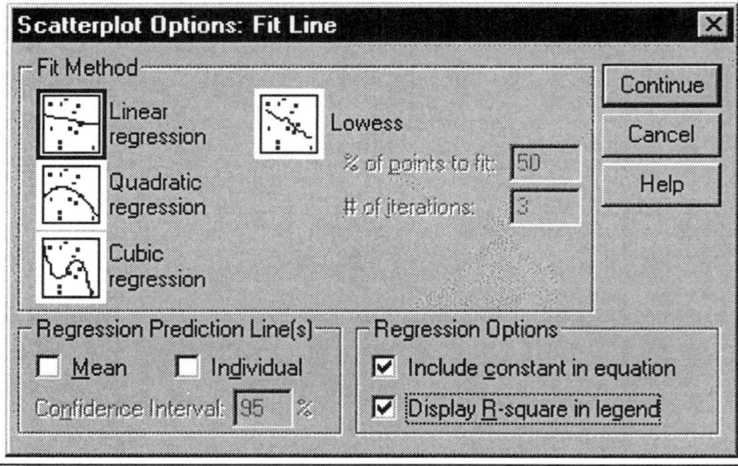

Fig. 9.10. Chart: Scatterplot.

Now try the following scatterplot by doing the same steps as Problem 3 for a new pair of variables. Don't forget to *change the title* before you run the scatterplot. Plot:

Math achievement (Y) with *mosaic* (X).

Do the two scatterplots in the output look like the ones in Output 9.3?

Output 9.3: Scatterplots

Graph

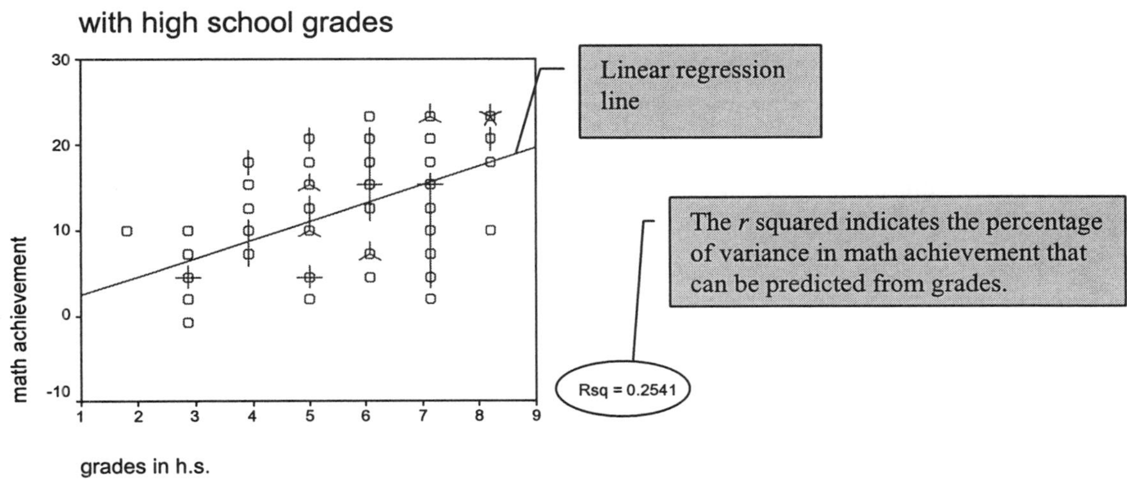

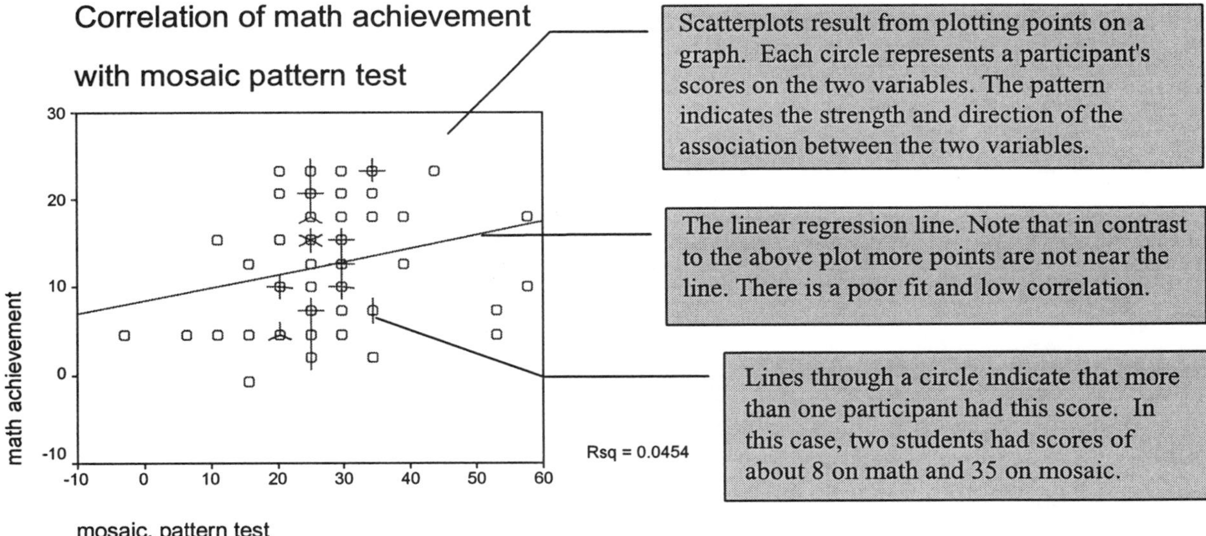

Correlation of math achievement
with mosaic pattern test
math achievement
30
20
10
0
-10
-10
0
10
20
30
40
50
60
mosaic, pattern test
Rsq = 0.0454
Scatterplots result from plotting points on a graph. Each circle represents a participant's scores on the two variables. The pattern indicates the strength and direction of the association between the two variables.
The linear regression line. Note that in contrast to the above plot more points are not near the line. There is a poor fit and low correlation.
Lines through a circle indicate that more than one participant had this score. In this case, two students had scores of about 8 on math and 35 on mosaic.

Interpretation of Output 9.3

The scatterplots shown in Output 9.3 show the best fit for a straight (linear) regression line (i.e., it minimizes the squared differences between the points and the line). To the right of the scatterplot is the r^2 that indicates the percentage of variance in the dependent variable (*math achievement)* that can be predicted from the independent variable. The r^2 is called the *coefficient of determination*. It is possible to have a statistically significant correlation that has very low *practical significance,* if the sample size is large. Note that the r^2 (.25) for the first scatterplot means that r is approximately .50, which is what Output 9.2 had for the same correlation. Note that the points fit the line moderately well. Cohen (1988) considers $r = .5$ to be a large effect, even though only 25% of the variance is shared or common. The r^2 (.05) for the second scatterplot is quite low, with only 5% common variance. Note this r^2 corresponds to the r of approximately .21 in Output 9.2, which was not statistically significant.

- ***Exit SPSS***

Interpretation Questions

1. In Output 9.1: a) What do the correlation coefficients tell us? b) What is r^2 for the Pearson correlation? What does it mean? c) Compare the Pearson and Spearman correlations on both correlation size and significance level. d) When should you use which type?

2. In Output 9.2, how many of the Pearson correlation coefficients are significant? Write an interpretation of a) one of the significant and b) one of the nonsignificant correlations in Output 9.2. Include whether or not the correlation is significant, your decision about the null hypothesis, *and* a sentence or two describing the correlations in nontechnical terms. Include comments related to the sign and to the effect size.

3. Using Output 9.3, inspect the scatterplots. a) What are the two r^2 and what do they mean? b) Why should one do scatterplots?

Extra Problems Using Class Data

Using your class data or the data from Appendix B, do the following problems. Print your outputs after typing your interpretations on them. Please circle the key parts of the output that you discuss.

1. What is the correlation between height and parent's height? Also produce a scatterplot. Interpret the results, including statistical significance, direction, and effect size.

2. Write a question that can be answered via correlational analysis with two *scale* type variables. Run the appropriate statistics to answer the question. Interpret the results.

3. Make a correlation matrix using at least four appropriate variables. Identify using the variable names, the two strongest and two weakest correlations. What were the r and p values for each correlation?

CHAPTER 10

Comparing Groups: *t* Tests and One-Way ANOVA

In this chapter you will learn how to compute two kinds of *t* tests and the one-way analysis of variance (ANOVA). The independent samples *t* is used to compare two groups (e.g., males and females). The one-way ANOVA is necessary if you want to compare three or more groups (e.g., three levels of father's education).

Lab Assignment F

Logon and Get Data

- Retrieve **HsbData** from your data file (your latest data).

Problem 1: Independent Samples *t* Test, Between Groups Design

Independent and Paired Samples t Tests

In this assignment, we shift our focus from the associational approach that we were using in the previous lab, to the comparative approach with difference questions and statistics. Problem 1 compares two independent groups (*between groups design*) such as boys and girls. In Problem 2 with a *within subjects or repeated measures design*, we see if the participants differ significantly on two comparable measures such as their father's and mother's education. Remember that chapter 7 discussed between groups and within subjects designs, which help determine the specific statistic to use.

The other determinant of which statistic to use has to do with statistical assumptions. If the dependent variable is approximately normally distributed, one can use the parametric *t* test. If these assumptions are markedly violated, you should use a nonparametric test. Chi-square, for nominal data, was the one discussed in chapter 8. There are also equivalent ordinal statistics (i.e., the Mann-Whitney U test), but we will not cover them in this book.

Problem/Research Question

Do boys and girls differ significantly in regard to their average math grades, math achievement, and overall grades in high school? Assume that the scores for the three dependent variables are normally distributed (i.e., scale data).

Let's determine if boys or girls do better on *math grades, math achievement,* and *grades in high school.*

Follow these commands:

- Click on **Analyze => Compare means => Independent Samples T Test.**
- Move *math grades, math achievement,* and *grades in high school,* to the **Test** (dependent) **Variable(s)** box and move *gender* to the **Grouping** (independent) **Variable(s)** box (see Fig. 10.1).

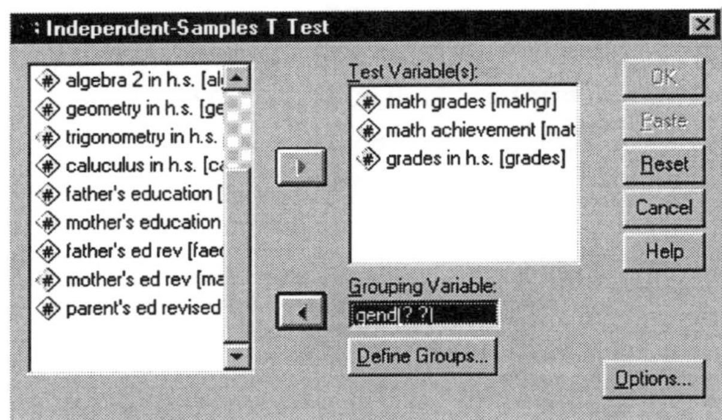

Fig. 10.1. Independent-samples *t* test.

- Next click on **Define Groups** in Fig. 10.1 to get Fig. 10.2.
- Type **1** (for males) in the **Group 1** box and **2** (for females) in the **Group 2** box (see Fig. 10.2).

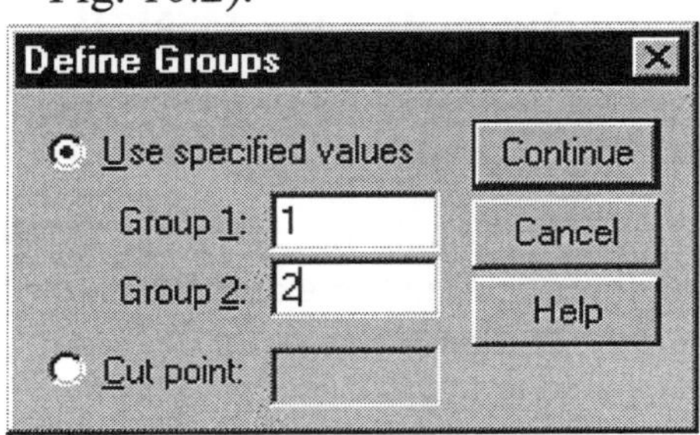

Fig. 10.2. Define groups.

- Click on **Continue** then on **OK**. Compare your output to Output 10.1.

Output 10.1: Independent Samples t Test--Between Groups Design

Means to be compared.

The Levene test in the next table indicates that these SDs Squared (Variances) are not equal.

Group Statistics

	gender	N	Mean	Std. Deviation	Std. Error Mean
math grades	male	34	.29	.46	7.93E-02
	female	39	.54	.51	8.09E-02
math achievement	male	34	14.7550	6.0315	1.0344
	female	39	10.8376	6.8578	1.0981
grades in h.s.	male	34	5.50	1.64	.28
	female	39	5.90	1.52	.24

For small numbers SPSS writes them in this format, which means that you should move the decimal 2 places to the left. Thus, these numbers are .0793 and .0809.

T-Test

Independent Samples Test

		Levene's Test for Equality of Variances		t-test for Equality of Means						
									95% Confidence Interval of the Difference	
		F	Sig.	t	df	Sig. (2-tailed)	Mean Difference	Std. Error Difference	Lower	Upper
math grades	Equal variances assumed	6.883	.011	-2.144	71	.035	-.24	.11	-.47	-1.71E-02
	Equal variances not assumed			-2.157	70.815	.034	-.24	.11	-.47	-1.85E-02
math achievement	Equal variances assumed	.947	.334	2.574	71	.012	3.9174	1.5220	.8826	6.9522
	Equal variances not assumed			2.597	70.992	.011	3.9174	1.5086	.9094	6.9255
grades in h.s.	Equal variances assumed	.720	.399	-1.076	71	.286	-.40	.37	-1.13	.34
	Equal variances not assumed			-1.070	67.883	.288	-.40	.37	-1.14	.34

Circled numbers are discussed in the Interpretation box.

Interpretation of Output 10.1

The first table shows descriptive statistics for the two groups (males and females) separately. Note that the means within each of the three pairs look somewhat different. Could this be due to chance?

The second table provides *two* statistical tests. In the left two columns is the Levene test for the *assumption* that the *variances* of the two groups are equal. This is *not* the *t* test; it only assesses an assumption! If this *F* test is *not* significant (as in the case of *math achievement* and *grades in high school*), the assumption is *not* violated and one uses the **equal variance assumed** line for the *t* test and related statistics. However, if Levene's *F* is statistically significant (sig $\leq$ .05), as with *math grades*, then variances are significantly different and the assumption of equal variances is violated. In that case, the **equal variances *not* assumed** line is used; *t* and *df* are adjusted.

Thus, for math grades, the appropriate $t = -2.16$, degrees of freedom (df) = 70.81, and p = .034. Because this *t* is statistically significant, we say that girls have higher math grades. We used *math grades* to provide an example where the assumption of equal variances was violated (Levene's *t* test was significant). However, you may remember that math grades, the dependent variable, was dichotomous (high or low) so the *t* test, while not wrong, is not the best choice of statistic. The chi-square test (chapter 8) would be more appropriate.

For *math achievement*, you should state the results as t (71)= 2.60, p= .012 (where the number in parentheses is the *df*) in a research report. Inspection of the two group means indicates that the average math achievement score for female students (10.84) is significantly lower than the score (14.76) for males. The difference between the means is 3.92 points on a 25-point test. The **95% confidence interval** tells us that if we repeated the study 100 times, 95 of the times the true (population) difference would fall within the confidence interval, which in this case is between +.88 points and +6.95 points. Note that confidence interval, which in this case is between +.88 points and +6.95 points. Note that if the "upper" and "lower" bounds have the same sign (either + and + or - and -) we know that the difference is statistically significant. On the other hand, if zero lies between the upper and lower limits, there could be no difference. For the HSB data, the lower limit of the confidence interval tells us that the difference between males and females on math achievement could be as small as .88 points out of 25, a pretty small difference.

Effect size measures for *t* tests are not provided in the printout but can be estimated relatively easily. See chapter 7 for the formula and interpretation of *d*. For *math achievement*, the difference between the means (3.92) would be divided by 6.5, an estimate of the pooled (weighted average) standard deviation. Thus, *d* would be approximately .60, which is, according to Cohen (1988), a medium to large size "effect". Because you need means and standard deviations to compute the effect size, you should include a table with means and standard deviations in your results section for a full interpretation of *t* tests (and ANOVAs).

Problem 2: Paired Samples *t* Test
Within Subjects Design With Two Levels

In this problem, you will compare the average scores of each HSB student on two related measures, namely education level of the father and mother. The paired samples *t* test is also used when the two scores are repeated measures. For example, each participant could be measured twice on the same visualization test to assess reliability or stability of participants' scores over a short time period. Another example is in an experimental study when the same assessment (perhaps an achievement test) is used as the pretest, before the intervention, and as the posttest.

Problem/Research Question

Do fathers of this group of students have more education than the mothers?

Now we will determine if the fathers of these students have more education than their mothers. Remember that the fathers and mothers are paired; that is, each child has a pair of parents. We would do a paired samples *t* test if the dependent variable data were approximately and normally distributed (i.e., scale data).

- Click on **Analyze => Compare means => Paired Samples T Test**.
- Click on both of the variables *Father's education* and *Mother's education* (not the revised) and move them simultaneously to the **Paired Variable(s)** box (see Fig. 10.3).
- Click on **OK**.
- Compare your output to Output 10.2.

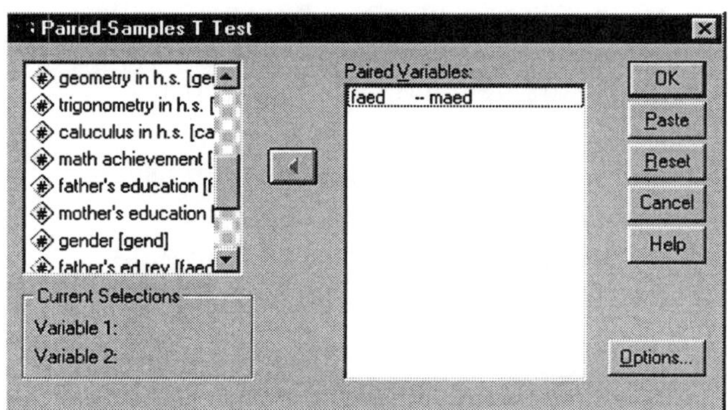

Fig. 10.3. Paired-samples *t* test.

Output 10.2: Paired Samples t Tests, Within Subjects Design With Two Levels

T-Test

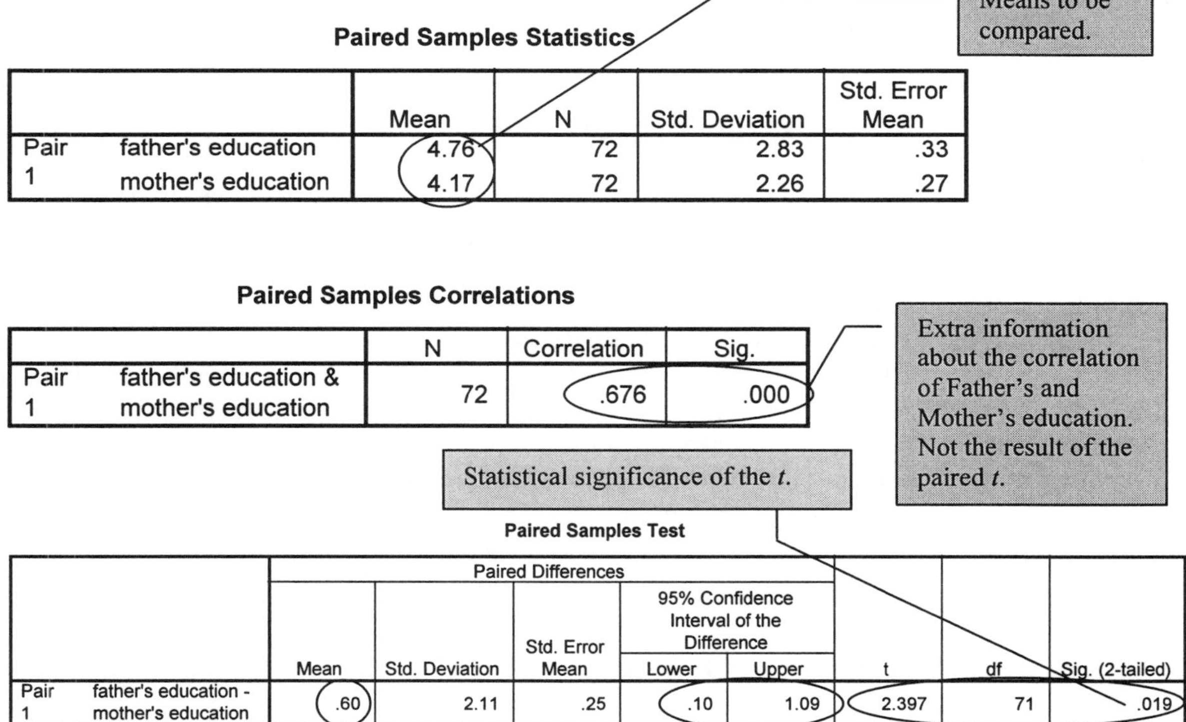

Means to be compared.
Extra information about the correlation of Father's and Mother's education. Not the result of the paired *t*.
Statistical significance of the *t*.

Paired Samples Statistics

		Mean	N	Std. Deviation	Std. Error Mean
Pair 1	father's education	4.76	72	2.83	.33
	mother's education	4.17	72	2.26	.27

Paired Samples Correlations

		N	Correlation	Sig.
Pair 1	father's education & mother's education	72	.676	.000

Paired Samples Test

		Paired Differences					t	df	Sig. (2-tailed)
					95% Confidence Interval of the Difference				
		Mean	Std. Deviation	Std. Error Mean	Lower	Upper			
Pair 1	father's education - mother's education	.60	2.11	.25	.10	1.09	2.397	71	.019

Interpretation of Output 10.2

The first table shows the descriptive statistics used to compare the average mother's and father's education. The second table provides correlations between the two paired scores.

We have already seen (chapter 9) that an r=.68 indicates that there is a relatively high positive association between mothers' and fathers' education. This means that women with a lot of education tend to marry men with a lot of education and visa versa.

The third table shows the paired samples *t* test. Note that the father's education score is .60 points higher than the mother's score and that this is a statistically significant difference: $t\ (71) = 2.40, p = .019$. This means that men tend to marry women with somewhat less education than they have. The confidence interval indicates that the difference in the education of these couples could be as small as .10 points or as large as 1.09 points. If we look at the HSB code book (Appendix C), we can see that the average mother in this group has less than two years of vocational education while fathers are close to two years of such education. One-tenth of a point seems like a small difference; so, even though it is statistically significant, it may not be of much practical importance. We can be confident that there is at least a little difference, on the average, in mother's and father's education.

Hopefully, you understand that the correlation between mother's and father's education provides you with different information than the paired *t*. If not, read this interpretation again and review chapter 9, if necessary.

Problem 3: One-Way (or Single Factor) ANOVA

In this lab, you also will examine a statistical technique for comparing two or *more* independent groups on the central tendency of the dependent variable. The appropriate statistic, called **one-way ANOVA** in SPSS, compares the *means* of the samples or groups in order to make inferences about the population means. As with the *t* test, ANOVA assumes that the dependent variable is scale data (i.e., approximately normally distributed in the population) and the variances of the groups are equal. One-way ANOVA is also called single factor analysis of variance, because there is only one independent variable. You might ask, why would you compute a *t* test when one-way ANOVA (F) can be used to compare *two* groups as well as three or more groups? Because $F = t^2$, they provide you with the same information, and the outputs look very similar. Thus, the choice is mostly a matter of personal preference. However, *t* tests can be either one tailed or two-tailed, while ANOVAs are always two tailed. Thus, if you have a clear directional hypothesis that predicts which group will have the higher mean, you may want to use a *t* test rather than one-way ANOVA when comparing two groups.

Problem/Research Question

Are there differences between the *three* fathers' education (revised) groups on grades and visualization scores?

We will use the **One-Way ANOVA** procedure because we have one independent variable with three values or levels to analyze. So, let's do these commands:

- **Analyze => Compare Means => One-Way ANOVA.**
- Move *grades in high school* and *visualization score* into the **Dependent List** box.
- Click on *father's education rev* and move it to the **Factor** box (independent variable).
- Finally, click on **Options** and choose **Descriptives** and **Homogeneity of variance**. See Fig. 10.4 through 10.5 for assistance.

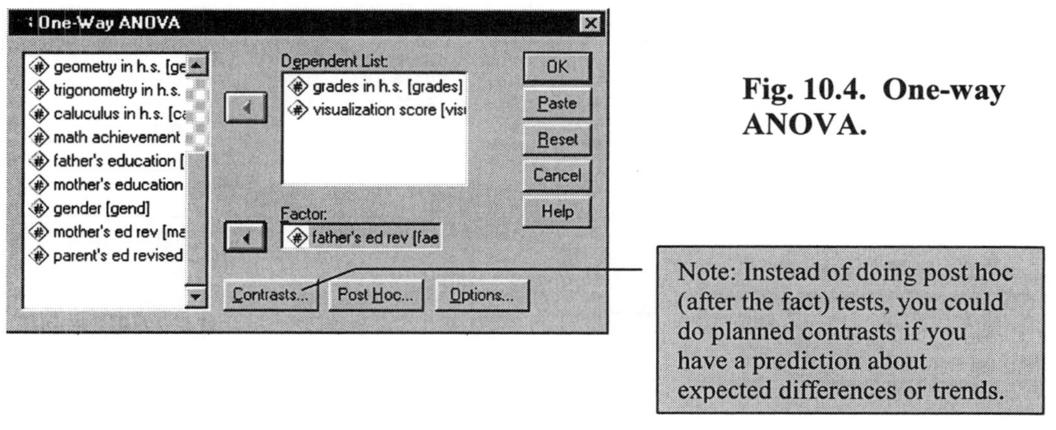

Fig. 10.4. One-way ANOVA.

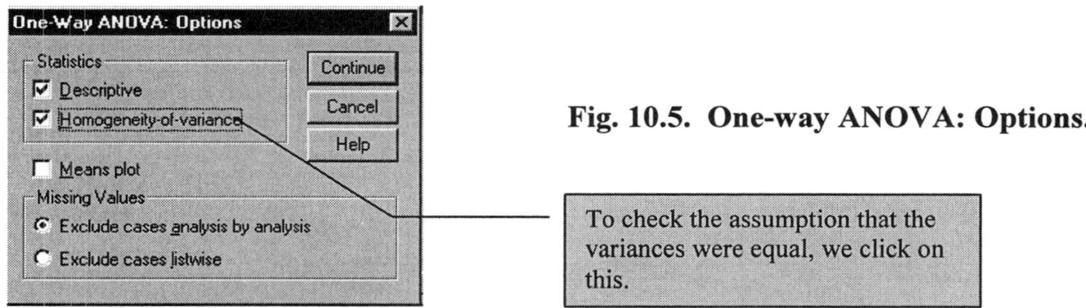

Fig. 10.5. One-way ANOVA: Options.

- Click on **Continue** then **OK**. Compare your output to Output 10.3.

Output 10.3: One-Way ANOVA
Oneway

Means to be compared.

Descriptives

		N	Mean	Std. Deviation	Std. Error	95% Confidence Interval for Mean		Minimum	Maximum
						Lower Bound	Upper Bound		
grades in h.s.	hs grad or less	37	5.35	1.49	.25	4.85	5.85	3	8
	some college	17	5.53	1.74	.42	4.64	6.42	2	8
	BS or more	19	6.53	1.22	.28	5.94	7.11	4	8
	Total	73	5.70	1.55	.18	5.34	6.06	2	8
visualization score	hs grad or less	37	4.7027	3.9886	.6557	3.3728	6.0326	-.25	14.75
	some college	17	5.9412	4.4261	1.0735	3.6655	8.2169	-.25	14.75
	BS or more	19	5.4605	2.7904	.6402	4.1156	6.8055	-.25	9.75
	Total	73	5.1884	3.8117	.4461	4.2990	6.0777	-.25	14.75

Test of Homogeneity of Variances

	Levene Statistic	df1	df2	Sig.
grades in h.s.	1.266	2	70	.288
visualization score	1.706	2	70	.189

These are not significant so the assumption is not violated.

ANOVA

		Sum of Squares	df	Mean Square	F	Sig.
grades in h.s.	Between Groups	17.965	2	8.983	4.046	.022
	Within Groups	155.405	70	2.220		
	Total	173.370	72			
visualization score	Between Groups	19.769	2	9.884	.674	.513
	Within Groups	1026.329	70	14.662		
	Total	1046.098	72			

Notice *grades in high school* are significant while *visualization* is not.

Interpretation of Output 10.3

The first table provides familiar descriptive statistics for the three fathers' education groups on each of the two dependent variables (*grades in high school* and *visualization score)* that we requested for this analysis. Note that although those two dependent variables appear together in the tables, we have really computed two separate one-way ANOVAs, just as we computed three *t*'s in problem 1. The second table is the Levene Test of the assumption of equal variances. It is not violated so we can proceed with the two one-way ANOVAs.

The ANOVA table in Output 10.3 is the key table because it shows whether the overall *F*s for these two ANOVAs were statistically significant. Note that the three fathers' education groups differ significantly on grades but not visualization. When reporting these findings one should write, for example, F (2, 70)=4.05, p=.022, for grades. The 2, 70 are the degrees of freedom (*df*). *F tables* also usually include the mean squares, which indicates the amount of variance (sum of squares) for that "effect" divided by the degrees of freedom for that effect. You should report the means and standard deviations so that one can see which groups were high and low and other researchers can compute effect sizes. Note that we put "effect" in quotes to remind you that unless you have a randomized experiment (which we do not here) the statistical terms effect and effect size do not mean that the independent variable caused the dependent variable to change. It is better to just say that the three groups differ. However, if you have three or more groups you will not know which specific pairs of means are significantly different, unless you do a post hoc or an a prior test.

Problem 4: Tukey Post Hoc Multiple Comparison Tests

Now, we will introduce the concept of **post hoc multiple comparisons**, sometimes called follow-up tests. When you compare *three or more group means*, you will know that there will be a statistically significant difference somewhere if the **ANOVA *F*** (sometimes called the **overall** or **omnibus *F***) is significant. However, we would usually like to know which specific means are different from which other ones. In order to know this, you can use *one* of several post hoc tests that are built into the SPSS one-way ANOVA program. The **LSD** post hoc test is quite liberal and the **Scheffe** test is quite conservative so many statisticians recommend a middle of the road test such as the **Tukey HSD** (honestly significant differences) test. Ordinarily, you *do post hoc tests only if the overall F is significant*. For this reason, we have separated Problems 4 and 5, which could have been done in one step. Fig. 10.6 shows the steps one should use in deciding whether to use post hoc multiple comparison tests.

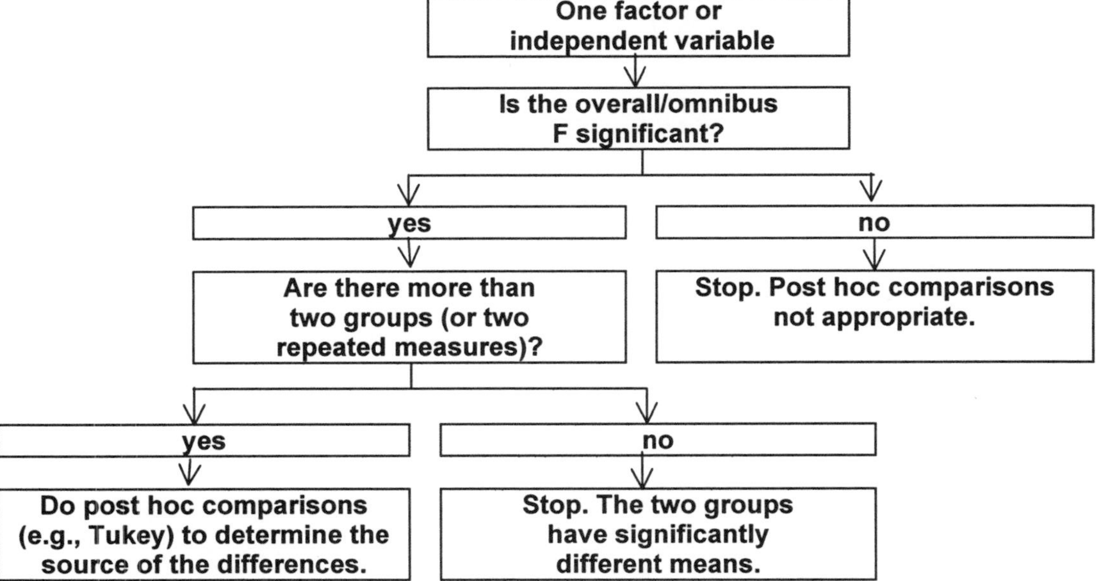

Fig. 10.6. Schematic representation of when to use post hoc multiple comparisons with a one-way ANOVA.

Problem/Research Question

If the overall *F* is significant, which pairs of means are significantly different? We will use the **Tukey** HSD.

After you have examined Output 10.3 to see if each overall or omnibus *F* was significant, you will do appropriate post hoc multiple comparisons. To do these, get the **One-Way ANOVA** dialog box *again* by doing the following:

- Select **Analyze** => **Compare Means** => **One-Way ANOVA** to see Fig. 10.4 again.
- Move *visual* out of the **Dependent List** by highlighting it and clicking on the arrow pointing left. (The reason is that the overall *F* for *visual* was not significant. See interpretation for Output 10.3.)
- Keep *grades* in the **Dependent List** because it had a significant *F*.
- Insure that *father's educ rev* is in the **Factor** box.
- Next, click on **Options** and *remove* the check for **Descriptive** (in Fig. 10.5) because we do not need to do them again.
- Then click on **Continue**.
- In the main dialogue box (Fig. 10.4), press **Post Hoc** to get Fig. 10.7.
- Check on **Tukey**.
- Click on **Continue** and then **OK** to run this post hoc test.

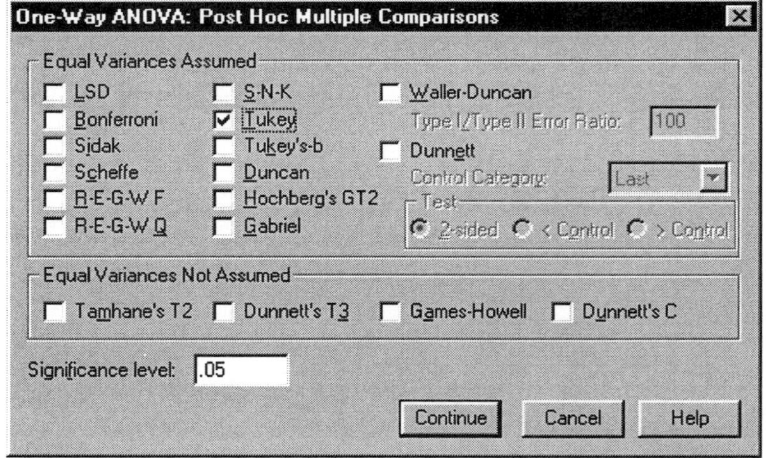

Fig. 10.7. One-way ANOVA: Post hoc multiple comparisons.

- Compare your output to Output 10.4.

Output 10.4: Tukey Multiple Comparison Test

Oneway

ANOVA

Grades in high school

	Sum of Squares	df	Mean Square	F	Sig.
Between Groups	17.965	2	8.983	4.046	.022
Within Groups	155.405	70	2.220		
Total	173.370	72			

Post Hoc Tests

Multiple Comparisons

Dependent Variable: Grades in high school
Tukey HSD

The Tukey HSD is a common post hoc test to use when variances are equal.

(I) Father's educ rev	(J) Father's educ rev	Mean Difference (I-J)	Std. Error	Sig.	95% Confidence Interval Lower Bound	Upper Bound
HS grad or less	Some College	-.18	.44	.913	-1.22	.87
	BS or More	-1.17*	.42	.018	-2.18	-.17
Some College	HS grad or less	.18	.44	.913	-.87	1.22
	BS or More	-1.00	.50	.119	-2.19	.19
BS or More	HS grad or less	1.17*	.42	.018	.17	2.18
	Some College	1.00	.50	.119	-.19	2.19

*. The mean difference is significant at the .05 level.

These are the differences between the means and the significance levels. Ignore duplicates.

Homogeneous Subsets

Grades in high school

Tukey HSD[a,b]

Father's educ rev	N	Subset for alpha = .05: 1	2
HS grad or less	37	5.35	
Some College	17	5.53	5.53
BS or More	19		6.53
Sig.		.918	.078

Means for groups in homogeneous subsets are displayed.

a. Uses Harmonic Mean Sample Size = 21.663.

b. The group sizes are unequal. The harmonic mean of the group sizes is used. Type I error levels are not guaranteed.

Another way of computing and displaying the post hoc tests. Groups listed in the same subset are not significantly different.

Interpretation of Output 10.4

The first table repeats the ANOVA for *grades in high school*. The next table shows the **Tukey HSD** test for *grades*. Note that we have added arrows to the table to show which groups were being compared. The top arrow and line indicates that students whose fathers were high school grads or less were compared to those whose fathers had some college in terms of average high school grades. Each comparison is presented twice; do not interpret both lines that involve the comparison of the same two means. You would report that there is only a small **mean difference** (-.18) between the mean grades of students whose fathers were high school grads or less (M = 5.35 from Output 10.3) and those fathers who had some college (M = 5.53). This difference is not significant (p = .913) using the Tukey test. Similarly, we can say that there *was* a statistically significant difference between the grades of students with low (M = 5.35) and high (M = 6.53) fathers' education (p = .018), but the medium versus high education difference was not significant (p = .119). The computation of effect size is more complex with three groups so we will not do that in this book, but note that you do have 95% confidence intervals that are interpreted like we did for Output 10.1 and 10.2.

Note also that we did not do a Tukey test for visual because the overall (ANOVA) F was not statistically significant. Thus, it could have been due to chance variation.

- ***Exit SPSS***

Interpretation Questions

1. In Output 10.1: a) Are the *variances* equal or significantly different for the three dependent variables? b) List the appropriate t, df, and p (significance level) for each t test as you would in an article. c) Which t tests are statistically significant? d) Write sentences interpreting the gender difference between the means of *grades* and of *math grades*. e) Interpret the 95% confidence interval for these two variables. f) Comment on the effect sizes.

2. In Output 10.2: a) What does the paired samples correlation for mother's and father's education mean? b) Interpret/explain the results for the t test. c) Explain how the correlation and the t test differ in what information they provide. d) Describe the results if the r was .90 and the t was zero. e) What if r was zero and t was 5.0?

3. In Output 10.3: a) List the F, df, and p values for each dependent variable as you would in an article. b) Describe the results in nontechnical terms for visualization and grades. Use the group means in your description.

4. In Outputs 10.4 what pairs of means were significantly different?

Extra Problems Using Your Class Data

Using your class data or the data from Appendix B, do the following problems. Print your outputs after typing your interpretations on them. Please circle the key parts of the output that you use for your interpretation.

1. Is there a significant difference between the genders on average student height? Explain. Provide a full interpretation of the results.

2. Write a question that can be answered from the data using a paired sample *t* test. Run the *t* test and provide a full interpretation.

3. Identify an example of a variable measured at the scale/normally distributed level for which there is a statistically significant overall difference (*F*) between the three marital status groups. Complete the analysis and interpret the results.

CHAPTER 11

Complex Statistics: Factorial ANOVA and Multiple Regression

In this chapter we will introduce two complex statistics: factorial ANOVA and multiple regression. Both factorial ANOVA and multiple regression tell you whether considering more than one independent variable at a time gives you additional information over and above what you would get if you did the appropriate *basic* inferential statistics for each pair of independent and dependent variables. Both of these inferential statistics have two or more independent variables and one scale (normally distributed) dependent variable. Factorial ANOVA is used when there are a small number of independent variables (usually 2 or 3) and each of these variables has a small number of values or categories (usually 2 to 4). For multiple regression, there can be more than 2 or 3 independent variables if the sample is large. These variables can have many ordered levels (scale data) or can be dichotomous.

Lab Assignment G

Logon and Get Data

- Retrieve **HsbData** from your data file (your latest data).

Problem 1: Factorial (2-Way) ANOVA

In chapter 10, we compared two or more groups based on the levels of *one* independent variable or factor using *t* tests and one-way ANOVA. These were called single factor designs. In this lab, we will compare groups based on *two* independent variables. The appropriate statistic for these problems is called a two factor or 2-way or factorial ANOVA. This statistic is used when there are two independent variables (each with a few categories or values) and a between groups design.

Problem/Research Question

Do *math grades* and also *father's education revised* seem to have an effect on *math achievement,* and do *math grades* and *father's education revised* interact?

Follow these commands:

- **Analyze => General Linear Model => Univariate**
- Move *math achievement* to the **Dependent** (variable) box.

- Move the first independent variable, *math grades* to the **Fixed Factor(s)** box and then move the second independent variable, *father's education rev,* to the **Fixed Factor(s)** box. (See Figure 11.1.)

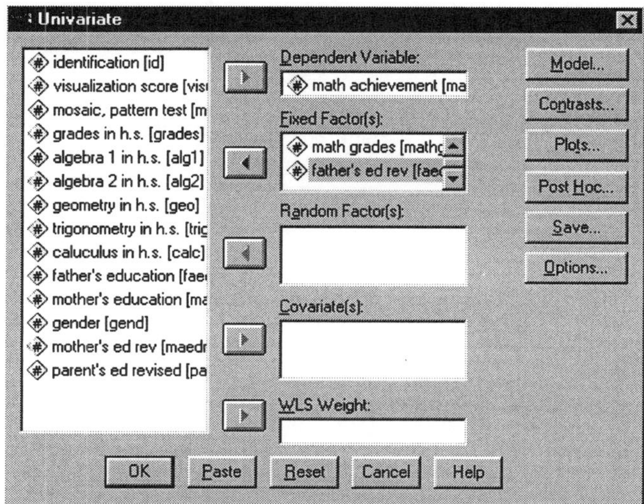

Fig. 11.1. GLM: Univariate.

Now that we know the variables we will be dealing with, let's determine our options.

- Click on **Plots** and move *faedr* to the **horizontal axis** and *mathgr* to the **Separate Lines** box (see Fig. 11.2). Note, the plots will be easier to interpret if you put *faedr* with its three values on the horizontal axis.
- Then press **Add**. You will see that *mathgr* and *faedr* have moved to the **Plots** window as shown in Fig. 11.2.
- Click on **Continue** to get back Fig. 11.1.

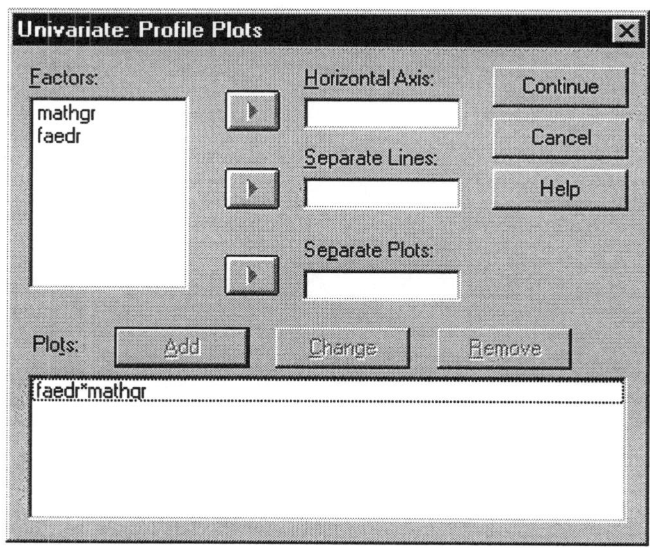

Fig. 11.2. Univariate: Profile plots.

Select **Options** and check **Descriptive statistics** and **Estimates of effect size** in Fig. 11.3.

- Click on **Continue**. This will take you back to Fig. 11.1
- Click on **OK**. Compare your output to Output 11.1.

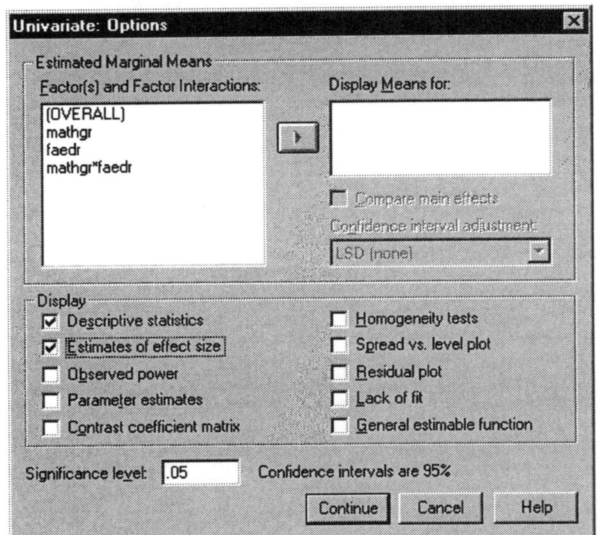

Fig. 11.3. Univariate: Options.

Output 11.1: GLM General Factorial (2-Way) ANOVA – Math Achievement by Math Grades and Father's Education Revised

Between-Subjects Factors

		Value Label	N
math grades	0	less A-B	43
	1	most A-B	30
father's ed rev	1	hs grad or less	37
	2	some college	17
	3	BS or more	19

Descriptive Statistics

Dependent Variable: math achievement

math grades	father's ed rev	Mean	Std. Deviation	N
less A-B	hs grad or less	9.5000	5.6247	22
	some college	12.5667	4.8306	10
	BS or more	12.3636	7.1841	11
	Total	10.9457	5.9460	43
most A-B	hs grad or less	10.4889	6.5657	15
	some college	16.4284	3.4306	7
	BS or more	21.8335	2.8452	8
	Total	14.9000	7.0064	30
Total	hs grad or less	9.9009	5.9550	37
	some college	14.1568	4.6235	17
	BS or more	16.3509	7.4092	19
	Total	12.5708	6.6508	73

Tests of Between-Subjects Effects

Dependent Variable: Math achievement

Source	Type III Sum of Squares	df	Mean Square	F	Sig.	Eta Squared
Corrected Model	1063.495[a]	5	212.699	6.718	.000	.334
Intercept	12119.816	1	12119.816	382.792	.000	.851
MATHGR	359.237	1	359.237	11.346	.001	.145
FAEDR	669.793	2	334.896	10.577	.000	.240
MATHGR * FAEDR	219.272	2	109.636	3.463	.037	.094
Error	2121.330	67	31.662			
Total	14720.540	73				
Corrected Total	3184.824	72				

a. R Squared = .334 (Adjusted R Squared = .284)

Eta squared indicates that 24% of the variance in math achievement can be predicted from father's education.

Percent of variance in math achievement predictable from both independent variables and the interactions.

Focus on these three *F*s, especially the *Mathgr x Faedr* interaction.

Estimated Marginal Means of Math Achievement

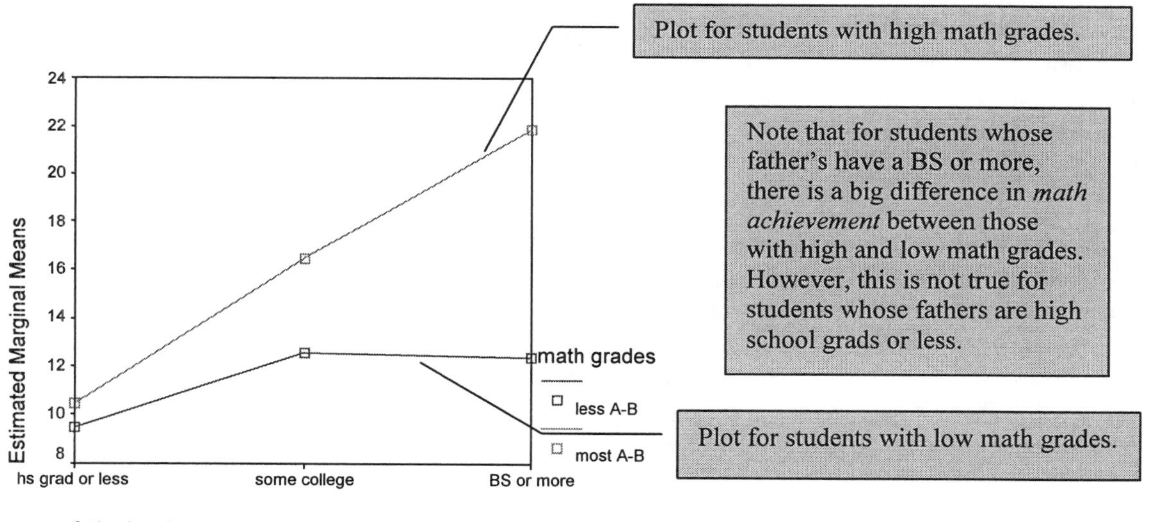
Plot for students with high math grades.
24
22
20
18
16
14
12
10
8
Estimated Marginal Means
Note that for students whose father's have a BS or more, there is a big difference in *math achievement* between those with high and low math grades. However, this is not true for students whose fathers are high school grads or less.
math grades
less A-B
most A-B
Plot for students with low math grades.
hs grad or less
some college
BS or more
father's ed rev

Interpretation of Output 11.1

The **GLM General Factorial** program allows you to print the means and counts, provides measures of effect size (eta), and plots the interaction, which is helpful in interpreting it. The first table in Output 11.1 shows that 73 participants (43 with low math grades and 30 high grades) are included in the analysis because they had data on all three of these variables. The second table shows the cell and marginal (total) means; they are very important for interpreting the ANOVA table and explaining the results of the test for the interaction.

The ANOVA table, called **Tests of Between Subjects Effects**, is the key table. Note that the word "effect" in the title of the table can be misleading because this study was not a randomized experiment. Thus, you cannot say in your report that the differences in the dependent variable were *caused* by the independent variable. Usually you will ignore the corrected model and intercept lines and skip down to the interaction *F* (***mathgr* * *faedr***) which is statistically significant, $F(2,67)=3.46$, $p=.037$. Thus, the "effect" of *math grades* on *math achievement* depends on the level of father's education. We would say that the "effect" of math grades depended on which father's education level is being considered. If you find a significant interaction you should examine the **profile plots** of cell means to visualize the differential effects. If there is a significant interaction the lines on the profile plot will not be parallel.

When the interaction is statistically significant, you should analyze the differences between cell means (the simple effects). In this case, the plot indicates that *math achievement* is relatively low for both groups of students whose fathers had relatively low *education* (high school grad or less), both those students with high and with low math grades. However, for students whose fathers have a high education level, differences in math grades seem to have a large "effect" on math achievement. This interpretation, based on a visual inspection of the plots, needs to be checked with inferential statistics. We will illustrate one method for statistically analyzing the simple effects in Problem 2.

Now, examine the main effects of *math grades* and of *father's education* (revised). Note that both are statistically significant, but because the interaction is significant this is somewhat misleading. For example, although overall those with high math grades did better in math achievement, this does not seem to be true for those whose fathers had the least education.

Note also the callout boxes about the adjusted *R* squared and eta squared. Eta is a type of correlation that is used when the independent variable is *nominal* and the dependent variable (math achievement in this problem) is *scale* data. Adjusted R^2 refers to the multiple coefficient squared correlation, which we will discuss in Problem 3. Like r^2, these statistics indicate how much variance (or variability) in the dependent variable can be predicted if you know the independent variable scores. In this problem, the eta^2 percentages vary from 9% to 24%.

Because eta and *R*, like *r*, are indexes of association, they can be used to interpret the effect size. In this example, eta for *math grades* is about .38 ($.38^2 = .145$) and, thus, according to Cohen (1988) a medium to large effect. Eta for *father's education* (revised) is about .49, a large effect. The interaction eta is about .31, a medium effect. The overall adjusted *R* is about .52, a large effect, but not much bigger than for father's education alone. Notice that the adjusted R^2 is lower than the unadjusted (.28 versus .33). The reason for this is that the adjusted R^2 takes into account (and adjusts for) the fact that not just one but three factors (*mathgr, faedr*, and the interaction) were used to predict *math achievement*.

An important point to remember is that statistical significance depends heavily on the sample size so that with 1000 subjects a much lower F or r will be significant than if the sample is 10 or even 100. Statistical significance just tells you that you can be quite sure that there is at least a tiny relationship between the independent and dependent variables. Effect size measures, which are more independent of sample size, tell you how strong the relationship is and, thus, give you an indication of its importance.

Problem 2: Post Hoc Analysis of a Significant Interaction

We have described, in the interpretation of Output 11.1 how to visually inspect and interpret the Profile Plots when there is a statistically significant interaction. In this problem we will illustrate one way to test the simple main effects statistically, using the Tukey test. In the interpretation of Output 11.1, we indicated that you should examine the interaction F first. If it is statistically significant, it provides important information and means that the results of the main effects may be misleading. Figure 11.4 is a decision tree that illustrates this point and guides to the analysis in this section.

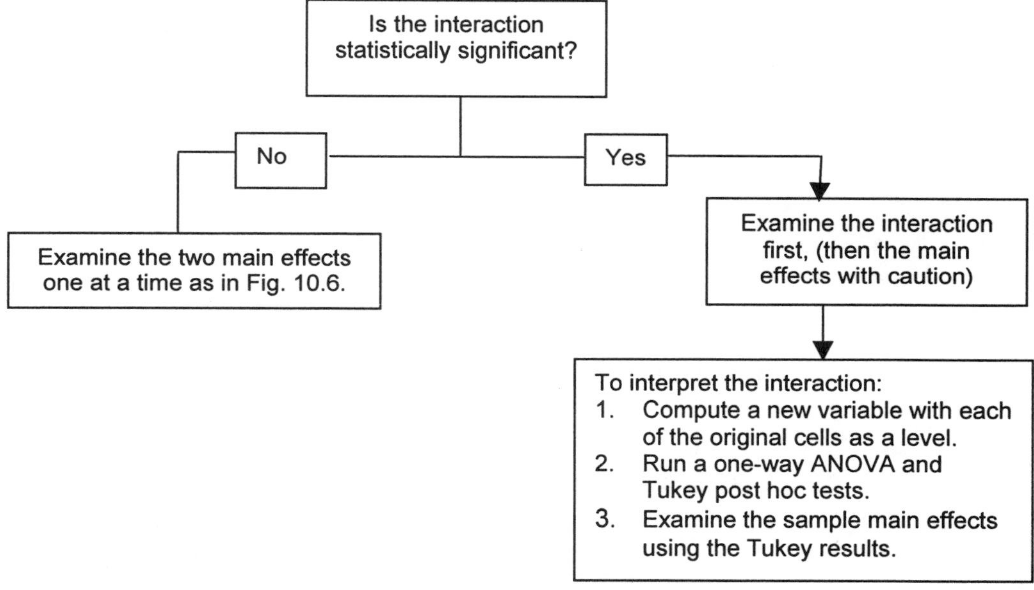

Fig. 11.4. Steps in analyzing a two-way factorial ANOVA.

Problem/Research Question

Which meaningful differences between cell means are statistically significant?

- Select **Transform=>Compute**. You will see the **Compute Variable** window (Fig. 11.5).

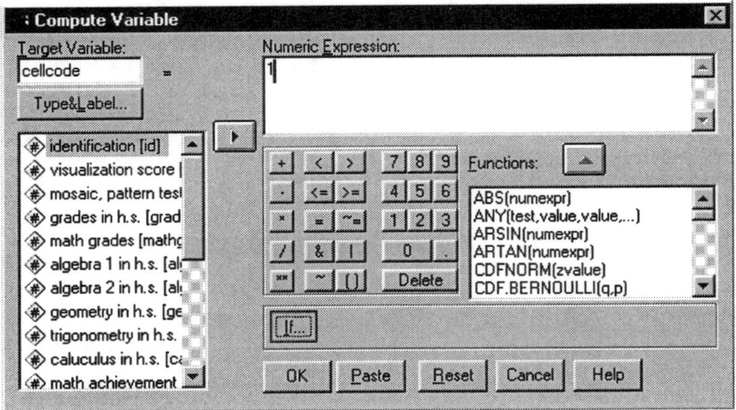

Fig. 11.5. Compute variable window.

- Under **Target Variable**, type *cellcode*. This is the name of the new variable you will compute.
- Click on **Type and Label**. You will see the **Compute Variable: Type and Label** window (Fig. 11.6).
- Type *six new cell codes* in the label box.

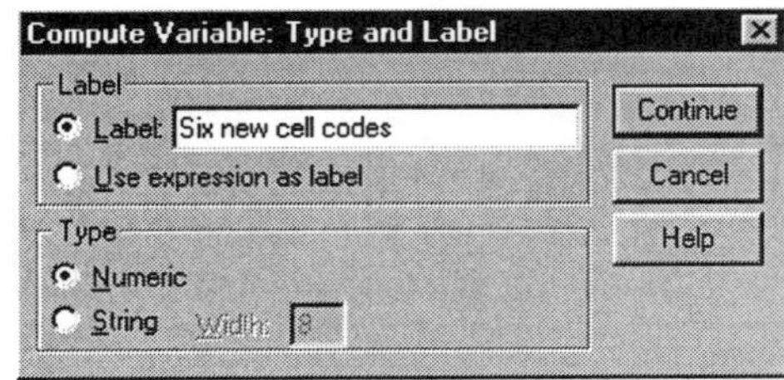

Fig. 11.6. Compute variable: Type and label.

- Click on **Continue**. You will see the **Compute Variable** window (Fig. 11.5) again.
- In the **Numeric Expression** box type *1*. This will be the first value or level for this new variable.
- Next, click on the **If...** button in Fig. 11.5 to produce Fig. 11.7.
- Select **Include if case satisfies condition.**
- Type *mathgr=0 & faedr=1* in the window. You are telling SPSS to compute level 1 of the new variable, *cellcode,* so that it combines the first level of *math grades* and the first level of *father's education revised*. See Fig. 11.7.
- Click on **Continue**.

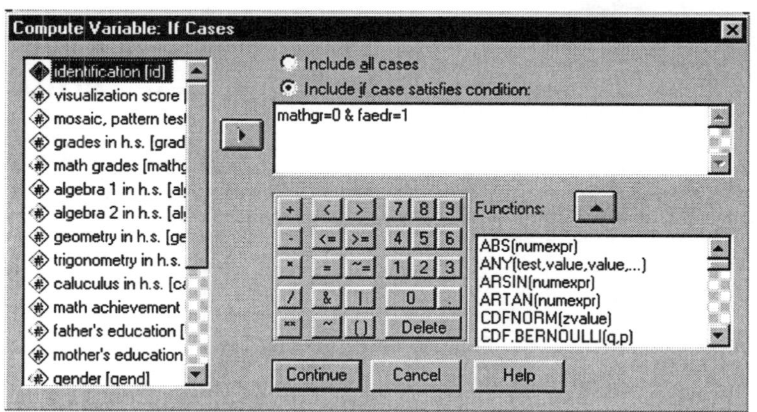

Fig. 11.7. Compute variable: If cases.

- Click on **OK**. If you look at your Data View or Variable View screen, you will see a new variable called *cellcode*. In the **Data View** screen, you should also notice that several of the cases now show a value of 1. Those are the cases where the original variables of *math grades* and *father's education revised* met the requirements you just computed.

You will need to repeat this process for the other 5 levels of this new variable. We will walk you through the process once more.

- Select **Transform=>Compute** to see the **Compute Variable** window (Fig. 11.5).
- Ensure that *cellcode* is still in the target variable box.
- Type *2* in the **Numeric Expression** box.
- Click on the **If...** button.
- Ensure that **Include if case satisfies condition** is selected.
- Type *mathgr=1 & faedr=1* in the box. You are now telling SPSS to use the other (higher) level of *math grades* with the first level of *father's education revised.*
- Click on **Continue**.
- Click on **OK**.
- SPSS will ask you if you want to change the existing variable. Click on **OK**. This means that you want to add this 2nd level to the *cellcode* variable. If you look at the **Data View** screen, you will notice that some of the cases now indicate a value of 2.
- Complete the above steps for the remaining 4 levels: *mathgr=0 & faedr=2*; *mathgr = 1 & faedr = 2*; *mathgr = 0 & faedr = 3; and mathgr = 1 & faedr = 3.*

Next, you will use this new variable *cellcode* to examine the statistical significance of differences among the six cells using one-way ANOVA and the Tukey test as described in chapter 10. This will help us to interpret the simple effects that we discussed above.

- Select **Analyze=>Compare Means=>One Way ANOVA....** You will see the **One Way ANOVA** window. Fig. 11.8.
- Move *math achievement* into the **Dependent List:** box by clicking on the top **arrow** button.
- Move *six new cell codes* into the **Factor:** box by clicking on the bottom **arrow** button.

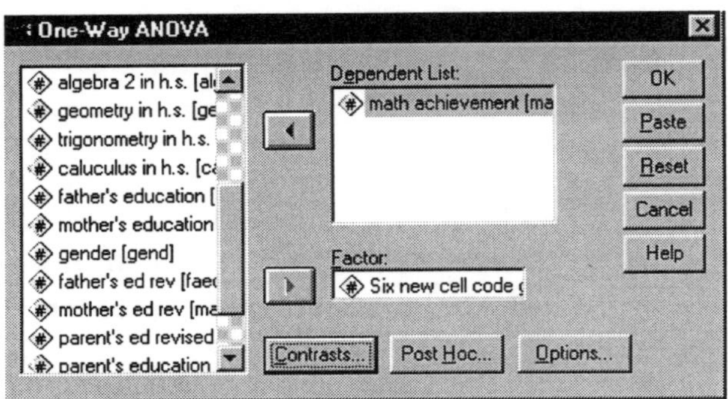

Fig. 11.8. One-way ANOVA.

- Click on the **Post Hoc...** button to see the **One-Way ANOVA: Post Hoc Multiple Comparisons** window (Fig. 11.9).
- Select the **Tukey** test under **Equal Variances Assumed.**
- Click on **Continue**.

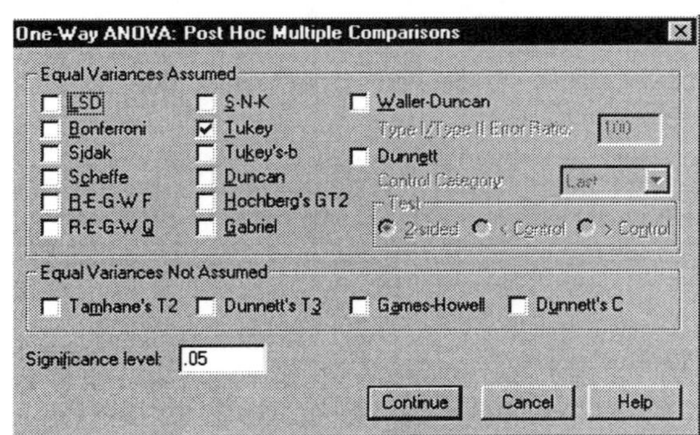

Fig. 11.9. One-way ANOVA: Post hoc multiple comparisons.

- Click on **Options...**
- Check the **Descriptive** box.
- Click on **Continue**.
- Click on **OK**.

Output 11.2: One-Way ANOVA for Comparing New Cell Means

Oneway

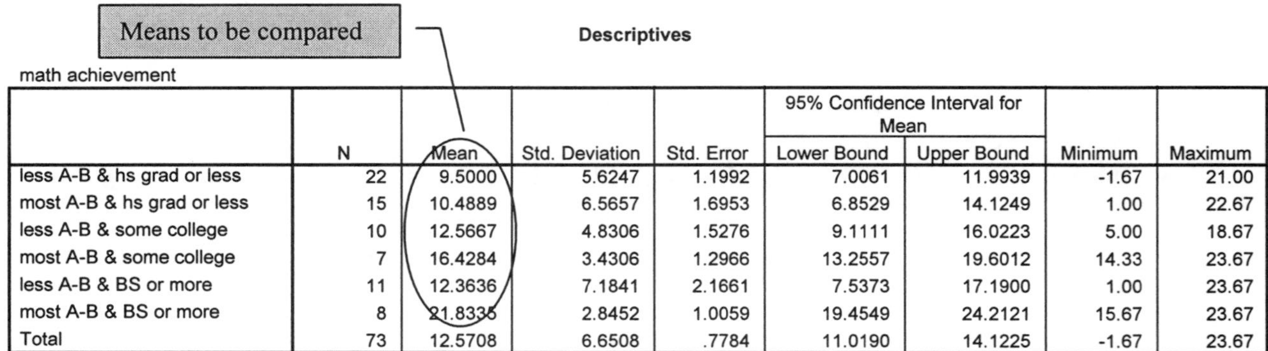

Descriptives

math achievement

	N	Mean	Std. Deviation	Std. Error	95% Confidence Interval for Mean		Minimum	Maximum
					Lower Bound	Upper Bound		
less A-B & hs grad or less	22	9.5000	5.6247	1.1992	7.0061	11.9939	-1.67	21.00
most A-B & hs grad or less	15	10.4889	6.5657	1.6953	6.8529	14.1249	1.00	22.67
less A-B & some college	10	12.5667	4.8306	1.5276	9.1111	16.0223	5.00	18.67
most A-B & some college	7	16.4284	3.4306	1.2966	13.2557	19.6012	14.33	23.67
less A-B & BS or more	11	12.3636	7.1841	2.1661	7.5373	17.1900	1.00	23.67
most A-B & BS or more	8	21.8335	2.8452	1.0059	19.4549	24.2121	15.67	23.67
Total	73	12.5708	6.6508	.7784	11.0190	14.1225	-1.67	23.67

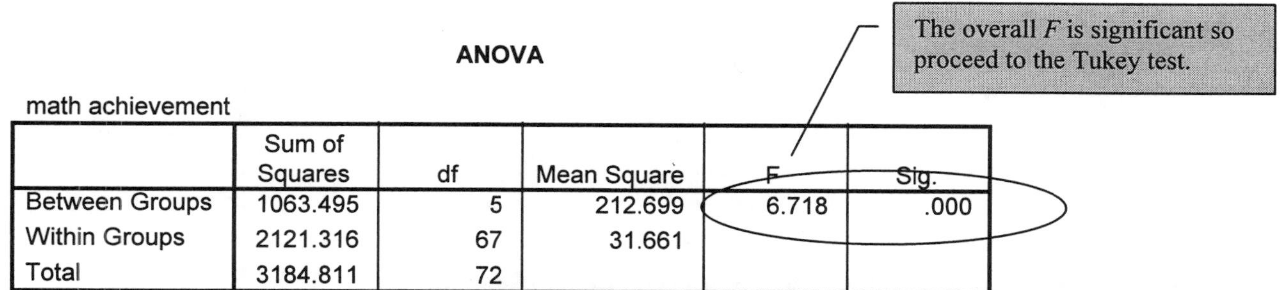

The overall F is significant so proceed to the Tukey test.

ANOVA

math achievement

	Sum of Squares	df	Mean Square	F	Sig.
Between Groups	1063.495	5	212.699	6.718	.000
Within Groups	2121.316	67	31.661		
Total	3184.811	72			

Post Hoc Tests

The circles below indicate the three simple main effects shown with arrows in Fig. 11.10. For now, ignore the lines without circles. Half are duplicates; others are not meaningful.

Multiple Comparisons

Dependent Variable: math achievement
Tukey HSD

(I) Six new cell code groups	(J) Six new cell code groups	Mean Difference (I-J)	Std. Error	Sig.	95% Confidence Interval Lower Bound	95% Confidence Interval Upper Bound
less A-B & hs grad or less	most A-B & hs grad or less	-.9889	1.8841	.995	-6.5166	4.5388
vs	less A-B & some college	-3.0667	2.1460	.709	-9.3627	3.2293
	most A-B & some college	-6.9284	2.4418	.064	-14.0922	.2353
	less A-B & BS or more	-2.8636	2.0779	.740	-8.9597	3.2324
	most A-B & BS or more	-12.3335*	2.3231	.000	-19.1491	-5.5179
most A-B & hs grad or less	less A-B & hs grad or less	.9889	1.8841	.995	-4.5388	6.5166
	less A-B & some college	-2.0778	2.2972	.944	-8.8173	4.6616
	most A-B & some college	-5.9396	2.5756	.206	-13.4960	1.6169
	less A-B & BS or more	-1.8748	2.2336	.959	-8.4278	4.6783
	most A-B & BS or more	-11.3446*	2.4634	.000	-18.5719	-4.1174
less A-B & some college	less A-B & hs grad or less	3.0667	2.1460	.709	-3.2293	9.3627
vs	most A-B & hs grad or less	2.0778	2.2972	.944	-4.6616	8.8173
	most A-B & some college	-3.8617	2.7729	.731	-11.9971	4.2736
	less A-B & BS or more	.2031	2.4585	1.000	-7.0099	7.4160
	most A-B & BS or more	-9.2668*	2.6690	.011	-17.0973	-1.4363
most A-B & some college	less A-B & hs grad or less	6.9284	2.4418	.064	-.2353	14.0922
	most A-B & hs grad or less	5.9396	2.5756	.206	-1.6169	13.4960
	less A-B & some college	3.8617	2.7729	.731	-4.2736	11.9971
	less A-B & BS or more	4.0648	2.7205	.669	-3.9168	12.0464
	most A-B & BS or more	-5.4051	2.9122	.438	-13.9489	3.1387
less A-B & BS or more	less A-B & hs grad or less	2.8636	2.0779	.740	-3.2324	8.9597
	most A-B & hs grad or less	1.8748	2.2336	.959	-4.6783	8.4278
vs	less A-B & some college	-.2031	2.4585	1.000	-7.4160	7.0099
	most A-B & some college	-4.0648	2.7205	.669	-12.0464	3.9168
	most A-B & BS or more	-9.4699*	2.6146	.007	-17.1406	-1.7991
most A-B & BS or more	less A-B & hs grad or less	12.3335*	2.3231	.000	5.5179	19.1491
	most A-B & hs grad or less	11.3446*	2.4634	.000	4.1174	18.5719
	less A-B & some college	9.2668*	2.6690	.011	1.4363	17.0973
	most A-B & some college	5.4051	2.9122	.438	-3.1387	13.9489
	less A-B & BS or more	9.4699*	2.6146	.007	1.7991	17.1406

*. The mean difference is significant at the .05 level.

Interpretation of Output 11.2

This output is the result of doing the first two steps, shown in Fig. 11.4, for interpreting a statistically significant interaction. Using Output 11.2, we can examine the simple main effects statistically. The first table, **Descriptives**, provides the means of the *six new cell code* groups that will be compared, two at a time, with the **Tukey HSD** (Honestly Significant Difference) test, which is in the third table, **Post Hoc Tests**. This table is big and complex because there are 15 possible paired comparisons and each is given twice, using the SPSS matrix format. Several of these comparisons are not meaningful to us, so, for now, ignore the lines that do not have circles on them. We will focus on one set of simple main effects in our interpretation. Note that we have circled three **mean differences** and the corresponding **sig.** (significance level or *p*). These correspond to three simple main effects shown with **arrows** in the following interaction plot (Fig. 11.10). For example, the left hand arrow (and the top line of the post tests table) compares math achievement scores for both groups of students whose fathers have a relatively low education level; that is, such students with high math grades are compared to those with low math grades.

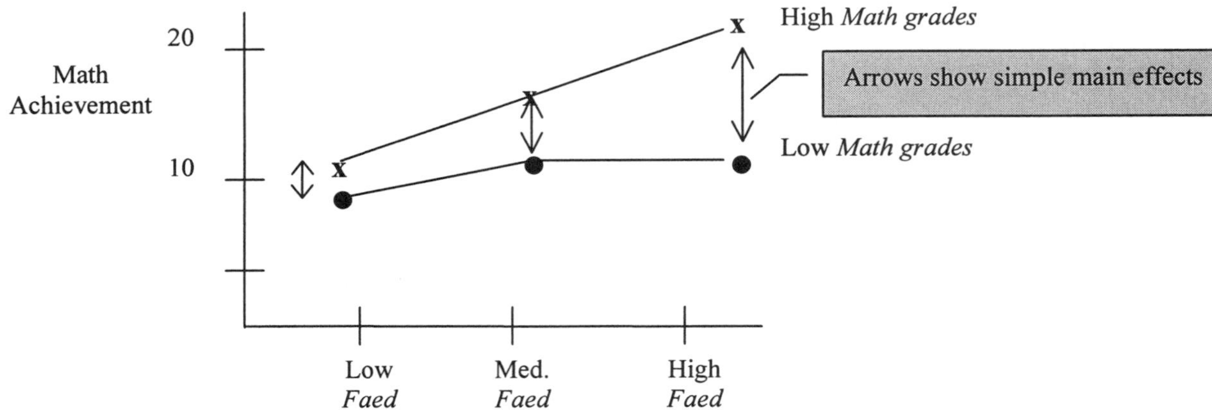

Fig. 11.10. Interaction plot showing three simple main effects.

We can now confirm statistically what we thought from visual inspection of the profile plot in Output 11.1. As you can see in Fig. 11.10 and the circled parts of the **Post Hoc** table, there is almost no difference (.99 points, $p = .995$) in *math achievement* between students with high and low *math grades* when their *father's education* is low. Likewise this difference, while bigger (3.26 points), is not statistically significant ($p = .731$) when their *father's education* is medium (some college). However, when *father's education* is high, students with high (mostly As and Bs) *math grades* do much better (9.47 points) on the achievement test than those with low grades ($p = .007$). Thus, *math achievement* depends on both a student's *math grades* and their *father's education*. It would also be possible to examine the sample main effects for high and low math grades separately (the two lines), but this is usually not necessary to understand the interaction.

Problem 3: Using Multiple Linear Regression

Multiple linear regression is one of several complex statistical methods based on the associational approach. Multiple regression is based on a correlation matrix of all the variables to be considered in a problem. It has the general purpose of predicting a dependent or criterion variable from *several* independent or predictor variables. For multiple regression, the *dependent* or outcome variable should be scale data which is normally distributed in the population from which it is drawn. The *independent* variables can be scale or dichotomous variables, which are also called "dummy" variables. Dummy variables are nominal categories that have been given numerical codes, usually 1 and 0. The 0 stands for whatever the 1 is not, and is thus said to be "dumb" or silent. In our study, when we use gender as a dummy variable in multiple regression, we're really using it as 2 = female and 1 = not female (i.e., male).

To reiterate, the purpose of multiple regression is to predict a *scale* level or type dependent variable from a combination of several *scale* and/or *dichotomous* independent or predictor variables. In this assignment, we will see if *math achievement* can be predicted better from a combination of several of our other variables than from any one alone. We will assume that all of the predictor variables are important and that we want to know the multiple correlation of all these variables with *math achievement*. For this purpose, we will use the method that SPSS calls **Enter**, which tells the computer to consider all the variables at the same time. This method is called *simultaneous multiple regression* as contrasted with stepwise or hierarchical, which we will not use in this book.

Problem/Research Question

How well can you predict *math achievement* from a combination of four variables: *mosaic, grades in high school*, and *mother's* and *father's education*? Which of these four predictors contribute significantly to the multiple correlation/regression?

Let's predict *math achievement* from the *grades in high school, mosaic pattern test,* and *mother's* and *father's education.*

- Click on the following: **Analyze => Regression => Linear** to see Fig 11.11.
- Select *math achievement* and click it over to the **Dependent** (variable) box.
- Next select the variables *mosaic, grades, mother's education,* and *father's education* (not revised) and click them over to the **Independent(s)** box (Independent variables).

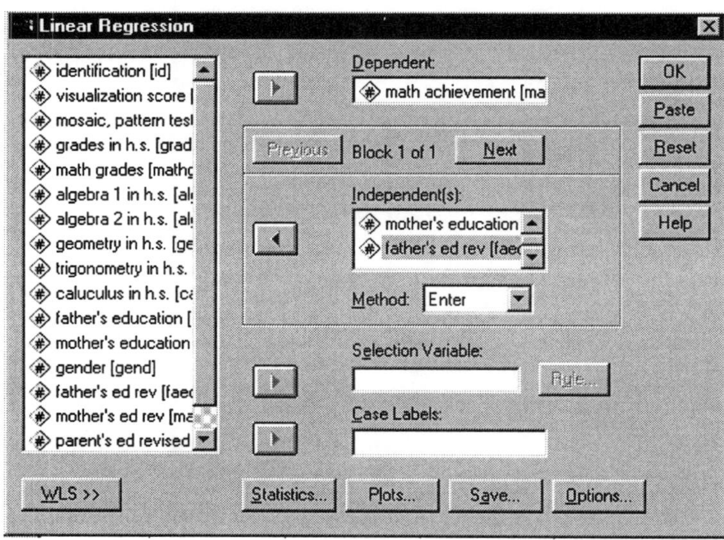

Fig. 11.11. Linear regression.

- Under **Method**, select **Enter**.
- Click on **Statistics** to get Fig. 11.12.
- Then check on **Descriptives** and ensure that **Estimates** (under **Regression coefficients**) and **Model fit** are also checked.
- Click on **Continue**.
- Click on **OK**.

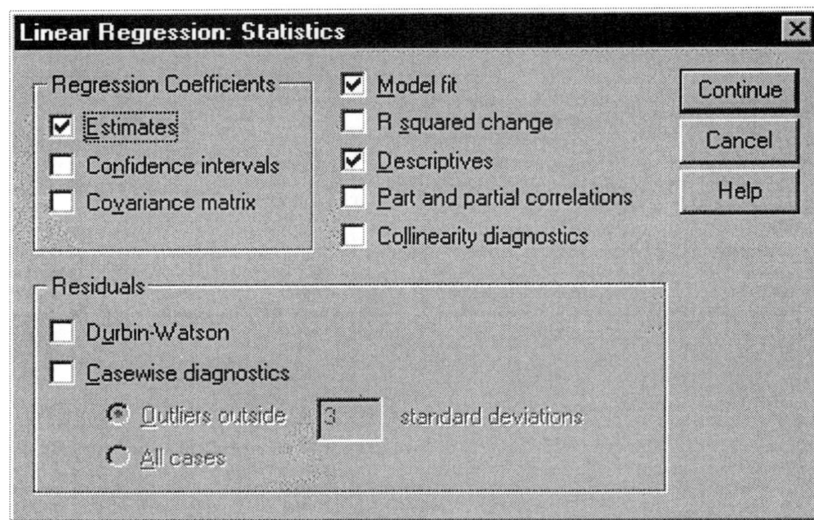

Fig. 11.12. Linear regression: Statistics.

Compare your output to Output 11.3.

Output 11.3: Multiple Linear Regression, Predicting Math Achievement

Regression

Descriptive Statistics

	Mean	Std. Deviation	N
math achievement	12.6019	6.6922	72
mosaic, pattern test	27.014	9.111	72
grades in h.s.	5.71	1.56	72
mother's education	4.17	2.26	72
father's education	4.76	2.83	72

Bivariate correlations with math achievement.

Their significance levels.

Correlations

		math achievement	mosaic, pattern test	grades in h.s.	mother's education	father's education
Pearson Correlation	math achievement	1.000	.229	.485	.342	.379
	mosaic, pattern test	.229	1.000	-.015	.043	.106
	grades in h.s.	.485	-.015	1.000	.185	.265
	mother's education	.342	.043	.185	1.000	.676
	father's education	.379	.106	.265	.676	1.000
Sig. (1-tailed)	math achievement	.	.027	.000	.002	.001
	mosaic, pattern test	.027	.	.452	.360	.187
	grades in h.s.	.000	.452	.	.060	.012
	mother's education	.002	.360	.060	.	.000
	father's education	.001	.187	.012	.000	.
N	math achievement	72	72	72	72	72
	mosaic, pattern test	72	72	72	72	72
	grades in h.s.	72	72	72	72	72
	mother's education	72	72	72	72	72
	father's education	72	72	72	72	72

High correlations (e.g., >.50) between variables can cause collinearity problems.

Variables Entered/Removed[b]

Model	Variables Entered	Variables Removed	Method
1	Father's education, Mosaic pattern test score, Grades in high school, Mother's education[a]		Enter

a. All requested variables entered.

b. Dependent Variable: Math achievement

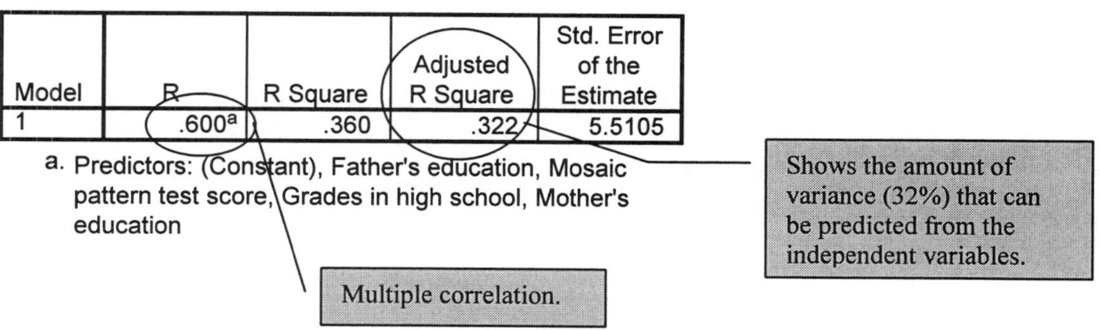

Model Summary

Model	R	R Square	Adjusted R Square	Std. Error of the Estimate
1	.600[a]	.360	.322	5.5105

a. Predictors: (Constant), Father's education, Mosaic pattern test score, Grades in high school, Mother's education

Shows the amount of variance (32%) that can be predicted from the independent variables.
Multiple correlation.

ANOVA[b]

Model		Sum of Squares	df	Mean Square	F	Sig.
1	Regression	1145.259	4	286.315	9.429	.000[a]
	Residual	2034.475	67	30.365		
	Total	3179.734	71			

a. Predictors: (Constant), Father's education, Mosaic pattern test score, Grades in high school, Mother's education

b. Dependent Variable: Math achievement

Indicates there is one or more significant predictors.

Coefficients[a]

Model		Unstandardized Coefficients		Standardized Coefficients	t	Sig.
		B	Std. Error	Beta		
1	(Constant)	-5.496	3.252		-1.690	.096
	mosaic, pattern test	.157	.072	.214	2.172	.033
	grades in h.s.	1.810	.435	.422	4.159	.000
	mother's education	.485	.392	.164	1.235	.221
	father's education	.316	.322	.134	.982	.329

a. Dependent Variable: math achievement

Indicates which variables are significant predictors when all are used together to predict math achievement.

Interpretation of Output 11.3

This output provides the usual **descriptive statistics** for all five variables in the first table. Note that the *N* is 72 because three participants were missing a score on one or more of the variables. Multiple regression uses only the participants who have complete data. The next table is a **correlation matrix**. The first column shows the correlations of the other variables with *math achievement.* Note that all of them (*mosaic, grades in high school,* and *mother's* and *father's education*) are significantly correlated *with math achievement*. Also notice that two of the predictor/independent variables (*mother's education* and *father's education*) are highly correlated with each other *(r*=.68). All the others have relatively low correlations with each other. The **variables entered/removed** table shows that all the variables were entered simultaneously.

The *model summary* table shows that the multiple correlation coefficient (***R***), using all the predictors simultaneously, is .60 and the **adjusted R^2** is .32, meaning that 32% of the variance in math achievement can be predicted from the four variables (*mosaic, grades,* and *mother's* and *father's* education) combined. Note that the adjusted R^2 is lower than the unadjusted R^2. This is, in part, related to the number of variables in the equation. An adjustment is necessary because several independent variables were used. You can use *R* based on the adjusted R^2 (square root of .32 = .57) as a rough estimate of the effect size. An *r* of .57 is a large effect according to Cohen (1988).

The ANOVA table shows that ***F* = 9.43** and is statistically significant. This indicates that one or more of the independent variables is a significant predicator of *math achievement* when used in this combination. This *F* is usually significant if any of the correlations were statistically significant.

The most important table is the **coefficients** table. It shows the unstandardized and the standardized beta coefficients. The **unstandardized coefficients** and the constant can be used to predict a person's math achievement score given his or her scores on mosaic, grades, mother's and father's education. The **standardized coefficients** are interpreted like correlation coefficients. The ***t*** and **Sig.** opposite each predictor or independent variable indicates whether that variable makes a significant addition to the prediction of math achievement *over and above* the contribution of all other variables; i.e., does it add anything new? Thus, *mosaic* and *grades*, in this example, each help the prediction when the other three variables are already considered. Because high intercorrelations among independent/predictor variables (called *collinearity)* causes a problem in the interpretation of multiple regression, neither *mother's* nor *father's education* adds significantly to the prediction. They sort of cancel out each other. One way to handle this is to combine variables that are highly related, if that makes conceptual sense. In this case we could compute a *parent's education* score. When we computed an average *parent's education* score, we found that it contributed significantly to the prediction of *math achievement*, but *mosaic* was no longer a significant predictor.

- ***Exit SPSS***

Interpretation Questions

1. In Output 11.1: a) Is the interaction significant? b) Examine the profile plot of the cell means that illustrates the interaction. Describe it in words. c) Is the main effect of father's education significant? Interpret the eta squared. d) How about the "effect" of math grades? e) Why did we put the word effect in quotes? f) How might focusing on the main effects be misleading?

2. In Output 11.3: a) What combination of the four variables contributes significantly to the prediction of math achievement? b) What is the multiple *R*? c) What is the adjusted R^2, and what does it mean?

Extra Problems Using Class Data

Using your class data or the data from Appendix B, do the following problems. Print your outputs after typing your interpretations on them. Please circle the key parts of the output that you use for your interpretation.

1. Do gender and marital status seem to have an effect on student's height and do gender and marital status interact? Run the appropriate SPSS analysis and interpret the results.

2. Design and run another appropriate factorial ANOVA. Interpret the results.

3. Is there a combination of gender and same sex parent's height that predict student's height better than either one of these variables alone?

4. Design and run another appropriate multiple regression. Interpret the results.

More Extra Problems

For the following problems, you must decide on an appropriate inferential statistic from chapters 8-11. Run the statistics and interpret the output using the data from Appendix B.

1. Are there differences between males and females in regard to the average number of hours they a) study, b) work, and c) watch TV?

2. Are there differences between the age groups in regard to the average number of hours they a) study, b) work, and c) watch TV?

3. Is there an association between having children or not and watching TV sitcoms?

4. Is there a difference between students who have children and those who do not in regard to their age group?

5. Is there a combination of hours of TV watching, hours of studying, and hours of work that predicts current GPA?

6. Do gender and having children interaction and do either seem to affect current GPA?

7. Is there a difference between the number of hours students study and the hours they work? Also, is there an association between the two?

8. Is there an association between the students' evaluation of their institution's social activities and their evaluation of their current program of study (major)?

APPENDIX A

WRITING RESEARCH PROBLEMS AND QUESTIONS

Frameworks for Stating Research Problems

Although a common definition of a research problem is that it is a statement that asks what relationship exists between two or more variables, most research problems are more complex than this definition implies. The research problem should be a broad statement that covers the several more specific research questions to be investigated, perhaps by using terms that stand for several variables. One way to state the problem that can help you determine the independent and dependent variables, is as follows (underlines indicate that you fill in the appropriate name for the variable or group of variables):

Format

If your study is randomized experimental, you could phrase the problem as follows: The research problem is to investigate the effect of (put independent variable 1 or group of variables here) (and independent variable 2, if any, here) (and independent variable 3, if any) on (dependent variable 1, here) (and dependent variable 2, if any) in (population).

Except in a totally descriptive study, there always must be at least two variables (we call one the independent and one the dependent variable). However, there can be two or more of each, and there often are. In the statement of the problem, in contrast to the research questions/hypotheses, it is desirable to use broad descriptors for groups of similar variables. For example, demographics might cover four variables: gender, mother's and father's education, and ethnicity. Spatial performance might include a mosaic pattern test score and a visualization score. Likewise, grades and mathematics attitudes could refer to more than one variable. Concepts such as self-esteem or teaching style have several aspects that usually result in more than one variable. The first example below is in the above format. The second and third are suggested variations when the approach is quasi-experimental, comparative or associational.

Examples

1. The research problem is to investigate the effect of a new curriculum on grades, math attitudes, and quantitative/spatial achievement in high school students.

This format is most appropriate for studies that use the *randomized experimental approach*. For other studies that compare groups or associate/relate variables, you could phrase the problem as follows:

2. The problem is to investigate the relationships of gender and grades to mathematics attitudes achievement in high school students.

If you have *more than two or three independent variables* it may be best to say:

3. The problem is to investigate whether demographics, mathematics courses, grades, spatial scores, and mathematics attitudes are predictors of mathematics achievement. More generally, we could say the problem is to investigate the factors that predict or *seem* to influence mathematics achievement.

This latter format is especially useful when the approach is a complex (many independent variables) associational one that will use multiple regression.

Framework for Stating Research Questions/Hypotheses

Although it is okay to phrase a randomized experimental research problem (in the format of the first example above) as a "study of the effect of...," we think it is best to phrase your research questions or hypotheses so that they do not appear to imply cause and effect (i.e., as *difference* or *associational* questions/hypotheses and/or as *descriptive* questions). The former is answered with inferential statistics and the latter with descriptive statistics. There are several reasonable ways to state research questions. We show below one way to state each type of question, which we have found useful and, hopefully, clear for our students.

Descriptive Questions

Basic descriptive questions. These questions are about some aspect of one variable. Descriptive questions ask about the central tendency, frequency distribution, percentage in each category, variability, or shape of the distribution. Some descriptive questions are intended to test assumptions. Some questions simply describe the sample demographics. Some *examples* are as follows:

1. What percentage of participants are of each gender?
2. What is the mean, mode, and median of the mathematics achievement scores?
3. Is mathematics achievement distributed approximately normally?

Complex descriptive questions. These questions deal with two or more variables at a time, but do not involve inferential statistics. Cross-tabulations of two categorical variables, factor analysis, and measures of reliability (e.g., Cronbach's alpha) are examples.

An *example* is:
1. What is the reliability of the visualization score?

Difference Questions/Hypotheses

Basic difference questions. The *format* is as follows:

Are there differences between the (insert number) levels of (put the independent variable name here) (you could name the levels here) in regard to the average (put the dependent variable name here) scores?

An *example* is as follows:

1. Are there differences between the three levels (high, medium, and low) of father's education in regard to the average mathematics achievement scores of the students?

Analysis: One-way ANOVA (see Output 10.3 and 10.4). A *t* test would be used if there were only two levels of the independent variable (see Output 10.1).

Complex difference and interaction questions. When you have two categorical independent variables considered together, you will have *three* research questions or hypotheses. There are advantages of considering two or three independent variables at a time. See chapter 11 for how to interpret the *interaction* question. Sample *formats* for a set of three questions answered by *one* 2-way ANOVA are as follows:

1. Is there a difference between the levels of the (insert independent variable 1) in regard to the average (put dependent variable 1 here) scores?

2. Is there a difference between the levels of the (insert independent variable 2) in regard to the average (dependent variable 1) scores?

3. Is there an interaction of (independent **variable 1**) and (independent **variable 2**) in regard to the (**dependent** variable 1)?

(Repeat these three questions, for the second dependent variable, if there is more than one.) An *example* is as follows:

1. Is there a difference between students having high versus low math grades in regard to their average mathematics achievement scores?

2. Is there a difference between male and female students in regard to their average math achievement scores?

3. Is there an interaction between mathematics grades and gender in regard to math achievement?

Note that the first question states the *levels* or categories of the first independent variable; that is, it states the groups that are to be compared (high vs. low math grade students). The second question does the same for the second independent variable; that is, states the *levels (*male and female) to be compared. However, in the third (interaction) question, it is asked whether the first *variable* itself (mathematics grades) interacts with the second variable (gender). No mention is made, at this point, of the values/levels/groups.

Analysis: Factorial ANOVA (see Outputs 11.1 and 11.2).

Associational/Relationship Questions/Hypotheses

Basic associational questions. When both the independent and dependent variables are ordered and essentially continuous (i.e., have five or more ordered categories) the approach and research question are considered to be associational. The *format* is as follows:

Is there an association between (independent variable 1) and (dependent variable 1)?

If there is more than one independent variable and/or dependent variable, which is common, and each pair of variables is associated separately, you can have a series of questions asking whether there is an association between *each* independent variable and *each* dependent variable. If it is arbitrary which variables are independent or antecedent or predictors and which are dependent or outcome variables, one might ask whether every variable is related to every other variable. This would produce a *correlation matrix.*

An *example* for a single association/relationship is as follows:
1. Is there an association between grades in high school and mathematics achievement?

An *example* that would produce a correlation matrix is as follows:
2. Are there associations among the three mathematics attitude scale scores?

Note that what is said to be associated in these questions is the variable itself; no mention is made of the levels or values here.

Analysis: Pearson or Spearman correlation, depending on the type or level of measurement of the variables.

Complex associational questions. In the associational approach, when two or more *independent* variables are considered together, rather than separately, as in the basic format above, you get a new kind of question. The *format* can be phrased something like:

Is there a combination of factors (list the several specific independent variables here) that predict (put dependent variable here) better than any one alone?

An *example* is as follows:

1. Is there a combination of number of mathematics courses taken, gender, and father's education that predicts mathematics achievement better than any predictor variable alone?

Analysis: Multiple regression (see Output 11.3).

This complex question can also be expanded into a set of questions. This set first asks about the association of each of the predictors (or independent) variables and the dependent (or outcome) variable and then states the complex or combination question as above.

For *example*:

1. Is there an association between the number of mathematics courses taken and mathematics achievement test scores?

2. Is there an association between gender and mathematics achievement?

3. Is there an association between father's education and mathematics achievement?

4. Is there combination of the number of mathematics courses taken, gender, and father's education that predicts mathematics achievement test scores better than any one of them alone?

Analysis: The multiple regression output will provide you with the three bivariate, Pearson correlations in a matrix as well as the multiple regression statistics (see, for example, Output 11.3).

APPENDIX B

Developing a Questionnaire and a Data Set for Assignment A

Nancy L. Leech

Questionnaires are commonly used in research to collect data that provide information about knowledge, perceptions, and attitudes. The information collected reflects the subject's attitudes, knowledge, and so on at the time that the questionnaire is completed. This appendix provides a brief overview about developing a questionnaire, but may include recollection of past or predictions of future behavior. A more complete discussion is provided by Salant and Dillman (1994).

Deciding What Information You Want

Before writing any questions for a questionnaire, it is important to think through how you will analyze the data. For example, you might want to know what cars are the most popular among your peers. An open-ended question to answer this would be: "What is your favorite vehicle?" Your classmates may simply write the name of their favorite *vehicle*. The following might be responses to this question:

Volkswagen
Ford
Truck
Corvette
Yacht
Ski lift
Convertible

The use of the word "vehicle" allowed responses like "ski lift" and "yacht". Thus, the way in which a researcher words a question can greatly impact the type of answers respondents provide.

Wording questions in a vague manner can cause other problems. As a researcher you have to decide how to input the data into SPSS. The vagueness of this "vehicle" example leaves the researcher with many different responses, some of which are not appropriate or the type of response that the question was intended to generate. It can be helpful to have peers read your questionnaire before proceeding. Many unclear questions or problems with wording can be found and changed before you end up with meaningless data.

Methods of Administration

After creating your questionnaire, the next step is to decide how to give or administer it to the subjects. Questionnaires can be administered using several different methods. The researcher could collect information via the telephone, mail, e-mail, individual face-to-face, or group administration. The face-to-face method usually is used when obtaining in-depth information requires more time or explanation than is possible using mail or telephone. The group method can be used in situations such as a club meeting or a college classroom where a researcher or a surrogate administers and collects the questionnaires from the group.

If your class is being taught via distance education the class questionnaire data will most likely be collected via e-mail or mail. If your class is being offered in the traditional classroom format, then the data will most likely be collected via the group method.

Sampling Techniques

There are a variety of sampling techniques that can be used. There are two broad kinds of sampling: probability, and non-probability. This appendix does not allow for a full explanation of these methods. You can find more information about sampling in a research methods book such as Gliner and Morgan (2000).

A probability sample is defined as a selection of participants where every person in a population has a known, nonzero chance of being chosen. There are four probability sampling techniques: simple random, systematic with a random start, cluster, and stratified. These techniques are the most powerful in that the data collected from samples using these methods are more likely to be generalizable to larger populations.

A nonprobability sample is defined as a sampling technique where there is not an equal chance for a participant to be chosen. Thus, bias is usually introduced into the study. There are several types of non-probability sampling techniques. Quota, convenience, and purposive are three. Unfortunately, most student research, including the class questionnaire suggested in chapter 4, use nonprobability sampling. With nonprobability sampling, making generalizations beyond the group of study may be problematic.

Writing Good Questions

In this section, we will describe briefly some of the main types of questionnaire (or survey) items and questions.

Likert scales. One of the most common types of items used to collect quantitative data is the Likert scale, which is sometimes referred to as an "ordered response scale". Most likely you have used Likert scales many times. An example of a Likert scale, which might have been used for the class questionnaire is:

- Research Methods is my favorite subject. Circle the response which most represents your feelings:

Strongly Agree Agree Undecided Disagree Strongly Disagree

When using a Likert scale the researcher has some choices. The first choice is whether the Likert scale should include a middle choice like undecided or should the question be written in a manner that forces the respondent to either agree or disagree. Another decision that needs to be made, is whether to provide a numerical scale under the wording. For example, the question as stated above could be used with a numerical scale added.

Strongly Agree	Agree	Undecided	Disagree	Strongly Disagree
5	4	3	2	1

Researchers disagree about whether this type of numerical addition is desirable. Sometimes researchers add the numerical scale when they input the data but do not show this numbering on the questionnaire. In standardized questionnaires it is common to have a number of Likert type items and often the words are at the top of the column and only the numbers are opposite each item.

Semantic Differential scales. Another way to collect quantitative data is with a semantic differential scale, which uses bipolar adjectives (adjectives that are opposite of one another). These adjectives can be Activity pairs, Evaluative pairs or Potency pairs. An example of an Activity pair would be "active – passive," or "fast – slow." Evaluative pairs include words such as "good – bad," or "dirty – clean." Examples of Potency pairs include comparisons such as "large – small," or "hot – cold." The evaluative type is used most often in quantitative research.

An example of part of a semantic differential scale, which might be used for your class questionnaire is:

- The research course I am currently taking is: (circle the number that best reflects your view)

Bad	1	2	3	4	5	6	7	Good
Large	1	2	3	4	5	6	7	Small
Worthless	1	2	3	4	5	6	7	Valuable

When creating a semantic differential scale, it is best to switch some of the positive choices from the right side to the left side. Notice in the above example, the right side includes positive words, such as "good" and "valuable." The left side includes words that are thought of as being more negative, such as "bad" and "worthless." The middle pair is switched, with the more negative word, "small," on the right and the more positive word, "large," on the left. Switching the words will help ensure that the subject reads the words, and does not just circle "7" for each answer.

Checklists. Another type of data collection for surveys is a checklist. Checklists are words that are listed so the subject can mark the ones that apply. Usually subjects are asked to mark all that apply, thus there can be multiple words selected. An example of a checklist is:

- What type of television shows do you watch? Please check all that apply.

❑ Sitcoms
❑ Movies
❑ Sports
❑ News

Rankings. Rankings are another type of survey question. With ranking questions subjects are asked to rank or place in order a number of choices. Ranked items are relatively easy to make and for participants to answer as long as they are asked to rank only a few (for example three or four) items. However, ranking items are not so easy to handle statistically. Two problems that may occur are 1) the respondents may not rank all the items and 2) they produce ordinal data which eliminates the use of parametric statistics (such as *t* test and correlation). An example of a ranking scale is:

- Rank the following types of television shows in terms of how much you would like to watch them (1 = most preferred, 4 = least preferred). Please use each number only once and use all four numbers.

  Sitcoms ______
  Movies ______
  Sports ______
  News ______

Open-ended. The last type of survey question discussed in this appendix is the open-ended question. Unlike the other types of survey questions discussed earlier, open-ended questions do not provide choices for the subject to select. Each question is worded so that the subject must generate an answer. An example of an open-ended question would be:

- Do you have additional comments?

"How many hours a week do you watch television?" and "What is your height in inches," are also technically open–ended questions, but they require only a single number for an answer. There are also partially open-ended questions, which list several possible response choices to pick from but also include an open-ended choice such as:

- Other, please specify________________________________

Open-ended questions can be difficult to code. Also, respondents may find open-ended questions to be more difficult than other types of questions, because they require more thinking, so they may skip them. There are also advantages to using open-ended questions. On the positive side, open-ended questions give subjects the opportunity to write whatever they want, giving them more freedom to answer how they really feel about a topic. Also, open-ended questions can give the researcher more in-depth insight into how the subjects actually feel in a more in-depth manner.

Sample Questionnaire, Codebook, and Data

The following figure and two tables include data to be used if you did not develop a questionnaire and collect data in your class as recommended in chapter 4. Figure B.1 is a sample of how such a printed questionnaire might look. Table B.1 is the codebook and Table B.2 is the raw data.

About You and Your Family

What is your height in inches?______

What is the estimated height of your same sex parent? ______

What is your gender? (circle one number)
1. Male
2. Female

What is your marital status? (circle one number)
1. Single, never married
2. Married
3. Divorced, separated, or widowed

What age group are you in? (circle one number)
1. Less than 22
2. 22-29
3. 30 or more

Do you have children?
1. Yes
2. No

How many hours a week do you watch television? ______

What type of television shows do you watch? Please check all that apply.
- ❑ Sitcoms
- ❑ Movies
- ❑ Sports
- ❑ News

How many hours a week do you study? ______

What is your current grade point average? ______

Please mark the following statements according to how much you agree with them.

I feel that the institution I am attending is great.
1. Strongly disagree
2. Disagree
3. Neutral
4. Agree
5. Strongly agree

I feel that the current program in which I am enrolled is meeting my needs.
1. Strongly disagree
2. Disagree
3. Neutral
4. Agree
5. Strongly agree

I feel the institution I am attending has good physical facilities.
1. Strongly disagree
2. Disagree
3. Neutral
4. Agree
5. Strongly agree

I feel that the institution I am attending provides mostly horrible social activities.
1. Strongly disagree
2. Disagree
3. Neutral
4. Agree
5. Strongly agree

How many hours a week do you work? ______

Fig. B.1. Sample questionnaire.

Table B.1. ***Codebook***

```
List of variables on the working file

Name                                                         Position

HEIGHT      student height in inches                           1
            Measurement Level: Scale
            Column Width: 8  Alignment: Right
            Print Format: F8.2
            Write Format: F8.2

PHEIGHT     same sex parent's height                           2
            Measurement Level: Scale
            Column Width: 8  Alignment: Right
            Print Format: F8.2
            Write Format: F8.2

GENDER      gender of student                                  3
            Measurement Level: Nominal
            Column Width: 8  Alignment: Right
            Print Format: F8
            Write Format: F8

            Value    Label

                1    males
                2    females

MARITAL     marital status                                     4
            Measurement Level: Nominal
            Column Width: 8  Alignment: Right
            Print Format: F8
            Write Format: F8

            Value    Label

                1    single
                2    married
                3    divorced

AGE         age group                                          5
            Measurement Level: Ordinal
            Column Width: 8  Alignment: Right
            Print Format: F8
            Write Format: F8

            Value    Label

                1    less than 22
                2    22-29
                3    30 or more
```

```
CHILDREN  does subject have children                          6
          Measurement Level: Nominal
          Column Width: 8  Alignment: Right
          Print Format: F8
          Write Format: F8

          Value    Label

              0    no
              1    yes

HRSTV     amount of tv watched per week                       7
          Measurement Level: Scale
          Column Width: 8  Alignment: Right
          Print Format: F8
          Write Format: F8

TVSITCOM  television shows-sitcoms                            8
          Measurement Level: Nominal
          Column Width: 8  Alignment: Right
          Print Format: F8
          Write Format: F8

          Value    Label

              0    no
              1    yes

TVMOVIES  television shows-movies                             9
          Measurement Level: Nominal
          Column Width: 8  Alignment: Right
          Print Format: F8
          Write Format: F8

          Value    Label

              0    no
              1    yes

TVSPORTS  television shows-sports                             10
          Measurement Level: Nominal
          Column Width: 8  Alignment: Right
          Print Format: F8
          Write Format: F8

          Value    Label

              0    no
              1    yes
```

TVNEWS television shows-news shows 11
Measurement Level: Nominal
Column Width: 8 Alignment: Right
Print Format: F8
Write Format: F8

Value	Label
0	no
1	yes

HRSSTUDY hours of study per week 12
Measurement Level: Scale
Column Width: 8 Alignment: Right
Print Format: F8
Write Format: F8

CURRGPA student's current gpa 13
Measurement Level: Scale
Column Width: 8 Alignment: Right
Print Format: F8.1
Write Format: F8.1

EVALINST evaluation of current institution 14
Measurement Level: Ordinal
Column Width: 8 Alignment: Right
Print Format: F8
Write Format: F8

Value	Label
1	strongly agree
2	agree
3	neutral
4	disagree
5	strongly disagree

EVALPROG evaluation of major program of study 15
Measurement Level: Ordinal
Column Width: 8 Alignment: Right
Print Format: F8
Write Format: F8

Value	Label
1	strongly agree
2	agree
3	neutral
4	disagree
5	strongly disagree

```
EVALPHYS  evaluation of physical facilities of institution  16
          Measurement Level: Ordinal
          Column Width: 8  Alignment: Right
          Print Format: F8
          Write Format: F8

          Value     Label

              1     strongly agree
              2     agree
              3     neutral
              4     disagree
              5     strongly disagree

EVALSOCL  negative evaluation of social life                17
          Measurement Level: Ordinal
          Column Width: 8  Alignment: Right
          Print Format: F8
          Write Format: F8

          Value     Label

              1     strongly agree
              2     agree
              3     neutral
              4     disagree
              5     strongly disagree

HRSWORK   hours per week spent working                      18
          Measurement Level: Scale
          Column Width: 8  Alignment: Right
          Print Format: F8
          Write Format: F8
```

Table B.2. ***Appendix B Data***

	height	pheight	gender	marital	age	children	hrstv	tvsitcom
1	67	66	2	.	1	0	18	1
2	72	72	1	2	3	1	4	0
3	61	62	2	3	3	1	25	1
4	71	71	1	1	2	0	6	0
5	65	63	2	1	1	0	8	1
6	67	68	1	1	2	0	10	0
7	69	74	1	1	2	0	24	1
8	75	73	1	2	3	1	14	0
9	62	65	2	3	3	0	5	1
10	61	64	2	2	3	1	5	1
11	64	63	2	2	2	1	10	1
12	64	64	1	3	2	1	6	0
13	70	65	1	1	2	0	20	0
14	63	62	2	2	3	0	7	1
15	64	60	2	1	2	0	4	1
16	63	60	2	2	3	1	10	1
17	65	58	2	2	3	1	10	1
18	71	76	1	2	3	1	6	1
19	72	75	1	2	3	1	9	0
20	68	65	2	1	2	0	8	1
21	75	73	1	1	1	0	20	0
22	67	66	2	3	1	1	4	1
23	69	74	1	1	1	0	10	1
24	67	68	1	1	1	0	8	0
25	64	63	2	1	1	0	14	1
26	64	62	2	3	2	1	8	1
27	70	65	1	3	2	1	17	0
28	64	64	1	1	1	0	8	0
29	70	75	1	1	1	0	14	0
30	72	75	1	3	1	1	12	0
31	64	62	2	2	2	1	15	1
32	71	73	1	3	3	1	10	0
33	67	66	2	2	3	1	8	1
34	63	60	2	2	3	1	6	0
35	69	68	1	1	1	0	20	1
36	68	66	1	3	2	1	15	1
37	64	63	2	1	1	0	15	1
38	70	68	1	1	1	0	7	1
39	71	74	1	2	3	1	6	0
40	72	73	1	1	1	0	20	1
41	60	62	2	3	2	1	10	1
42	65	63	2	2	1	1	15	1
43	72	72	1	1	1	0	24	1
44	63	62	2	1	2	0	18	1
45	75	74	1	2	2	1	10	1
46	71	68	1	1	1	0	24	1
47	65	59	2	2	2	1	5	0
48	69	67	1	2	2	1	15	1
49	63	62	2	2	2	1	10	0
50	67	66	2	3	3	0	22	1

tvmovies	tvsports	tvnews	hrsstudy	currgpa	evalinst	evalprog	evalphys	evalsocl	hrswork
1	0	0	5	3.2	3	3	4	2	0
0	1	0	24	2.6	3	.	3	2	43
1	0	0	20	3	4	4	4	4	.
0	1	1	17	3.1	3	4	3	3	37
1	0	1	18	3	3	3	4	4	35
0	1	0	10	3	3	2	3	4	38
0	1	1	12	3	4	4	4	5	0
0	1	0	10	3.6	3	3	3	5	20
1	0	1	8	3.4	3	4	3	4	40
1	0	1	17	3.5	2	2	2	3	38
1	0	1	38	3	4	3	3	2	28
0	1	0	35	2.4	2	3	3	4	40
0	1	0	20	3	4	4	4	5	0
1	0	1	10	3.8	3	4	3	2	30
1	0	0	12	3.3	3	4	5	3	45
1	0	0	35	3.7	3	3	3	2	43
0	0	1	30	3.4	3	3	3	4	34
0	1	0	22	3.7	4	4	4	4	36
0	1	0	20	3.6	4	3	4	5	30
1	0	0	12	3	3	3	3	4	29
0	1	1	2	2.5	3	4	2	4	0
1	0	0	30	3	2	2	2	3	21
0	1	1	12	3.4	2	2	2	4	23
0	1	1	10	2.5	4	3	3	3	26
1	0	0	15	3	2	2	2	3	12
1	0	0	30	3.1	2	2	3	3	15
0	1	1	18	2.4	4	3	2	3	5
0	1	1	12	2.9	2	1	3	4	35
0	1	0	4	3	3	3	2	3	7
0	1	1	8	2.9	2	2	5	2	10
1	0	0	15	3.2	3	3	3	3	40
0	1	1	20	3.8	2	3	5	3	42
0	0	0	12	3.8	1	1	5	1	40
0	0	1	22	4	1	2	3	3	35
0	0	0	7	2.8	2	2	1	2	0
0	1	1	12	2.9	3	3	2	2	28
1	0	0	18	3.2	2	2	4	2	0
0	1	0	13	3	2	3	3	4	40
0	0	1	10	3.6	1	2	3	1	50
0	1	0	8	2.8	4	4	1	4	40
1	1	0	20	3.2	2	2	5	1	20
0	0	0	10	3.4	2	3	3	1	15
0	1	1	8	2.9	1	1	3	2	38
1	0	0	15	3.2	2	2	5	1	10
0	1	0	10	3	2	2	3	2	20
0	1	1	5	2.9	4	5	2	3	37
0	0	1	12	3.6	1	2	5	1	40
0	1	1	18	3.3	2	2	3	2	35
0	0	1	10	3.1	3	2	5	3	10
1	1	0	20	3.9	1	1	4	1	20

APPENDIX C

Developing the HSB Codebook

The purpose of a codebook is to identify clearly each variable so that both you and other investigators will know what the data represent. *Tables C.1 and C.2 are the HSB codebook that can be generated from the HsbData file by clicking on* ***Utilities*** *and then* ***File Info,*** *while the data file is showing on your screen.* We have edited the codebook to make it more compact and typed in the transformation formulas (in middle column) of Table C.2 to make the codebook more complete.

The left column gives the *variable names* in 8 characters or less. Notice that these names are the same as those across the top of the data editor (see Table 6.1). The second column in Table C.1 provides several pieces of information for each variable. First, there is a longer name called the *variable label*. Second is the Print and Write formats, which indicate the number of columns and decimal places. Third, the *values* and their *labels* for each variable are specified. Thus, for example, grades can take on values between 1 and 8; 1 indicates grades of less than a D, 8 is a grade average that is mostly A, and numbers 2 through 7 being grade averages in between. Likewise, the values for math grades are zero for less than A-B and one for mostly A-B. These values are categories or levels of the variable (see chapter 2).

Certain variables are considered to be essentially continuous and thus do not have labels for each value. Visual mosaic and math achievement are such variables in this data set. We have however, identified the highest and lowest value for each of these variables, indicating the range of possible scores for these continuous variables. For example, visualization scores could range from -4 to 16 and mosaic from -28 to 56. Math achievement, the variable in position 11, can range from -8.33 to 25. The minus scores are probably due to an adjustment for guessing so that a person who is just making wild guesses would get a score of less than zero.

The *print format* and *write format* are always the same and indicate the possible number of columns the variable can fill, for example, an identification number can be 3 columns, any number between 000 and 999. The visualization score format is 6.2 which means that it can be up to six columns with two places after the decimal point.

Table C.2 provides a codebook for the new or transformed variables. It is important to keep track of such new variables and label them appropriately. The middle column shows how these variables were recoded.

Table C.1. *File Information - Codebook*

List of variables on the working file

Name	Variable label, format, and Value label	Position
ID	identification	1
	Measurement Level: Nominal	
	Column Width: 8 Alignment: Right	
	Print Format: F3	
	Write Format: F3	
VISUAL	visualization score	2
	Measurement Level: Scale	
	Column Width: 8 Alignment: Right	
	Print Format: F6.2	
	Write Format: F6.2	
	Value Label	
	16.00 high	
	-4.00 low	
MOSAIC	mosaic, pattern test	3
	Measurement Level: Scale	
	Column Width: 8 Alignment: Right	
	Print Format: F6.1	
	Write Format: F6.1	
GRADES	grades in h.s.	4
	Measurement Level: Scale	
	Column Width: 8 Alignment: Right	
	Print Format: F1	
	Write Format: F1	
	Value Label	
	1 less than D	
	2 mostly D	
	3 half CD	
	4 mostly C	
	5 half BC	
	6 mostly B	
	7 half AB	
	8 mostly A	

MATHGR   math grades 5
Measurement Level: Nominal
Column Width: 8 Alignment: Right
Print Format: F1
Write Format: F1

Value   Label

0   less A-B
1   most A-B

ALG1   algebra 1 in h.s. 6
Measurement Level: Nominal
Column Width: 8 Alignment: Right
Print Format: F1
Write Format: F1

Value   Label

0   not taken
1   taken

ALG2   algebra 2 in h.s. 7
Measurement Level: Nominal
Column Width: 8 Alignment: Right
Print Format: F1
Write Format: F1

Value   Label

0   not taken
1   taken

GEO   geometry in h.s. 8
Measurement Level: Nominal
Column Width: 8 Alignment: Right
Print Format: F1
Write Format: F1

Value   Label

0   not taken
1   taken

TRIG   trigonometry in h.s. 9
Measurement Level: Nominal
Column Width: 8 Alignment: Right
Print Format: F1
Write Format: F1

Value   Label

0   not taken
1   taken

CALC calculus in h.s. 10

Measurement Level: Nominal
Column Width: 8 Alignment: Right
Print Format: F1
Write Format: F1

Value	Label
0	not taken
1	taken

MATHACH math achievement 11

Measurement Level: Scale
Column Width: 8 Alignment: Right
Print Format: F7.2
Write Format: F7.2

Value	Label
25.00	high
-8.33	low

FAED father's education 12

Measurement Level: Ordinal
Column Width: 8 Alignment: Right
Print Format: F2
Write Format: F2
Missing Values: -1

Value	Label
2	< h.s. grad
3	h.s. grad
4	< 2 yrs voc
5	2 yrs voc
6	< 2 yrs coll
7	> 2 yrs coll
8	coll grad
9	master's
10	MD/PhD

MAED mother's education 13

Measurement Level: Ordinal
Column Width: 8 Alignment: Right
Print Format: F2
Write Format: F2
Missing Values: -1

Value	Label
2	< h.s.
3	h.s. grad
4	< 2 yrs voc
5	2 yrs voc
6	< 2 yrs coll
7	> 2 yrs coll
8	coll grad
9	master's
10	MD/PhD

GEND gender 14

Measurement Level: Nominal
Column Width: 8 Alignment: Right
Print Format: F1
Write Format: F1

Value	Label
1	male
2	female

Table C.2. *File Information for Transformed/New Variables*

Name List of variables on the working file — Transformation Position

FAEDR father's ed rev 15

Measurement Level: Ordinal
Column Width: 8 Alignment: Right
Print Format: F8
Write Format: F8

Value	Label
1	hs grad or less
2	some college
3	BS or more

MAEDR mother's ed rev 16
Measurement Level: Ordinal
Column Width: 8 Alignment: Right
Print Format: F8
Write Format: F8

Value	Label
1	hs grad or less
2	some college
3	BS or more

PAEDR parent's ed revised 17
Measurement Level: Ordinal
Column Width: 8 Alignment: Right
Print Format: F8
Write Format: F8

Value	Label
1	hs grad or less
2	some college
3	BS or more

APPENDIX D

Using Tables and Figures to Communicate Results

Don Quick

Tables and figures are used in most fields of study to provide a visual presentation of important information to the reader. They are used to organize the statistical results of a study, to list important tabulated information, and to allow the reader a visual method of comparing related items. Tables offer a way to detail information that would be difficult to describe in the text.

A figure may be just about anything that is not a table, such as a chart, graph, photograph, or line drawing. These figures may also include pie charts, line charts, bar charts, organizational charts, flow charts, diagrams, blueprints, or maps. Unless the figure can dramatically illustrate a comparison that a table cannot, use a table. A good rule is to use a table for numbers and text and to use figures for visual presentations.

The meaning and major focus of the table or figure should be evident to the readers without them having to make a thorough study of it. A glance should be all it takes for the idea of what the table or figure represents to be conveyed to the reader. By reading only the text itself, the reader may have difficulty understanding the data; by constructing tables and figures that are well presented, the readers will be able to understand the study results more easily.

The purpose of this appendix is to provide guidelines that will enhance the presentation of research findings and other information by using tables and figures. It will highlight the important aspects of constructing tables and figures using the *Publication Manual of the American Psychological Association, Fourth Edition* as the guide for formatting.

General Considerations Concerning Tables

Be selective as to how many tables are included in the total document. Determine how much data the reader needs to comprehend the material, and then decide if the information would be better presented in the text or as a table. A table containing only a few numbers is unnecessary, while a table containing too much information may not be understandable. Tables should be easy to read and interpret. If at all possible, combine tables that repeat data.

Keep a consistency to all of your tables throughout your document. All tables and figures in your document should use a similar format, with the results organized in a comparable fashion. Use the same designation measure or scale in all tables, figures, and the text.

Adjust the column headings or spacing between columns so the width of the table fits appropriately between the margins. Fit all of one table on one page. Reduce the data, change the type size, or decrease line spacing to make it fit. A short table may be on a page with text, as long as it follows the first mention of it. Each long table is on a separate page immediately after it is mentioned in the text. If the fit and appearance would be improved, turn the table sideways (landscape orientation, top of table toward the spine) on the page or use more than one page with logical breaks at the page end.

The table should reside as soon as possible after it is referred to in the text. An informative table will supplement but not duplicate the text. In the text, discuss only the most significant parts of the table. Make sure the table is understood by itself without the accompanying text; however, it is never independent of the text. There must be a reference in the text to the table.

Construction of the Table

Table D.1 is an example of an APA table for displaying simple descriptive data collected in a study. It also appears in correct relation to the text of the document. (Figure D.1 shows the same table with the table parts marked.) The major parts of a table are: the number, the title, the headings, the body, and the notes.

Table D.1. ***An Example of a Table in APA Format for Displaying Simple Descriptive Data***

Table 1

Means and Standard Deviations on the Measure of Self-Direction in Learning as a Function of Age in Adult Students

		Self-Directed Learning Inventory Score	
Age Group	n	M	SD
20-34	15	65	3.5
35-40	22	88	6.3
50-64	14	79	5.6
65-79	7	56	7.1
80+	--[a]	--	--

Note. The maximum score is 100.
[a] No participants were found for the over 80 group.

Table Numbering

Arabic numerals are used to number tables in the order in which they appear in the text. Do not write in the text "the table on page 17" or "the table above or below." The correct method would be to refer to the table number like this: (see Table 1). Left-justify the table number (see Table D1). In an article, each table should be numbered sequentially in the order of appearance. Do not use suffix letters with the table numbers. If the table appears in an appendix, identify it with the letter of the appendix capitalized, followed by the table number; for instance Table C.3 is the third table in Appendix C.

Table Titles

Include the variables for the data, the groups on whom the data were collected, the subgroups, and the nature of the statistic reported. The table heading or a title should concisely describe what is contained in the table. Abbreviations that appear in the body of the table can sometimes be explained in the title, however, it may be more appropriate to use a general note (see also comments below on *Table Headings*). The title must be underlined. Standard APA format requires double spacing throughout. However, tables in student papers should be single spaced for better presentation.

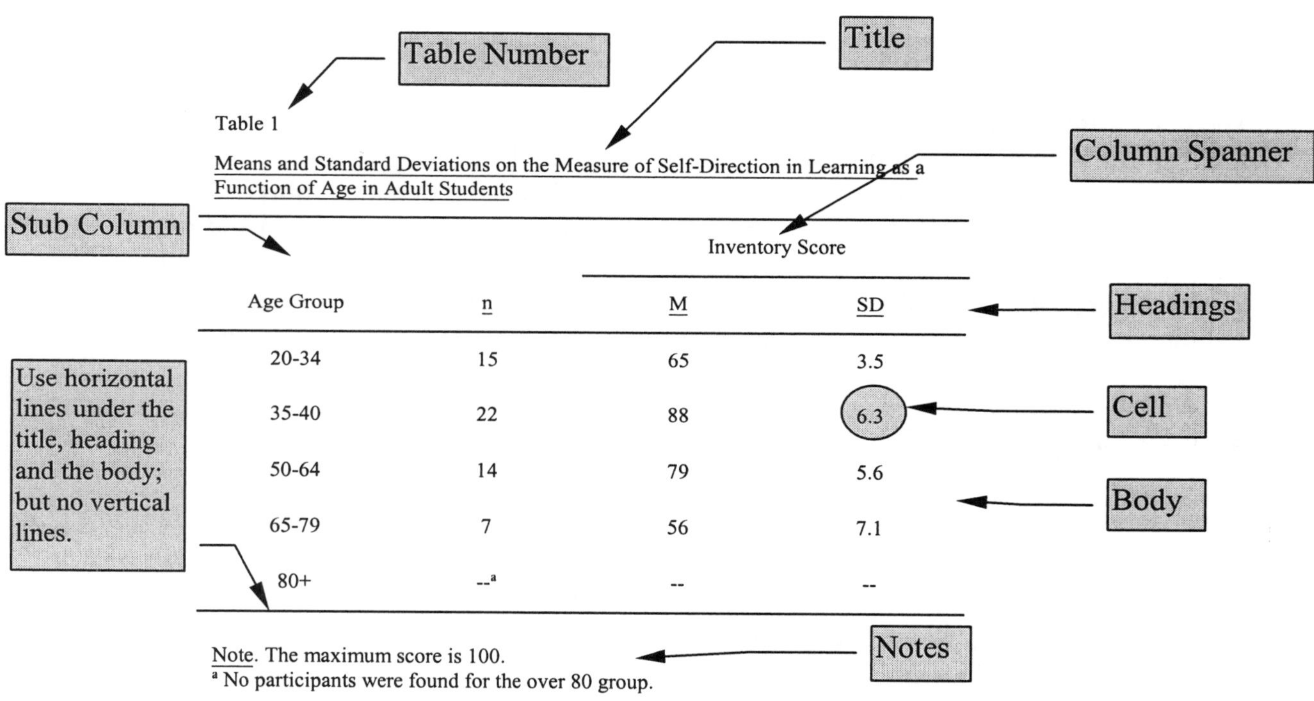
Table 1

Means and Standard Deviations on the Measure of Self-Direction in Learning as a Function of Age in Adult Students

Age Group	n	Inventory Score M	Inventory Score SD
20-34	15	65	3.5
35-40	22	88	6.3
50-64	14	79	5.6
65-79	7	56	7.1
80+	--[a]	--	--

Note. The maximum score is 100.
[a] No participants were found for the over 80 group.

Fig. D.1. The major parts of an APA table.

Table Headings

Headings are used to explain the organization of the table. You may use abbreviations in the headings, however, include a note as to their meaning if you use mnemonics, variable names, and scale acronyms. Standard abbreviations and symbols for non-technical terms can be used without explanation (e.g., *no.* for *number* or *%* for *percent*). Have precise title, column headings, and row labels that are accurate and brief. Each column must have a heading, including the *stub column*, or leftmost column. Its heading is referred to as the *stubhead*. The stub column usually lists the significant independent variables or the levels of the variable, as in Table D.1.

The *column heads* cover one column, and the *column spanners* cover two or more columns—each with its own column head (see Table D.1 and Figure D.1). Headings stacked in this manner are called *decked heads*. This is a good way to eliminate repetition in column headings but try to avoid using more than two levels of decked heads. Column heads, column spanners, and stubheads should all be singular, unless referring to a group (e.g., children). Table spanners, which cover the entire table, may be plural. Use title capitalization in all headings.

Notice that there are no vertical lines in an APA style table. The horizontal lines can be added by using a "draw" feature or a "borders" feature for tables in the computer word processor, or they could be drawn in by hand if typed. If translating from an SPSS Table or box, the vertical lines must be removed.

The Body of the Table

The body contains the actual data being displayed. Round numbers improve the readability and clarity more than precise numbers with several decimal places. Good rules of thumb are to report two digits more than the raw data. Percentages should have no decimal points at all. A reader can compare numbers down a column more easily than across a row. Column and row averages can provide a visual focus that allows the reader to inspect the data easily without cluttering the table. If a cell cannot be filled because the information is not applicable, then leave it blank. If it cannot be filled because the information could not be obtained, or was not reported, then insert a dash and explain the dash with a note to the table.

Notes to a Table

Notes are often used with tables. There are three different forms of notes used with tables: a) to eliminate repetition in the body of the table, b) to elaborate on the information contained in a particular cell, or c) to indicate statistical significance:

- A *general note* provides information relating to the table as a whole, including explanations of abbreviations used:

  Note. This could be used to indicate if the table came from another source.

- A *specific note* makes a reference to a specific row or column or cell of the table and is given superscript lowercase letters, beginning with the letter "a":

  [a]n = 50. Specific notes are identified in the body with superscript.

- A *probability note* is to be included when one or more inferential statistic has been computed. Asterisk(s) indicate the statistical significance of findings presented within the table. Try to be consistent across all tables, however, sometimes it is impossible. The important thing is to start with one asterisk and proceed to two within the same table:

  $*\underline{p} < .01. \quad **\underline{p} < .05.$

Notes should be listed with general notes first, then specific notes, and concluded with probability notes, without indentation. They may be single spaced for better presentation. Explain all uses of underlining, dashes, and parentheses. Abbreviations for technical terms, group names, and those of a similar nature must be explained in a note to the table.

Examples

Displaying Textual Information

Although tables are used generally to display data (see Table D.1), some tables are used to organize text information (see Table D.2). These can be helpful to consolidate the important pieces of information from a prose explanation. Use tables to present qualitative or descriptive information without repeating what is in the text.

Table D.2. ***An Example of a Table for Displaying Textual Information***

Table 2

Descriptions of SPSS Measurement Terms and How We Use Them

SPSS Term	Our Description
Nominal	Three or more unordered or qualitative categories. Also dichotomous (two category) variables.
Ordinal	Three or more ordered categories, but the responses are not normally distributed among the categories, or they are *ranks*.
Scale	Three or more ordered categories, and the responses are normally distributed among the categories.

Displaying SPSS ANOVA and Descriptive Outputs in APA Format

Figure D.2 is a standard SPSS output but is not an acceptable way of displaying data in APA format: the vertical lines must be removed, the stubs rearranged, the decimal places rounded, the lines double spaced, and the heading changed. Also, you may not want to include all of the information in the final table, only that which is pertinent to your study. In this example both SPSS tables are used to interpret the data. Tables D.3 and D.4 are examples of what this might look like in your report. Some authors include the *p* or significance in a column and some use asterisks and probability notes. We believe it to be a matter of preference. However, you must be consistent in all tables in your document, and it is not desirable to use both a column of *p* values and asterisks because they are redundant.

Descriptives

						95% Confidence Interval for Mean			
		N	Mean	Std. Deviation	Std. Error	Lower Bound	Upper Bound	Minimum	Maximum
Grades in high school	HS grad or less	37	5.35	1.49	.25	4.85	5.85	3	8
	Some College	17	5.53	1.74	.42	4.64	6.42	2	8
	BS or More	19	6.53	1.22	.28	5.94	7.11	4	8
	Total	73	5.70	1.55	.18	5.34	6.06	2	8

ANOVA

		Sum of Squares	df	Mean Square	F	Sig.
Grades in high school	Between Groups	17.965	2	8.983	4.046	.022
	Within Groups	155.405	70	2.220		
	Total	173.370	72			

Fig. D.2. An example of the type of tables generated from a SPSS ANOVA output.

Table D.3. ***An Example of Descriptive Statistics Converted from SPSS to APA Format***

Table 3

Mean and Standard Deviation for Grades in High School by Father's Education

Father's Education	n	M	SD
HS Grad or Less	37	5.35	1.49
Some College	17	5.53	1.74
BS or More	19	6.53	1.22

Table D.4. ***An Example of an ANOVA Table***

Table 4

One-Way Analysis of Variance of Grades in High School by Father's Education

Source	df	SS	MS	F	p
Between groups	2	17.97	8.98	4.05	.02
Within groups	70	155.41	2.22		
Total	72	173.37			

Displaying SPSS Correlation Outputs in APA Format

Another common table that is used in articles and dissertations is one for intercorrelations. (see Figure D.3). Table D.5 is the conversion to APA format of this table. This is the general format of the correlation table. For more variables you must add columns as needed. You may also abbreviate the names of the variables and use them at both the top and side of the table. You can also present the means and standard deviations on this table by adding those two columns to the left of the correlation data.

Correlations[a]

		Visualization score	Mosaic pattern test score	Grades in high school	Math achievement
Visualization score	Pearson Correlation	1.000	.030	.127	.423**
	Sig. (2-tailed)	.	.798	.279	.000
Mosaic pattern test score	Pearson Correlation	.030	1.000	-.012	.213
	Sig. (2-tailed)	.798	.	.920	.067
Grades in high school	Pearson Correlation	.127	-.012	1.000	.504**
	Sig. (2-tailed)	.279	.920	.	.000
Math achievement	Pearson Correlation	.423**	.213	.504**	1.000
	Sig. (2-tailed)	.000	.067	.000	.

**. Correlation is significant at the 0.01 level (2-tailed).

a. Listwise N=75

Fig. D.3. An example of the correlation table from a SPSS output.

Table D.5. ***An Example of a Correlation Matrix in APA Format***

Table 5

Intercorrelations of Visualization Score, Mosaic Pattern Test Score, Grades in High School, and Math Achievement

Measure	1	2	3	4
1. Visualization Score	--			
2. Mosaic Pattern Test Score	.03	--		
3. Grades in High School	.13	-.01	--	
4. Math Achievement	.42**	.21	.50**	--

Note. Listwise N = 75.
**p < .01, two tailed.

Displaying Several Inferential Statistics in One Table

Group Statistics

	Gender	N	Mean	Std. Deviation	Std. Error Mean
Math grades	male	34	.29	.46	7.93E-02
	female	39	.54	.51	8.09E-02
Math achievement	male	34	14.7550	6.0315	1.0344
	female	39	10.8375	6.8578	1.0981
Grades in high school	male	34	5.50	1.64	.28
	female	39	5.90	1.52	.24

Independent Samples Test

		Levene's Test for Equality of Variances		t-test for Equality of Means						
									95% Confidence Interval of the Difference	
		F	Sig.	t	df	Sig. (2-tailed)	Mean Difference	Std. Error Difference	Lower	Upper
Math grades	Equal variances assumed	6.883	.011	-2.144	71	.035	-.24	.11	-.47	-1.71E-02
	Equal variances not assumed			-2.157	70.81	.034	-.24	.11	-.47	-1.85E-02
Math achievement	Equal variances assumed	.947	.334	2.574	71	.012	3.9175	1.5220	.8826	6.9523
	Equal variances not assumed			2.597	70.99	.011	3.9175	1.5086	.9094	6.9255
Grades in high school	Equal variances assumed	.720	.399	-1.076	71	.286	-.40	.37	-1.13	.34
	Equal variances not assumed			-1.070	67.88	.288	-.40	.37	-1.14	.34

Fig. D.4. An example of SPSS outputs of multiple *t* tests.

Table D.6. ***An Example of Displaying Multiple t Tests in APA Format***

Table 6

Gender Differences in Math Grades, Math Achievement Scores, and Grades in High School

	Male		Female			
	M	SD	M	SD	t	p
Math Grades	.29	.46	.54	.51	-2.16[a]	.034
Math Achievement	14.76	6.03	10.84	6.86	2.57	.012
Grades in High School	5.50	1.64	5.90	1.52	-1.08	.286

[a] Because Levene's F was statistically significant ($p < .05$), the "equal variances not assumed" t was used for Math Grades.

Adjusting the SPSS Output to Approximate the APA Format

The preceding examples show how the standard SPSS output can be used to create a table in APA format. However, this does require some knowledge of your word processing program's table creation capabilities in order to accomplish this task. It also requires retyping the data into the table. You can adjust SPSS so that the output will approximate the APA format. We would not recommend submitting this to an APA journal, but it may be acceptable for student papers and some graduate program committees.

In SPSS follow these commands:

- Click **Edit => Options**.
- Under the **Pivot Tables** tab select **Academic (narrow).tlo** (see Figure D.5).
- Press **OK**.

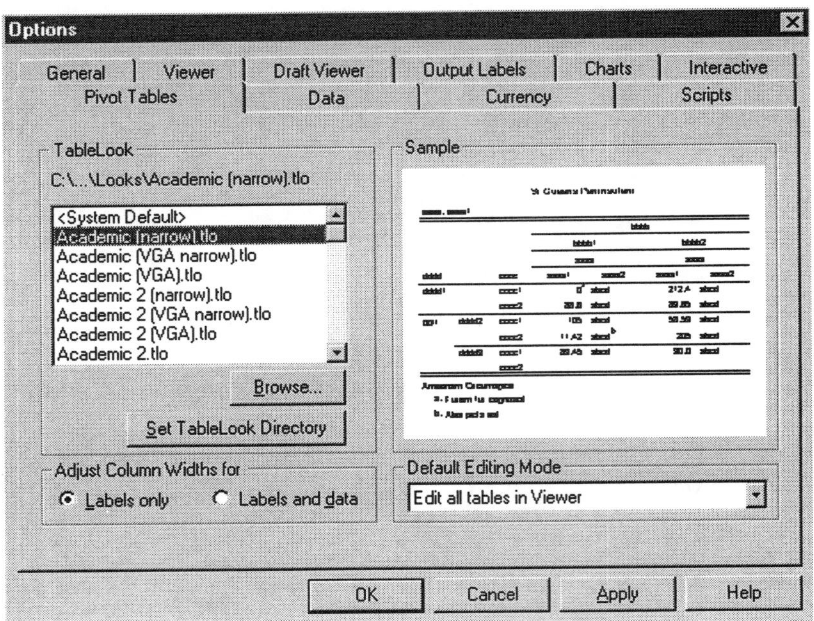

Fig. D.5. Setting SPSS for an approximate APA format output.

Table D.7. ***An Example of the SPSS "Academic" Output***

Table 7

<u>One-Way Analysis of Variance of Grades in High School by Father's Education</u>

ANOVA

grades in h.s.

	Sum of Squares	df	Mean Square	F	Sig.
Between Groups	17.965	2	8.983	4.046	.022
Within Groups	155.405	70	2.220		
Total	173.370	72			

Using Figures

Generally, the same concepts apply to figures as have been previously stated concerning tables: they should be easy to read and interpret, be consistent throughout the document when presenting the same type of figure, kept on one page if possible, and it should complement the accompanying text or table. Considering the numerous types of figures, I will not attempt to detail their construction in this document. However, one thing is consistent with all figures. The figure number and caption description are located below the figure and the description is detailed similar to that of the title of a table. See Figure D.6.

Some cautions in using figures include:

1) make it simple--complex diagrams that require lengthy explanation should be avoided unless it is an integral part of the research;
2) use a minimum number of figures for just your important points--if too many figures are used then your important points may be lost;
3) integrate text and figure -- make sure your figure compliments and enhances the accompanying text.

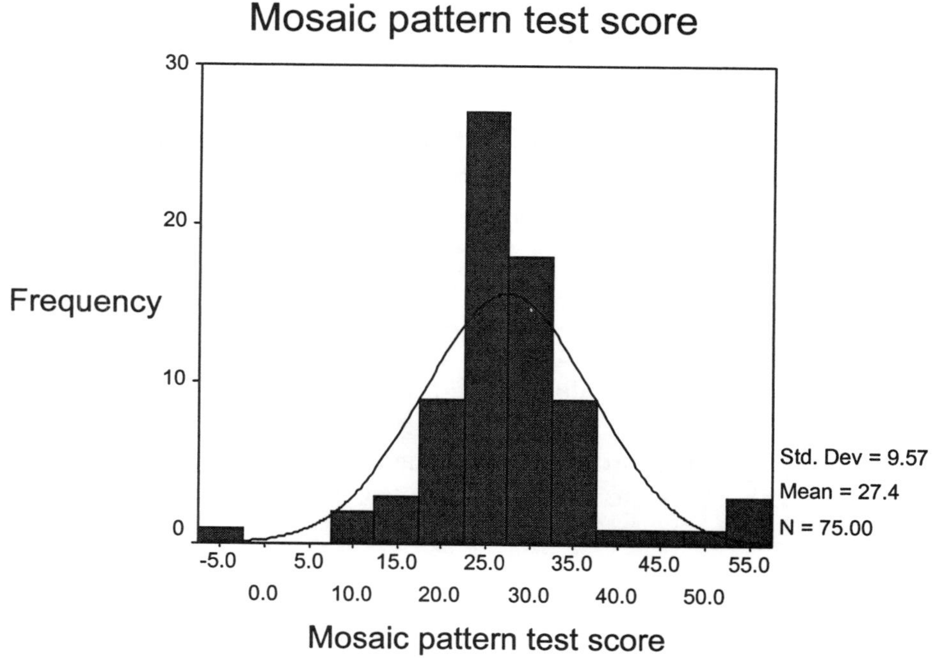

Fig. D.6. An example of a bar chart generated by SPSS.

APPENDIX E

Writing the Methods, Results, and Discussion Sections

Nancy L. Leech

After computing the statistics with SPSS, the next step is to write about the findings in a paper, thesis, or dissertation. This step is sometimes difficult. The purpose of this appendix is to provide an example of how this step can be done, using HSB data and outputs provided earlier. Appendix D provides examples of several tables using the same HSB data. Tables and figures are often used to supplement words in a research paper.

Method

Participants

The sample of 75 participants was randomly selected from 28,240 high school seniors who completed the survey. Thirty-four of the respondents were male and 39 were female. Two subjects did not supply gender information. Fifty percent of the male respondents reported that their fathers had not obtained more than a high school degree, 21% reported receiving 2 years or less of a vocational or college program, 25% reported receiving a college degree or higher, and 4% of the males did not report their father's education. Sixty-three percent of the female respondents reported that their fathers had not obtained more than a high school degree, 26% reported receiving 2 years or less of a vocational or college program, and 11% reported receiving a college or higher degree.

The respondents varied in background information regarding math classes taken. Twenty-one percent did not take algebra one, 53% did not take algebra two, and 52% did not take geometry. Only 26% took trigonometry and 11% took all math classes through calculus.

There was no sample selection bias because participants were randomly selected (In a thesis it would be appropriate to state the techniques used to assure results are not due to sample selection bias.)

Instruments

Data from three standardized instruments and a background information sheet was obtained. The background sheet contained the following variables: gender, education of mother, education of father, whether or not participants had enrolled in algebra one, algebra two, geometry, trigonometry, and calculus, student report of overall high school grades, and student report of grades in mathematics courses. The standardized instruments were a 25 item mathematics test, a 16 item test of visualization in three dimensions, and a 56 item test involving the detection of relationships in patterns of tiles. (In a thesis more information would be given regarding the instruments used. Information regarding reliability or validity would be placed here.)

Skewness was checked for the variables math achievement, mosaic pattern test score, grades in high school, and visualization score. Since none of these variables was markedly skewed, it is assumed that the data are normally distributed.

Procedure (The order in which instruments were given and instructions given to students would be presented here.)

Design and Analysis

(For a thesis or dissertation it is common to have a section describing the design, restating the research questions or hypothesis, and stating how each would be analyzed. This is less common in a journal article.)

This study used a non-experimental approach. Descriptive, difference, and associational research questions were investigated. There are no active or manipulated independent variables. The following research questions were examined.

1. Do boys and girls differ significantly on math achievement? OR Are there differences between the boys and girls (the two levels of gender) in regards to the average math achievement scores of the students?

   An independent samples or groups t test was chosen as the statistical method for this research because the design was between groups, included only two groups (girls versus boys), and had a normally distributed dependent variable (math achievement).

2. Are there differences between the two levels of gender (boys and girls) in regard to the average overall high school grades?

   An independent samples or groups t test was the statistic chosen. (see #1 above).

3. Do boys and girls differ on whether they receive high versus low math grades? OR Is there a relationship between gender and math grades?

   The chi-square statistic was chosen for this research question because it is comparing nominal (categorical) data on both the independent and dependent variables.

4. Are there differences between the three levels of fathers' education (high, medium, and low) in regard to average grades? And if so, what pairs of means are significantly different?

   A one-way ANOVA was the statistic used because there was one independent variable with two or more categories (high, medium, and low) and because there was a normally distributed dependent variable (grades). The Tukey Honestly Significant Difference (HSD) multiple comparison test was done to examine which specific pairs of means were significantly different.

5. Do math grades *seem* to have an effect on math achievement? Does father's education (revised) *seem* to have an effect on math achievement? Do math grades and father's education (revised) interact?

   Factorial (2-Way) ANOVA statistic was used because there were two independent variables (math grades and father's education) and a between groups design.

6. What are the associations among the four variables: visualization, mosaic, overall grades, and math achievement?

   Pearson correlation was used because the variables are normally distributed and other assumptions are not markedly violated.

7. How well can you predict math achievement from a combination of four variables: mosaic, overall grades in high school, and mother's and father's education? Which of these four predictors contribute significantly to the multiple correlation/regression? OR is there a combination of mosaic, grades in high school, and mother's and father's education that predicts math achievement better than any predictor variable alone?

   A linear multiple regression was utilized for this research question. This statistic was chosen because it predicts an interval scale dependent variable (math achievement) from a combination of several interval scale independent variables.

Data were checked for outliers before statistical analysis was done (Wilkinson et al., 1999).

Results

Two independent sample t tests were executed. The first, comparing genders on math achievement, was significant $t(71) = 2.60$, $p = .012$, indicating that the average math achievement score for female students (10.84) is significantly lower than the score (14.76) for males. (In a thesis effect sizes or information to compute effect sizes should be presented but SPSS does not provide effect sizes with the *t* test program. See discussion below of factorial ANOVA and multiple regression.)

The second t test compared males and females on overall high school grades. No significant difference was found between the two genders, $t(71) = -1.08$, $p = .286$. The average high school grade score for male students (5.50) is not significantly lower than the score (5.90) for females.

A 2 X 2 chi-square analysis was done with the variables math grades and gender. The result was not significant, $X^2(1, N=73) = 3.50$, $p = .062$. These results suggest that males and females do not differ in whether they receive high or low math grades because $p > .05$.

To analyze whether there was a difference between the three father's education (revised) groups on grades, a one-way analysis of variance was done. A significant difference was found, $\underline{F}$ (2,70)= 4.05, $\underline{p}$ = .022. This finding indicates that there is a significant difference somewhere between the mean grade scores for the levels of father's education. To examine which specific pairs of means were significant a Tukey Honestly Significant Difference (HSD) multiple comparison test was done. The only pair of means that had a significant difference ($\underline{p}$ = .018) was found between the mean score for father's who were HS grads or less ($\underline{M}$ = 5.35) and the mean score for those with a BS or more ($\underline{M}$ = 6.53).

A factorial (2-way) ANOVA was used to investigate whether math grades and father's education (revised) have an "effect" on math achievement. The interaction was found to be statistically significant, $\underline{F}$ (2,67) = 3.46, $\underline{p}$ = .037. The effect of math grades on math achievement depends on the level of father's education. Students with fathers who have relatively low education, tend to have relatively low math achievement whether or not they have low math grades. With students who have fathers with high education, there is a big difference in math achievement for those with high and low math grades. The magnitude of the effect size of the interaction (eta^2 = .172) is medium (Cohen, 1988), but only 17% of the variance in math achievement can be predicted from math grades.

To analyze what the associations were among visualization, mosaic, grades, and math achievement a correlation matrix was computed. Significant correlations were found between math achievement and visualization, $\underline{r}$ (73) = .42, $\underline{p}$ < .01, and between grades, $\underline{r}$ (73) = .50, $\underline{p}$ < .01 and math achievement. Students who have high math achievement scores generally have high visualization scores and high overall high school grades. Students who have low math achievement scores generally have low visualization and low overall high school grade scores. Similarly, this is true for math achievement and grades.

To analyze which of the following variables taken together: mosaic pattern test score, grades in high school, mother's education, and father's education are significant predictors of math achievement, a multiple regression was used. The combination of mosaic pattern test score, beta = .214, $\underline{p}$ = .033, and grades in high school, beta = .422, $\underline{p}$ < .001, were found to significantly predict math achievement ($\underline{R}$ = .60; adjusted $\underline{R}^2$ = .32). Due to high collinearity, non-significant betas were found with the variables of mother's education (.164) and father's education (.134). Variance predicted from a combination of these variables is 23% which is a large effect size (Cohen, 1988).

Discussion

Seven research questions were investigated in this study. Males and females were found to differ significantly on math achievement. Also, students who had fathers who had a BS or more had higher math achievement scores than students whose fathers were HS grads or less, but no significant relationship was found with overall high school grades and gender. In addition, math achievement depends on both father's education and math grades. Also males and females were found to not differ on whether they receive high or low math grades. Math achievement is related to both visualization and overall high school scores. The last research question addressed how well one can predict math achievement from a combination of four variables. Mosaic pattern test scores and grades in high school were found to significantly predict math achievement.

With respect to the results mentioned earlier, males were found to have higher math achievement scores than females. This result could be explained from the different expectations that parents have for different genders. Traditionally, male children are expected to excel in math and science. Teachers can contribute to this gender difference by calling on male students more often or by expecting less achievement from female students (Sadker, Sadker, & Klein, 1991).

Curiously, even though males and females were found to differ on math achievement, males and females were not found to have different overall high school grades. In other words, males did not receive higher overall high school grades than females. Grades in high school are not dependent totally on tests. Grades include extra credit, attendance, etc. This result could be explained by how girls are more conscientious and work harder by doing extra work. Teachers tend to like this behavior and reward it with good grades.

Males and females did not differ on whether they received high or low math grades. As stated in the results no significant difference was found. Whether a student receives high or low grades is not related to being male or female. According to these findings it appears that males and females can earn good or poor grades depending on their study skills and intelligence, not depending on their gender.

Another research question examined whether there was a difference between the three father's education (revised) groups on overall grades. Students whose fathers had a higher education degree had higher grades. Students whose fathers had only a high school education had lower grades. This could be explained because more educated parents place a higher value on their children's grades and may be able to help them more than do less educated parents

References

(A list of references, including all articles mentioned in this paper, would be provided next. The reference page(s) would follow APA format as shown below, but would be double spaced, as would all of the above text if submitted to a journal. In addition, all would be in the same size 12 point type with no bold or italics.)

Cohen, J. (1988). Statistical power analysis for the behavioral sciences (2nd ed.). Hillsdale, NJ: Lawrence Erlbaum Associates.

Sadker, M., Sadker, D., & Klein, S. (1991). The issue of gender in elementary and secondary education. In G. Grant (Ed.), Review of Research in Education, (pp. 269-334.) Washington, DC: American Educational Research Association.

Wilkinson, L., & The Task Force on Statistical Inference. (1999). Statistical methods in psychology journals: Guidelines and explanations. American Psychologist. 54, 594-604.

APPENDIX F

Transferring SPSS to and from Word, Power Point, and Excel

One of the nice features of SPSS 10.0 is the possibility of copying and pasting SPSS output files to word processing, graphic, and spread sheet applications like Microsoft Word, PowerPoint, and Excel. This appendix will explain what steps you can take to accomplish this task. More specifically it will explain:

- How to paste into Word.
- How to paste into PowerPoint.
- How to paste data into Excel.
- How to paste from Excel to SPSS.

Pasting into Microsoft Word: Option 1

There are two methods for pasting into Word. Let's look at the first approach. The easiest way to do this is have an output. Let's assume you ran a frequency distribution of gender and grades with a bar chart. Your output listings would look something like Fig. F.1a. To the right of the output listing (not shown) will be the tables and graphs you created.

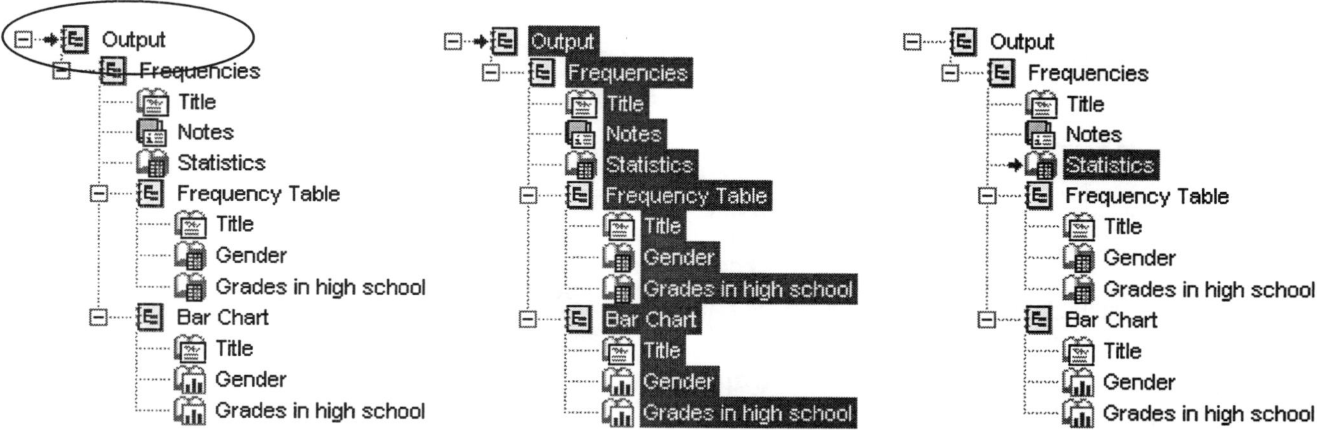

Fig. F.1a. Output listing. **Fig. F.1b. Output listing.** **Fig. F.1c. Output listing.**

To highlight the entire output at once, click once on the **Output** heading circled above in Fig. F.1a. All the subheadings below it will immediately turn blue (see Fig. F.1b) and the tables and graphs will have boxes around them. You can also highlight just one section by clicking on it. In Fig. F.1c, we have clicked on "Statistics." You can also highlight two or three areas if you hold the Control Key (CTRL) on your keyboard while clicking on your selections. Once your selection is made follow these steps:

- From the SPSS menu bar select **Edit => Copy Objects**.

- Open up Microsoft Word or toggle to it if it is already open. (The commands for Word are usually **Start => Programs => Microsoft Office => Microsoft Word**. However, each computer is set up differently).
- Once Word is open and a Word document is showing then follow these commands: **Edit => Paste Special** (see Fig. F.2 for an example).
- Under **Paste Special**, select **Formatted Text (RTF)**
- Click on **OK**

Statistics

		Gender	Grades in high school
N	Valid	73	75
	Missing	2	0

Fig. F.2. Example of output (not complete).

Important: Sometimes the directions above do not always work depending on which version of Word you are using and if you have Windows 95, 98, 2000, or NT. In some cases the right side of the table may be cut off. If you find this to be the case, follow the steps outlined below.

Pasting into Microsoft Word: Option 2

Have the output file you wish to copy showing.

- In your output, select only one area (i.e., title, table, chart) by clicking on it once. A red arrow and a box around the selection will appear like Fig. F.3.

Statistics

		GENDER	GRADES
N	Valid	73	75
	Missing	2	0

Fig. F.3. Singularly selected table.

- From the menu bar select **Edit => Copy**.
- Open up Microsoft Word.
- In Word select **Edit => Paste Special**
- Select **Picture** and then **OK**.

Copying and Pasting Output Files to PowerPoint

The steps are similar to copying and pasting into Microsoft Word. The first thing you want is an output file showing. With PowerPoint, it is rare you would paste an entire output file since the formatting doesn't lend itself to doing that well. Consequently, this part will deal with copying and pasting one object in the output file. Follow these commands.

- In your output select only one area (i.e., title, table, chart) by clicking on it once. A red arrow and a box around the selection will appear like Fig. F.3.
- From the menu bar select **Edit => Copy**.
- Open up Microsoft PowerPoint.
- In PowerPoint select **Edit => Paste Special**. You will get Fig. F.4.

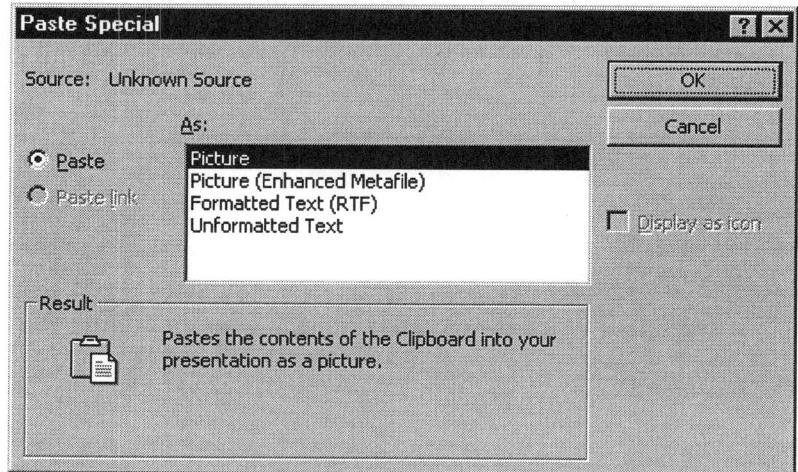

Fig. F.4. Paste special.

- Select **Picture** and then **OK**. You will get something like Fig. F.5. Your table or chart will be pasted into PowerPoint.

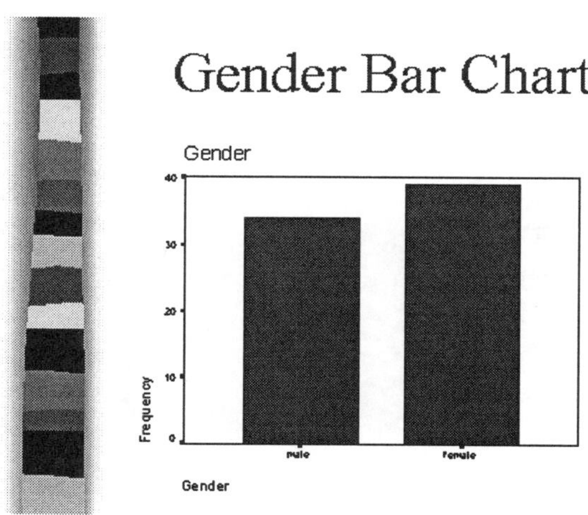

Fig. F.5. Chart pasted into PowerPoint.

- **Note**: You can also select **Formatted Text (RTF)** to avoid the white background but you will then have to reformat the table by hand. It can be cumbersome with large files. For advanced users with Microsoft PowerPoint 2000, look at your help menu on "Set Transparent Color" to eliminate the white background.

Copying and Pasting SPSS Data Files to Excel

Let's assume you put all your data into SPSS but now need to move it over to Microsoft Excel. To do that, follow these instructions.

- In your SPSS data file highlight the columns you wish to copy. Hold the mouse key down once on the gray variable column and slide it across until you have the variables you wish to copy highlighted. See Fig. F.6 as an example. In this case we selected ID, visual, mosaic, and grades. We omitted mathgr.

	id	visual	mosaic	grades
1	1	8.75	31.00	4
2	2	4.75	56.00	5
3	3	4.75	25.00	6
4	4	1.00	22.00	3
5	5	2.25	17.50	3
6	6	1.00	23.50	5

Fig. F.6. Highlighted data columns.

- From the SPSS menu bar select **Edit => Copy**.
- Open up **Microsoft Excel**.
- Select the cell where you want to paste the data (generally A1 or B1). In Excel select **Edit => Paste** (see Fig. F.7). Notice your data will appear with one exception—*you will lose your labels*. Consequently, you will need to insert those into Excel on your own.

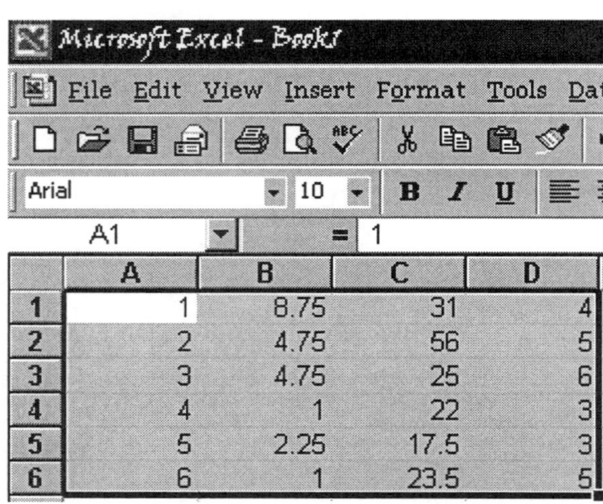

	A	B	C	D
1	1	8.75	31	4
2	2	4.75	56	5
3	3	4.75	25	6
4	4	1	22	3
5	5	2.25	17.5	3
6	6	1	23.5	5

Fig. F.7. Pasted data into Excel file.

Copying and Pasting Excel Data Into SPSS

Basically we do the opposite of what we just learned.

- In your Excel data file highlight the columns you wish to copy. Hold the left mouse button down once on the columns you wish to copy and slide it across until you have the data highlighted.
- From the Excel menu bar select **Edit => Copy**.
- Open up **SPSS**.
- Select the cell where you want to paste the data (generally var1 – cell 1). In SPSS select **Edit => Paste**. Your data will appear with one exception—no labels. You will need to define labels on your own.

APPENDIX G

Other Useful SPSS Commands

Lisa M. Vogel

Often additional manipulation is necessary to clearly understand and interpret the data. This chapter will review some supplementary SPSS commands that may help with further interpretation. Please use the data set provided in Appendix B to practice the commands in this chapter.

Recode

There are two different recoding options offered by SPSS. The first, "recode into same variable," should be utilized cautiously because it changes the existing data. Once this process is completed, the original data will be lost unless it is reentered. Therefore, unless you are sure that you are doing the recode properly and will never want to use the original data again, it is not wise to use this recode process. The second option, "recode into different variables," is often helpful because you can determine new values for the variable without losing the original data. This process will create an additional variable. Chapter 6, contains information about the steps you must take to complete this process.

Recode into Same Variables may be helpful when you want to reverse the original values of your variable. For example, when you look at the statement, "I feel that the institution I am attending provides only horrible social activities" you notice that this question is negatively phrased. For accurate analysis, these values will have to be reversed to fit with the other data and make sense logically. Note: This same process can be completed using the 'Recode into Different Variables' process if it would be useful to have the original value entries later.

Please note that this process is also useful when converting some values to 'system-missing'. For example if one had a data set where "not applicable" was coded as zero (0) or a six (6) when you had a 5-point Likert scale, it would be advisable to permanently change all those zeros (or 6s) to blanks. The reason is that they would provide misleading means if not changed.

To reverse the data, follow these directions:

- Open the data file in Appendix B, as shown in earlier chapters.
- Select **Transform=>Recode=> Into Same Variables**.

After selecting **Into Same Variables**, you will see the **Recode into Same Variables** box (Fig. G.1). You are now ready to reverse the variable values so they coincide with the rest of your data.

- In the box on the left, highlight the *evaluation of social life* variable, then click on the arrow to move variable into the **Numeric Variables** box. The window should look like Fig. G.1. Now, click on **Old and New Values**. You will then see the **Recode into Same Variables: Old and New Values** box (Fig. G.2).

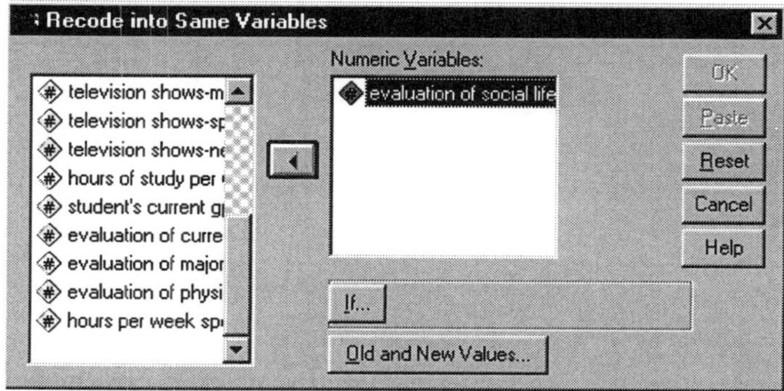

Fig. G.1. Recode into same variables.

- Click on **Value** under **Old Value**, then enter *1* in the box to its right.
- Next, click **Value** in the **New Value** box, then enter *5* in the box to its right.
- Then, under **Old=>New Value**, click **Add**.
- Do the same for the second value. Click **Value** in the **Old Value** box, then type *2* in the box to the right. Then click **Value** in the **New Value** box, and enter *4* to the box to the right. Finally, click **Add** under **Old=>New Value**. Continue this until all the values have been reversed. The box on your screen should resemble Fig. G.2.
- Click **Continue**, then **OK** in Fig. G.1.

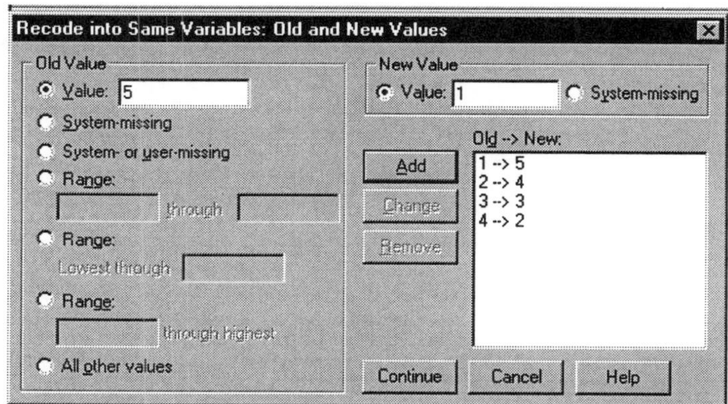

Fig. G.2. Recode into same variables: Old and new values.

Count

The **Count** process is used to count the number of occurrences for each respondent. For example, let's count the type of television shows that each respondent watches. Again use the Appendix B data file.

- Click **Transform=>Count**. You will see the **Count Occurrences of Values within Cases** window.

- Under **Target Variable**, type *numbertv*. This is a new variable you are creating to count the number of types of television shows each respondent watched.
- Under **Target Label**, type *number of types TV shows watched*. This is a description of the new variable you just created.
- In the box on the left with all of your variables, *highlight* each of the following variables and move them to the right using the arrow button: *television shows-sitcoms, television shows-movies, television shows-sports, and television shows-news*. (See Fig.G.3)

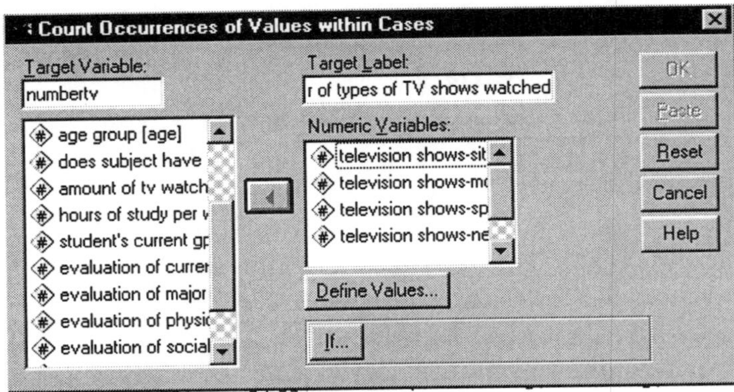

Fig. G.3. Count occurrences of values.

- Finally, click **Define Values**. You will now see the **Count Values within Cases: Values to Count** window.
- Click **Value** and enter *1* into the box to the right. This is the count value you wish to assign to each respondent answer.
- Next, click **Add** next to the **Values to Count** box. (See Fig. G.4)
- Click **Continue**, then **OK**.

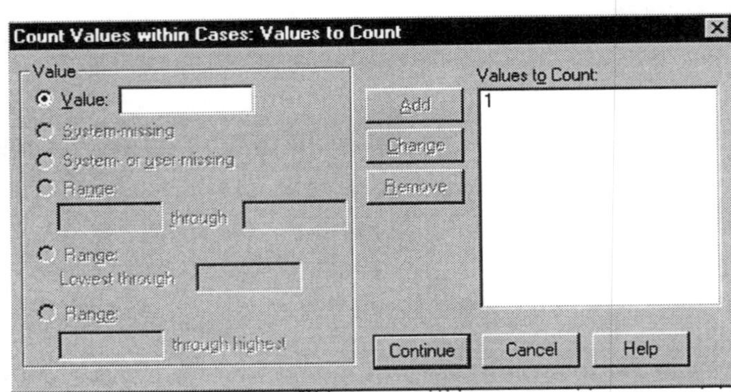

Fig. G.4. Count values with cases: Values to count.

- You will now see a new variable column at the end of your data editor called *numbertv*. Does it look the same as Fig. G.5?

numbertv
2.00
1.00
2.00
2.00
3.00
1.00
3.00
1.00
3.00
3.00
3.00
1.00

Fig. G.5. The *numbertv* variable.

Compute

The Compute command is used to create an average summated score from several variables. There are two types of compute commands that are quite useful. The first is to compute a score using only the respondents who did not have any missing data. After this computation, we will try the compute command using the MEAN function. This will include all respondents who have any data on the variables to be averaged.

For the first process we will compute a college evaluation score using the variables: *evaluation of institution*, *evaluation of program*, *evaluation of facilities*, and *evaluation of social activities*:

- Click on **Transform=>Compute**. You will see the **Compute Variable** window (Fig. G.6).
- In the **Target Variable** box, type *colleval.*
- Click **Type&Label** button and type in the label box your new variable c*ollege evaluation scale.*
- Click **Continue**.

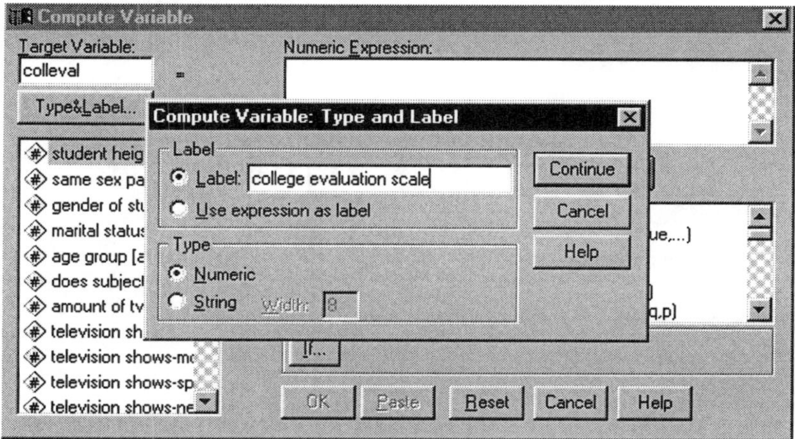

Fig. G.6. Compute variable: Type and label.

Next you will enter the Numeric Expression.

- Click on the **( )** button and set your cursor between the 2 parentheses.
- Select each of the college evaluation variables, one at a time. After you select a variable and move it over using the **arrow** button, press the + button. After all variables are selected and look as if they would add together, move your cursor to the right of the final parenthesis. Next, type /4. If you select the buttons instead, you will have to eliminate the spaces between the final) (end parentheses symbol), the / (forward slash) and the 4. Your equation should look *exactly* like Fig. G.7.

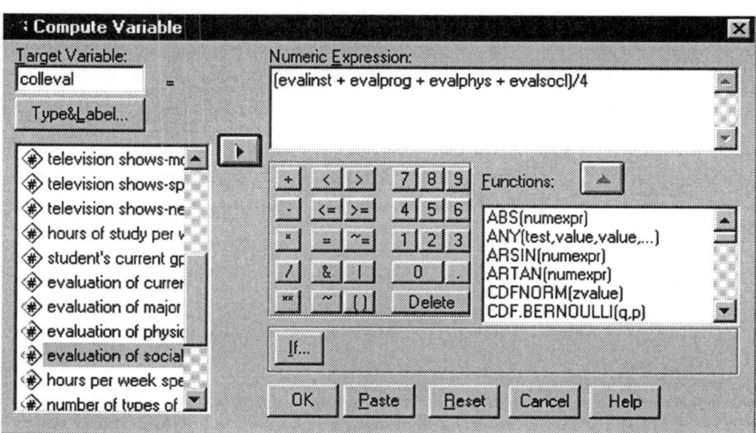

Fig. G.7. Compute variable box with algebraic numeric expression.

- Click **OK**
- Look at the end of your data editor. There now should be a variable column named *colleval.* It would be prudent to check a few of the new values by hand to be certain that you did the compute correctly.

The second compute command we will apply uses the MEAN function. This command includes all respondents regardless of whether they have missing data or not.

- Click on **Transform=>Compute**. You will then see the **Compute Variable** window.
- Click **Reset**
- In the **Target Variable** box, type *coleval2.*
- Click **Type&Label** button and label your new variable *college evaluation scale-2.*
- Click Continue.
- Select the **MEAN(numexpr, numexpr)** in the **Functions:** box and move it up to the **Numeric Expression** box using the **arrow** button. The window should resemble Fig. G.8.

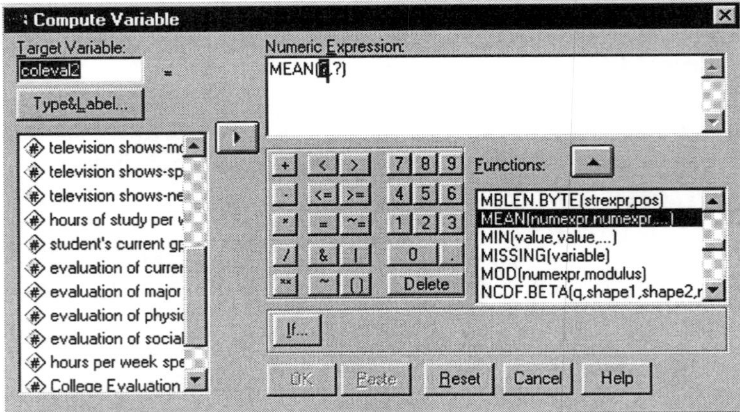

Fig. G.8. Compute variable: MEAN.

Next, move each of the *evaluation* variables to the **Numeric Expression** box with the arrow button. Between each of these variables, type a **,** (comma) for separation if it is not there already (see Fig. G.9). Notice the difference between the numeric expression in Fig. G.9 and that in Fig. G.7. It is this difference that creates the different end results we will see at the end of the command.

- Click **OK** and look to the last variable of your data set on the data editor. It should resemble Fig. G.10. Notice the differences between the two Compute commands even with the selection of the same variables.

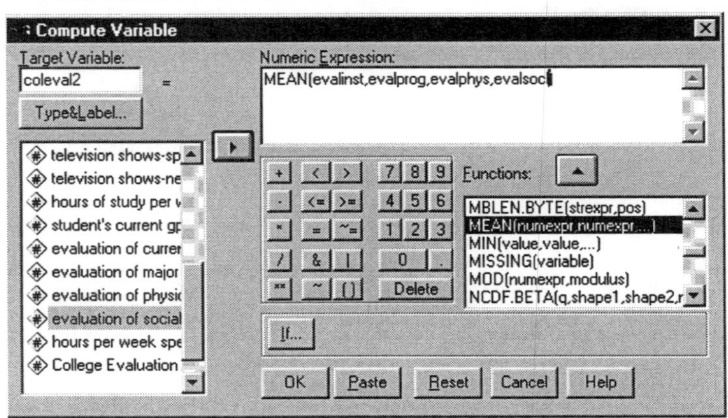

Fig. G.9. Compute variable with MEAN expression.

colleval	coleval2
3.00	3.00
.	2.67
4.00	4.00
3.25	3.25
3.50	3.50
3.00	3.00
4.25	4.25
3.50	3.50
3.50	3.50
2.25	2.25
3.00	3.00
3.00	3.00
4.25	4.25
3.00	3.00
3.75	3.75
2.75	2.75

Fig. G.10. Data editor with both compute variables.

Multiple Response

This process is helpful to look at how respondents answered a question that allowed for multiple responses. For example, let's look at television show types. Respondents were able to choose any or all of four different types of TV shows (e.g. sitcoms, etc.). These were originally entered as separate variables so that we could analyze each separately. They were entered 1=yes and 0=no for *tvsitcom*, *tvmovies*, *tvsports*, and *tvnews*.

Let's try viewing the multiple response output of these variables.

- Select **Analyze**, => **Multiple Response**, => **Define Sets**.You will then see the **Define Multiple Response Sets** window (Fig. G.11).
- From the **Set Definition** box, highlight the following variables and move them to the right with the **arrow** button: *television shows-sitcom, television shows-movies, television shows-sports, and television shows-news.* (See Fig. G.11)
- Note: You can highlight all of these variables together by pressing the **shift** key while selecting each variable.
- Select **Dichotomies** in the **Variables are Coded As** box, and type *1* in the **Counted Value** box. (You chose Dichotomies because each of the variables had a value label of either 1 or 0).
- Next you have to name the new **Multiple Response set** variable. Type *prteach* in the **Name** box, and then *percent watching each type of show* in the **Label** box.
- Finally click **Add** and you should see the variable *$prteach* in the **Mult Response Sets:** box.
- Click Close, and you will have defined the set from which you will create a Multiple Response table.

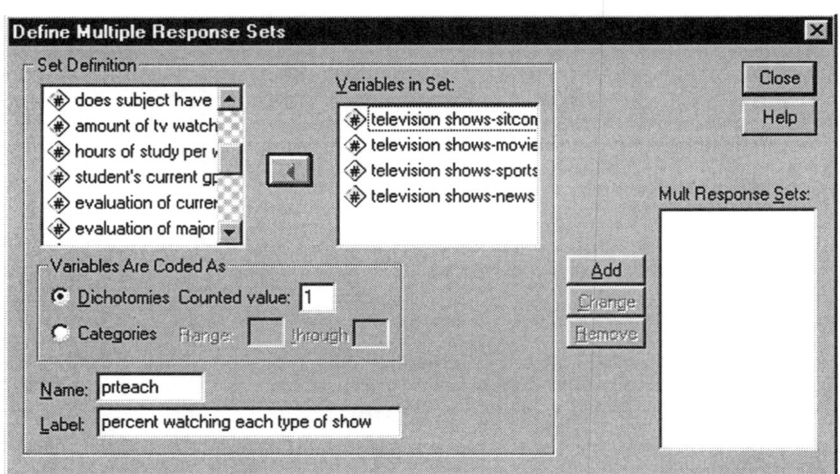

Fig. G.11. Define multiple response sets.

Once you have defined the set, you are ready to create a multiple response table, either for frequencies or crosstabs. We will show you a Multiple Response Frequency table. The steps are similar if you want to develop a crosstabulation table.

- Click **Analyze**, =>**Multiple Response**, =>**Frequencies**. You will then see the **Multiple Response Frequency** window (fig. G.12).
- You will see the set *Percent watching each type of show ($prteach)* in the box under **Multiple Response Sets:**.
- Highlight that variable, and click the **arrow** to move it to the box under **Table(s) for:**. (See Fig. G.12.)
- Click **OK**. (Note: you may have circumstances where you want to exclude all missing cases from the frequency table. In that situation, you would want to click on **Exclude cases listwise within dichotomies**.)

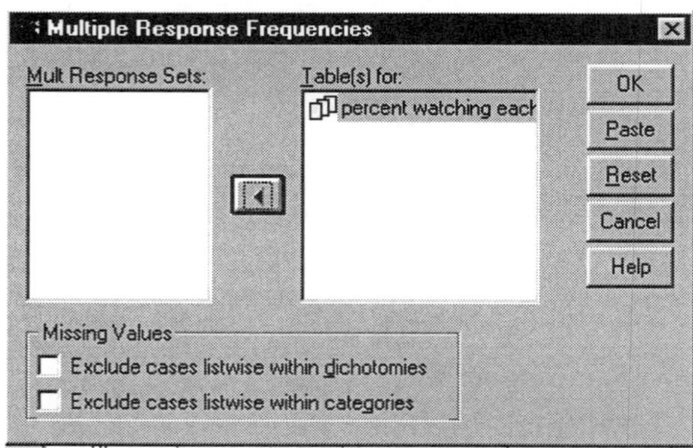

Fig. G.12. Multiple response frequencies.

An Output Window in the SPSS Viewer will appear entitled, "Multiple Response." It should look like Output G.1.

Output G.1: Multiple Response Frequencies

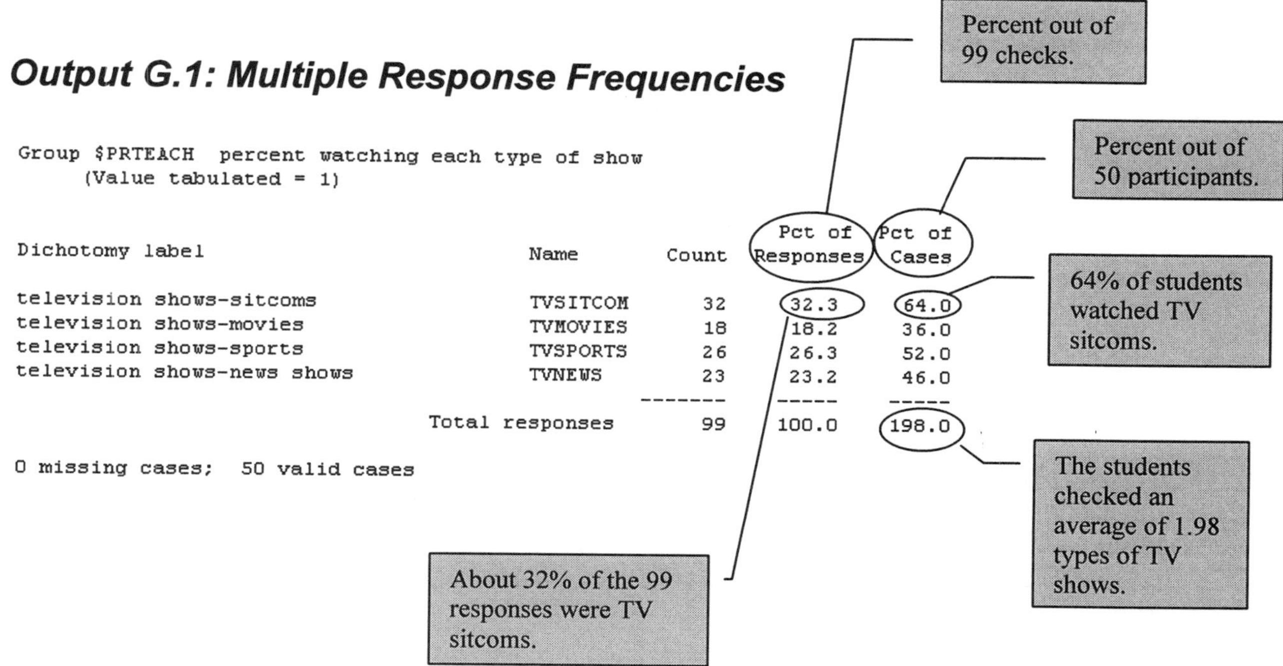

```
Group $PRTEACH  percent watching each type of show
     (Value tabulated = 1)
```

Dichotomy label	Name	Count	Pct of Responses	Pct of Cases
television shows-sitcoms	TVSITCOM	32	32.3	64.0
television shows-movies	TVMOVIES	18	18.2	36.0
television shows-sports	TVSPORTS	26	26.3	52.0
television shows-news shows	TVNEWS	23	23.2	46.0
	Total responses	99	100.0	198.0

0 missing cases; 50 valid cases

Split File

This next command allows you to split your data set by another variable. This is helpful when you wish to run the same statistics separately for two or more groups or values of a variable such as gender or school district.

- Select **Data=> Split File**. You should see the **Split File** window.
- At this point, you will have to determine whether you want to compare the groups that you are using to split the file, or to organize the output by those groups. For example, if you are using gender to split the file, you have to decide if you want to compare males and females to each other according to your dependent variables, or to see all the independent variables of the males in your data set, and then all of the independent variables of the females in your data set.
- Once you make these determinations, you should click on either **Compare groups**, or **Organize output by groups**. For our example, we will compare the groups (see Fig. G.13). On your own, see what happens when you choose to organize the output by groups.

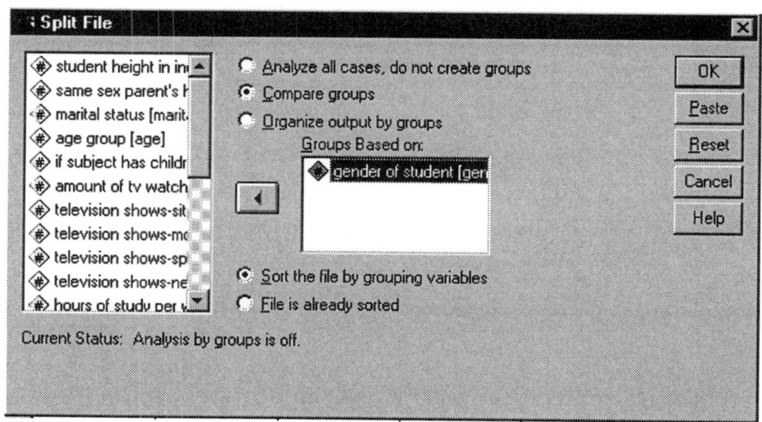

Fig. G.13. Split file.

- From the box on the left of the window, choose *gender of student*. Next, click the **arrow** to move gender to the **Groups Based on:** box. Click **OK**.
- Now, when you look at your data set, you will see that all of the males are grouped together and all of the females are grouped together (see Fig. G.14).

gender
1
1
1
1
1
1
1
1
1
2
2
2
2
2
2
2

Fig. G.14. Data set split by gender.

- You are now ready to run just about any statistical command that is appropriate for your data. For the sake of explanation, we will run a simple frequency distribution to illustrate the *Compare groups* command.
- Select **Analyze=>Descriptive Statistics=>Frequencies**. You should now see the **Frequencies** window.
- Select the variable *student height in inches* from the box on the left, and click the **arrow** button to move it over to the **Variable(s)** box (see Fig. G.15). Click **OK**.

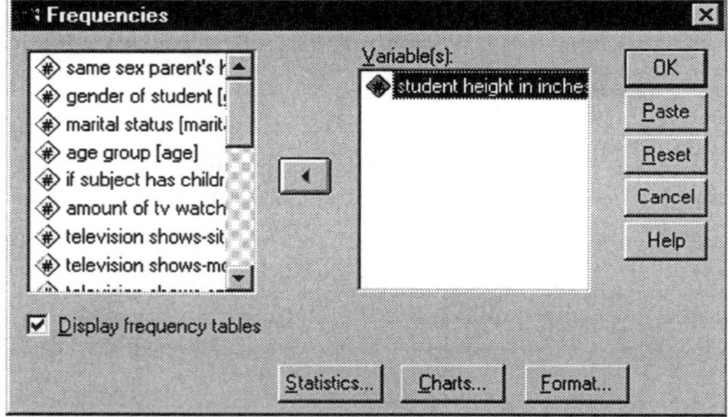

Fig. G.15. Frequencies.

- SPSS will now create a frequency table for you (See Output G.2). Notice that the variable *student height* is split by gender. This is the type of output that will result from a *Compare groups Split File*.

Output G.2: Split File Frequencies

student height in inches

gender of student			Frequency	Percent	Valid Percent	Cumulative Percent
males	Valid	64.00	2	7.7	7.7	7.7
		67.00	2	7.7	7.7	15.4
		68.00	1	3.8	3.8	19.2
		69.00	4	15.4	15.4	34.6
		70.00	4	15.4	15.4	50.0
		71.00	5	19.2	19.2	69.2
		72.00	5	19.2	19.2	88.5
		75.00	3	11.5	11.5	100.0
		Total	26	100.0	100.0	
females	Valid	60.00	1	4.2	4.2	4.2
		61.00	2	8.3	8.3	12.5
		62.00	1	4.2	4.2	16.7
		63.00	5	20.8	20.8	37.5
		64.00	6	25.0	25.0	62.5
		65.00	4	16.7	16.7	79.2
		67.00	4	16.7	16.7	95.8
		68.00	1	4.2	4.2	100.0
		Total	24	100.0	100.0	

Notice that the file is split by gender, and the two levels are compared to each other.

Pivot Tables

The Pivot Tables command allows you to switch the variable axes in your tables. This is helpful if switching the variable axes would make more sense when interpreting the table, or if you have many levels of one variable therefore creating a table that is too wide to fit on a page. To illustrate this command, we will run a cross-tabulation using the variables *gender* and *marital*.

Run the cross-tabulation as shown in Chapter 5.

- In the **Crosstabs** window, move *gender* into the Row(s) box, and *marital* into the Column(s) box.
- Click **OK**. You will see a table similar to that in Output G.3.

Output G.3: Gender of Student and Marital Status Crosstabulation

gender of student * marital status Crosstabulation

Count

		marital status			Total
		single	married	divorced	
gender of student	males	14	7	5	26
	females	6	11	6	23
Total		20	18	11	49

Notice that Marital Status is shown in the columns, and Gender is shown in the rows.

Consider that you want to discuss the different marital statuses in relation to gender, but that marital status is the dependent variable. It might be more helpful to present the cross-tabulation table so that marital status is along the vertical axis (in the rows) and that gender is on the horizontal axis (the columns). Instead of running the command again, you are able to pivot the table to fit your needs.

- In the SPSS Viewer, double click on the table you want to alter. You will see the **Pivoting Trays1** and the **Formatting Toolbar1** windows.
- Bring the **Pivoting Trays1** window to the front by clicking anywhere on that window. (See Figure G.16.)

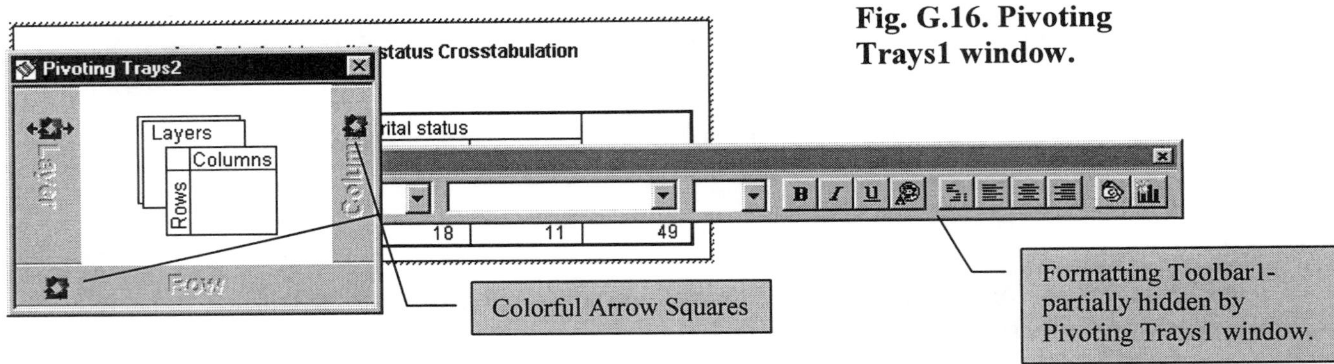

Fig. G.16. Pivoting Trays1 window.

Notice the 'grayed out' **Layer**, **Column**, and **Row** borders each with a colorful arrow square. You can move these squares to change the look of your table.

- Click on the **arrow square** on the **Column** side and, while continuing to hold your left mouse button down, move it to the **Row** side of the **Pivoting Trays1** window. (See Fig. G.17.)
- Do the same on the **Row** side…click and hold the arrow square on the **Rows** side and move it to the **Columns** side. If you had three variables, your table would essentially be three dimensions. The third dimension is called **Layers**.

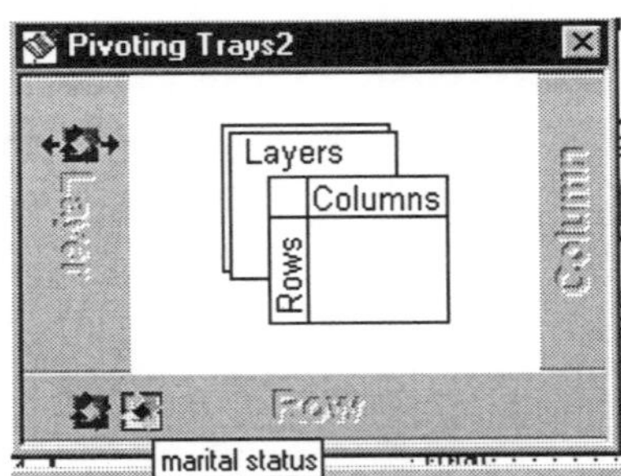

Fig. G.17. Column arrow square moved to Row side.

- You can see that your table changed to reflect these moves. Your table should now look similar to Output G.4.

Output G.4: Changed Table

gender of student * marital status Crosstabulation

Count

		gender of student		
		males	females	Total
marital status	single	14	6	20
	married	7	11	18
	divorced	5	6	11
Total		26	23	49

Appendix H

Creating 3-D Graphs and Charts with SPSS

The purpose of the appendix is to create 3-D graphs and charts. In this appendix we will take a step-by-step approach to creating graphs and charts using your SPSS software. We will focus on creating a bar chart. However, similar steps apply for creating pie charts, ribbons, and so forth.

First, let's create the following 3-D graph using the hsbdata so that it looks like Fig. H.1 below:

Gender of Participants

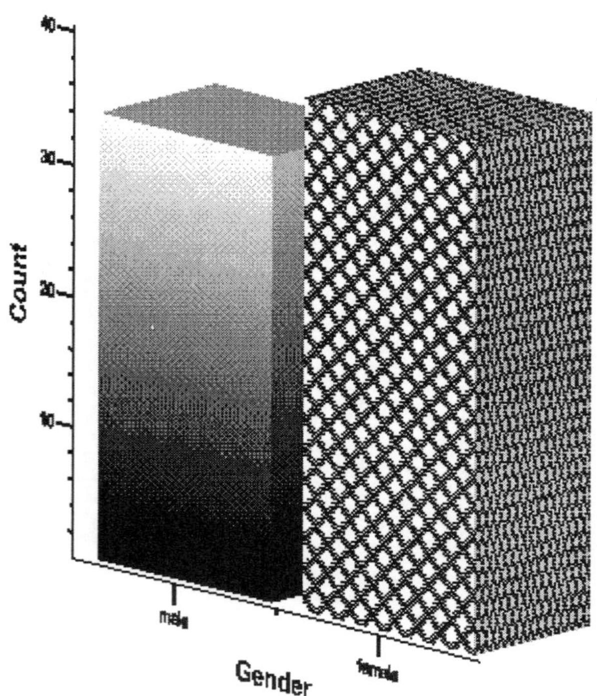

Fig. H.1. Sample bar chart.

Follow these commands:

- Open up your most recent **HsbData** file
- Select **Graphs** => **Interactive** => **Bar** to get a Fig. H.2

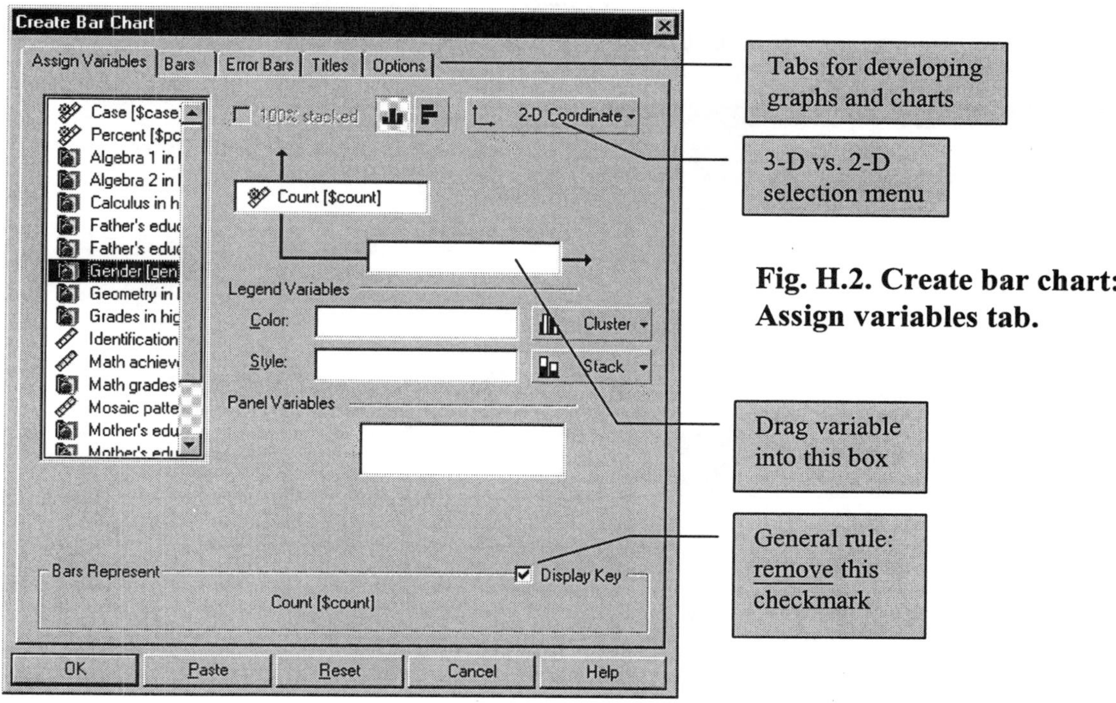

Fig. H.2. Create bar chart: Assign variables tab.

- Highlight *Gender*, hold the left mouse button down and *drag* it into the box noted in Fig. H.2.
- Now select **3-D Coordinate** from the 3-D vs. 2-D Coordinate menu.
- Remove the checkmark in the **Display Key** box by clicking on it.
- Click on the **Bars** tab at the top of the window noted in Fig. H.2 and you will get Fig. H.3.

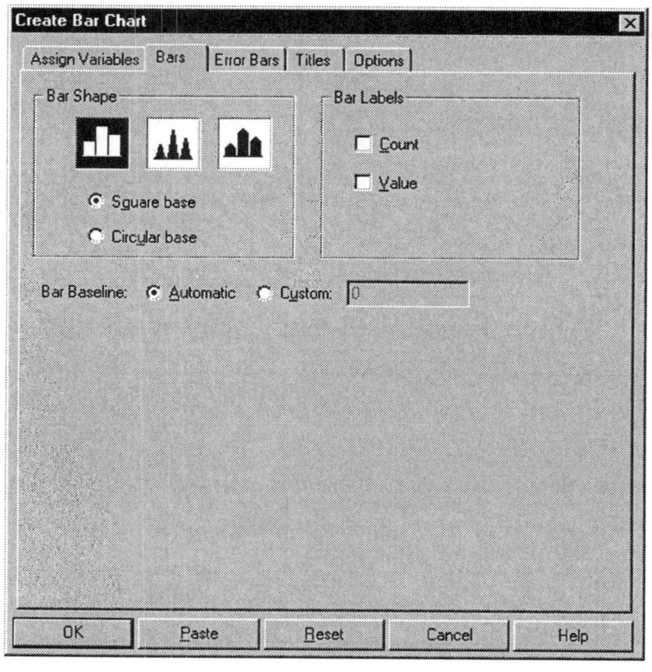

Fig. H.3. Create bar chart: Bars tab.

- Select the **bar shape** you desire. In this case, we have selected the first one.
- Click on the **Titles** tab and type in "**Gender of Participants**" as noted in Fig. H.4.

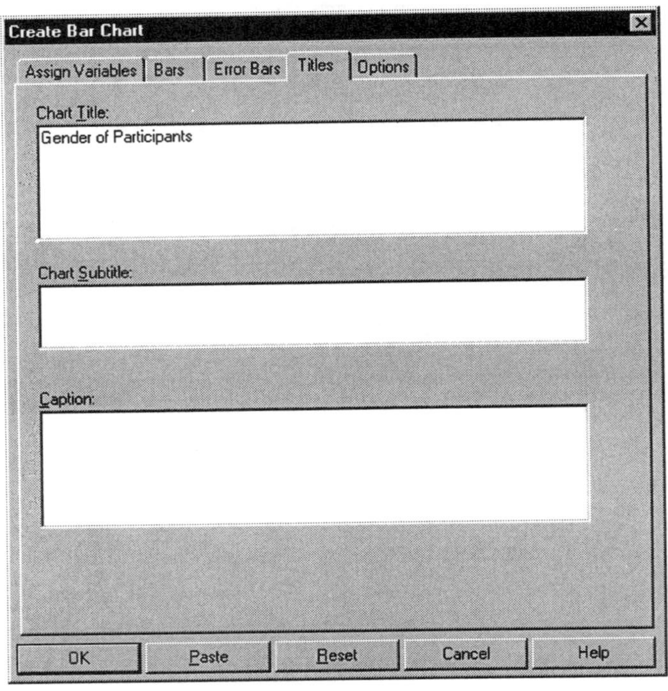

Fig. H.4. Create bar chart: Titles tab.

- Select the **Options** tab (to get Fig. H.5) and select *Gender* in the **Variable** box.
- Select **Grayscale** under **Chart look** (you can choose others in the future).
- Finally, click on **OK** to get your initial bar chart that looks like Fig. H.6.

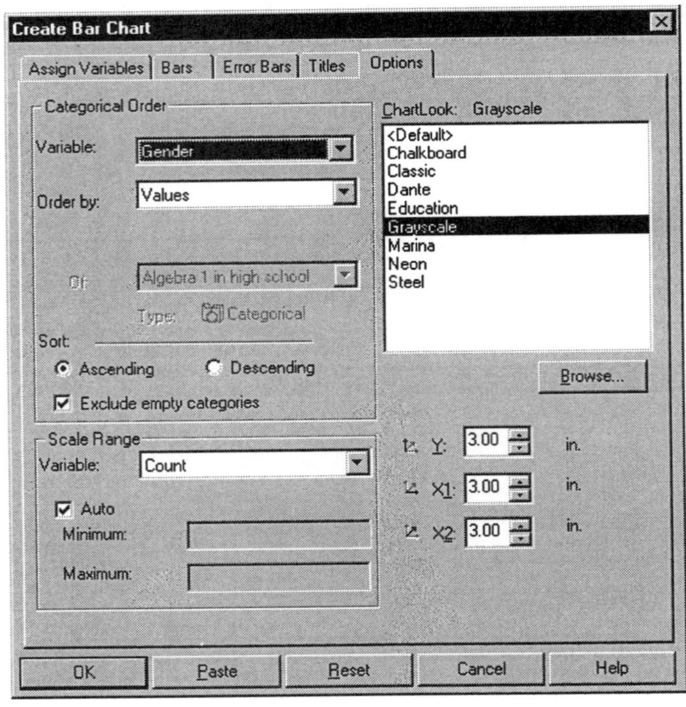

Fig. H.5. Create bar chart: Options tab.

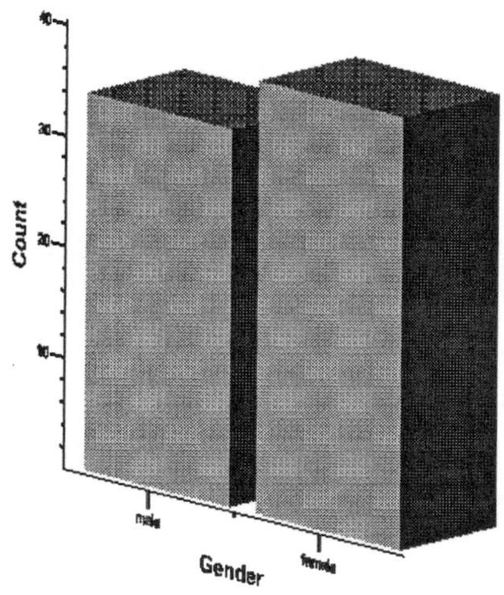

Fig. H.6. Initial bar chart.

Now, let's modify this chart using the various SPSS commands available. Follow these steps:

- In your Output mode, *double click* on the bar chart to get something like Fig. H.7. Note, the 3-D window may also show up to the left depending on your computer.

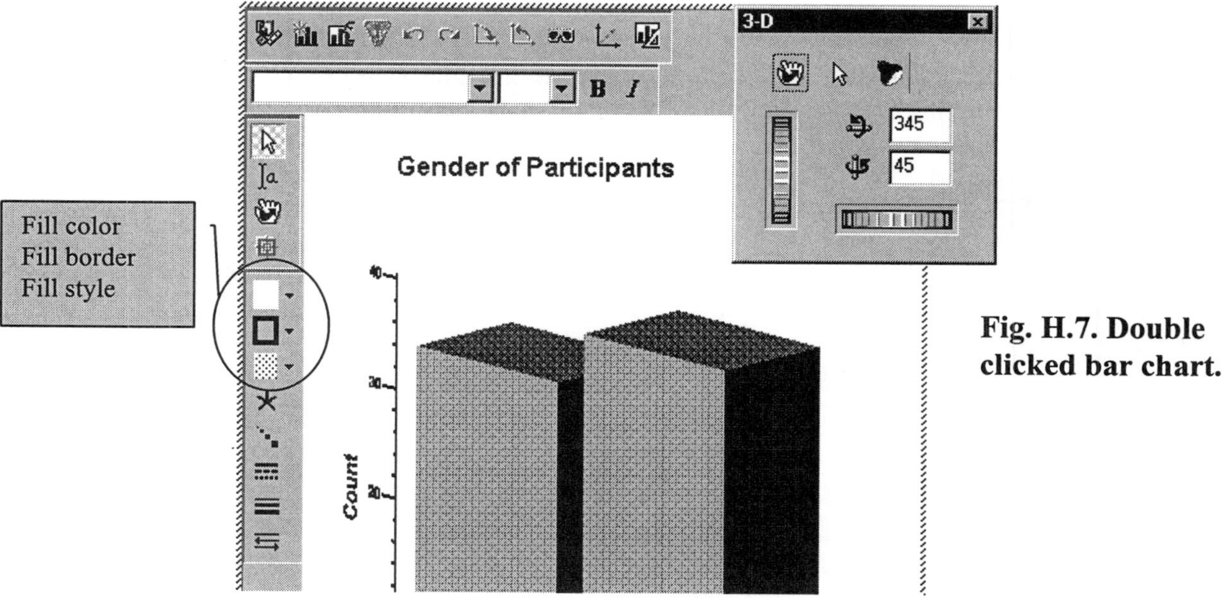

Fig. H.7. Double clicked bar chart.

- Now, click once on the first bar (males) and a blue dotted line will appear around it.
- Now click on the **Fill Style** noted in Fig. H.7 and select the one noted in H.8.

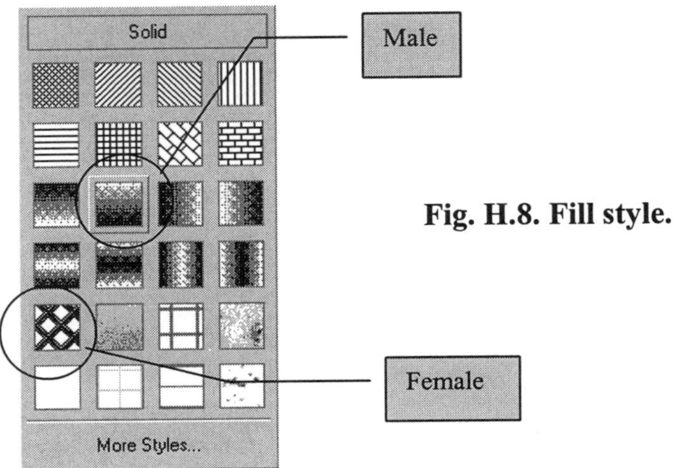

Fig. H.8. Fill style.

- Click once on the **female bar** and select the one noted by Fig. H.8.
- Congratulations! You've done it! Your bars should look like Fig. H.1.

Little notes to consider when creating 3-D charts and graphs. The best way to learn is to play, play, play. Start creating different charts and graphs with different designs and colors. Don't worry about creating anything for professional purposes. Rather, go with the intent that you will click on various buttons until you figure it out.

Review Appendix F to see how you can paste your 3-D graphs into Word, PowerPoint, and Excel.

You can use the 3-D menu bar shown in Fig. H.9 to rotate your 3-D graph or change the lighting highlights and light angles. These add more wiz-bang to the charts and graphs that you can eventually transfer to Microsoft Word, PowerPoint, Publisher, or other software.

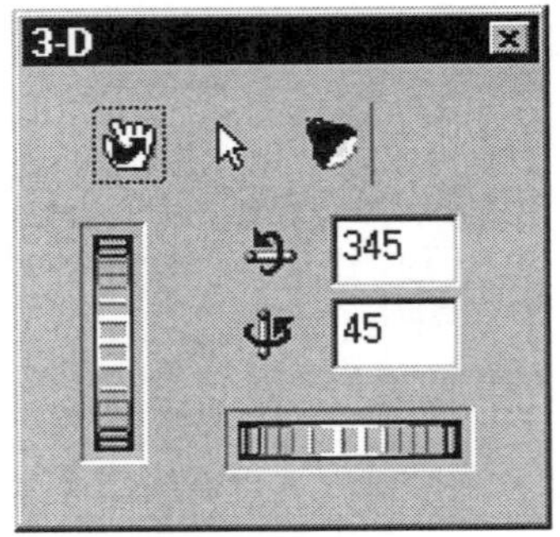

Fig. H.9. 3-D effect menu.

For further instruction, go to www.spss.com. SPSS has a tutorial on more advanced 3-D effects that is worth browsing.

APPENDIX I

Working with SPSS Syntax (Log) Files

Mei-Huei Tsay

It is possible to modify syntax files to run slightly different statistics and/or complex, customized statistics. Sometimes output files are too large to save on a disk or take up too much space on your hard drive. Therefore, it is a good idea to understand how to use the syntax or log files that contain SPSS commands. You can use the SPSS logs from your output file to run these commands.

It is possible to open a syntax window and type in commands, but sometimes it is easier to build your syntax file by using one of the following methods:

- Paste syntax commands from dialog boxes.
- Copy syntax from the output log.
- Copy syntax from the journal file.

Creating Syntax Commands From Dialog Boxes: Using Paste Instead of OK

The easiest way to generate a syntax command file is to make selections in dialogue boxes and paste the syntax of the selections into a syntax window. By pasting the syntax in the syntax window, you can generate a job file that allows you to repeat the analysis, edit it, save the syntax in a syntax file, and copy/cut it into an output log.

To paste syntax commands from a dialog box:

- Retrieve the data file.
- Open the dialog box and make desired selections. For example: **Analyze => Descriptive Statistics => Frequencies**.
- For this purpose we will select **Ethnic** and **Gender**. Now, click **Paste** instead of **OK** (see Fig. I.1). The syntax command is pasted to the syntax window. If you don't have an open syntax window, SPSS will open a new syntax window and paste the syntax there (see Fig. I.2).

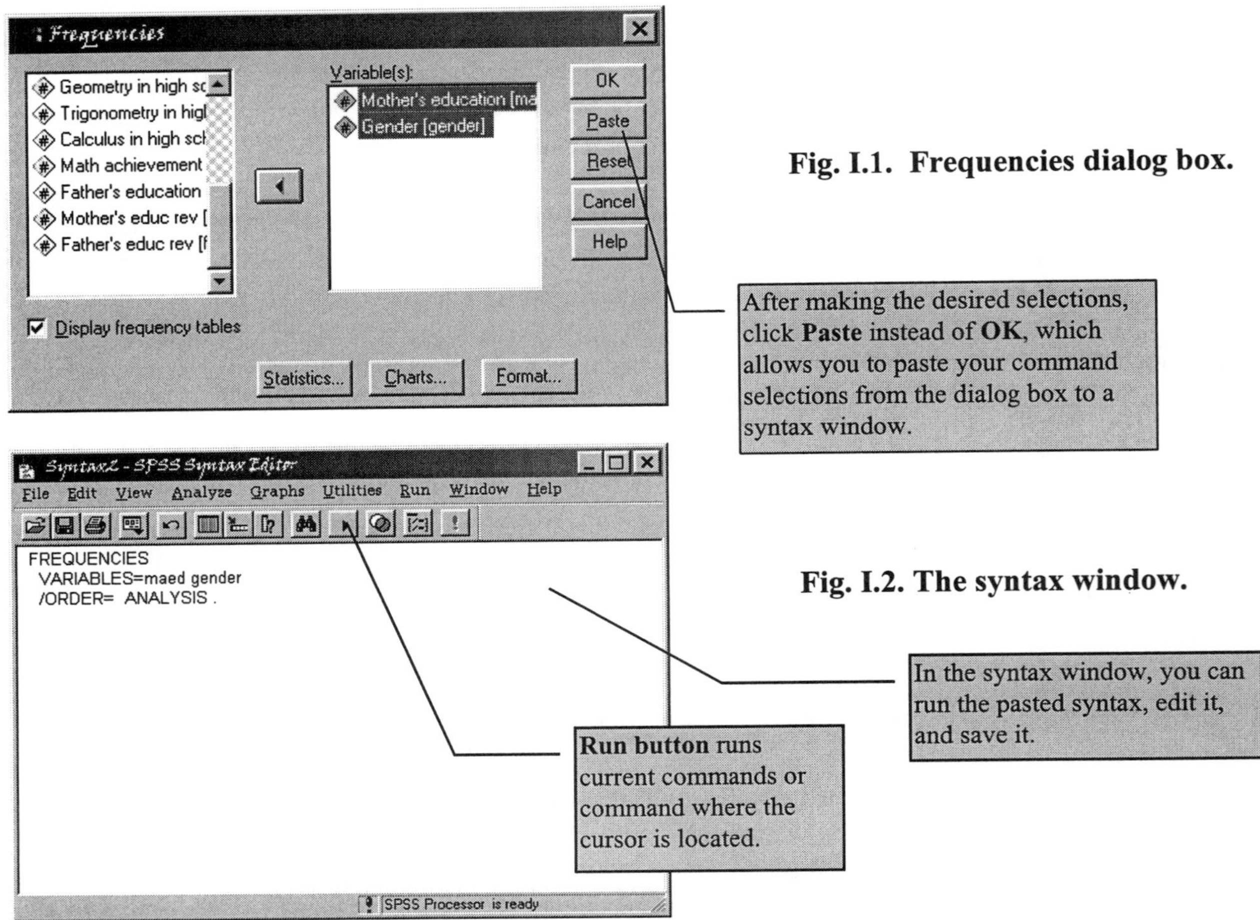

Fig. I.1. Frequencies dialog box.

Fig. I.2. The syntax window.

- To run/use a syntax file, when there is only one syntax file in the window, just simply click on **Run => All** in the menu bar.
- If there are many syntax files in the window, *highlight* the desired syntax first, then click **Run => Selection**. The output will show on the output window.

Using Syntax From the Output Log

This is useful when you don't have much room to spare on your computer or disk. You can save only the SPSS logs and delete all the output tables, charts, and other files that take up disk space. This allows you to store very small files and expand to larger files if needed.

You can build a syntax file by copying syntax commands from the SPSS output log in the Output Navigator. First follow these commands:

- Click on **Edit => Options** in the top menu.
- Click on the **Draft Viewer** tab to get a menu like Fig. I.3.
- Select **Display commands in the log** (circled area in Fig. I.3).
- Click on **OK**.

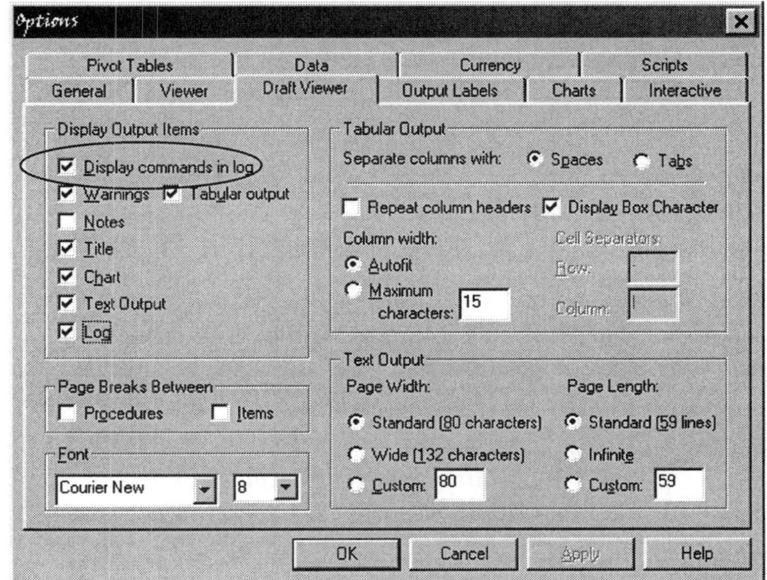

Fig. I.3. Options menu.

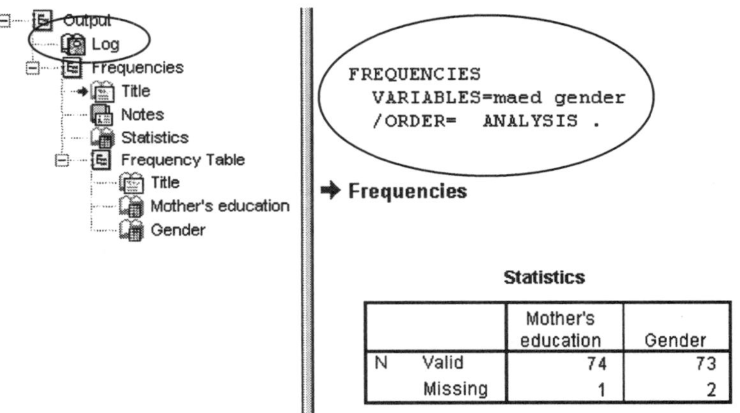

		Mother's education	Gender
N	Valid	74	73
	Missing	1	2

Fig. I.4. Output with syntax log.

To copy the syntax log from the Output file to the Syntax Editor follow these commands:

- First **highlight** the desired syntax file by clicking once on the **Log** or the **syntax commands** (see Fig. I.4 circled areas);
- Click on **Edit => Copy** from the Output menu bar.
- Now open a new **Syntax Editor** by choosing **File** => **New** => **Syntax** from the menu bar. A blank syntax editor like Fig. I.2 will appear.
- Now click on **Edit => Paste** from the **Syntax Editor** menu bar (see Fig. I.2).

Now you can run the pasted syntax as we showed you above.

Using Syntax Logs From the Journal File

This is a more complicated way of doing things, but it is worth mentioning here.

By default, SPSS records all commands executed during a session in a journal file named *spss.jnl* (set with **Options** on the **Edit** menu). You can edit the journal file and save it as a syntax file that you can use to repeat the previous analysis. The big problem is finding the journal file.

To find the journal file,

- From the Start menu choose Start menus choose **Start** => **Find** => **Files and Folder** (see Fig. I.5).
- Then choose *spss.jnl* from the file name box or enter **.jnl* in the **Named** part of the box (see Fig. I.6).
- Double click to open the file. Note, in most cases you may have more than spss.jnl file. Check the dates with the file you would like to open and use that one.

Warning! Sometimes with new installations of SPSS, the spss.jnl file is not associated with an application that opens it and you will get an **Open With** menu when you double click the spss.jnl file. Since the spss.jnl file is a small file, we suggest you select **Notepad** (alternatively, Wordpad or Winword) as the application to open the file.

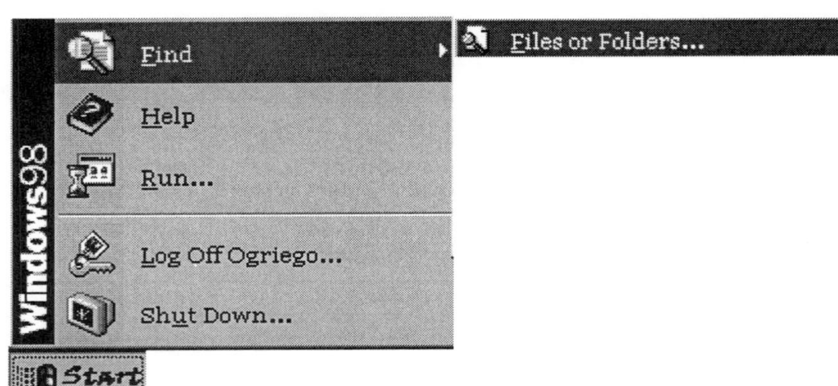

Fig. I.5. Start: Find files and folders menu.

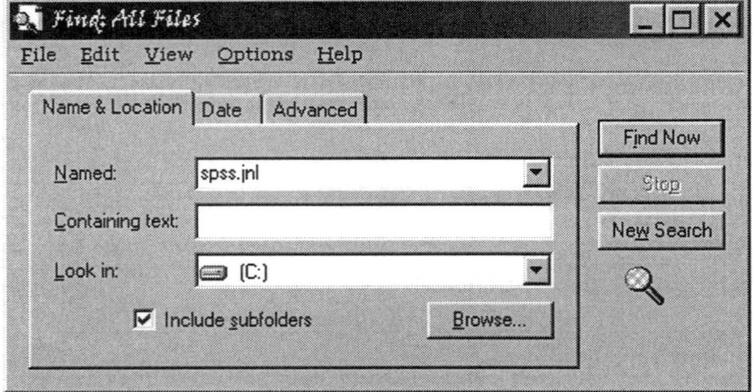

Fig. I.6. Find all files window.

The journal file is a text file that can be edited like any other text file. But notice, because *error* and *warning messages* are also recorded in the journal file along with your commands, you must **delete** any of these messages that appear before saving or running the syntax file (see Fig. I.7).

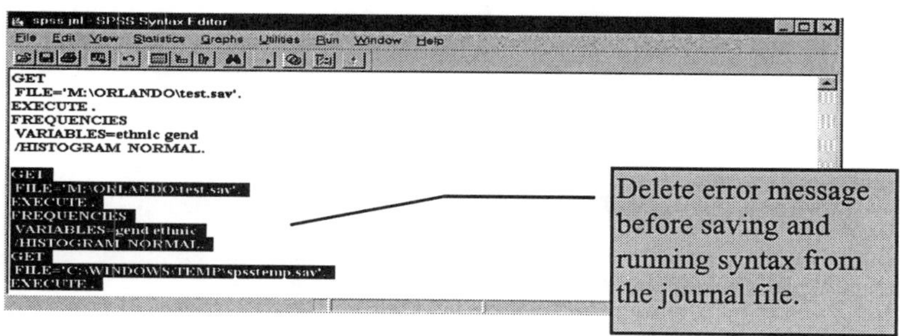

Fig. I.7. Editing the journal file.

Finally, to run or edit the journal file you need to highlight, copy, and paste them into a Syntax Editor (see above instructions on getting a <u>new</u> Syntax Editor). Also, it is important that you understand that all syntax commands start with **CAPITALIZED** words and end with **period** (.). That is where you begin and end highlighting. Here is what you need to do:

- With the spss.jnl displaying the text (see Fig. I.8), *highlight* the command or commands you want. In this case we selected **FREQUENCIES** for the variables mother's education (*maed*) and *gender*.
- Note that we highlighted the period also.
- Select **Edit** => **Copy**.
- Now open your new syntax editor (**File** => **New** => **Syntax**).
- Select **Edit** => **Paste** from your syntax editor.

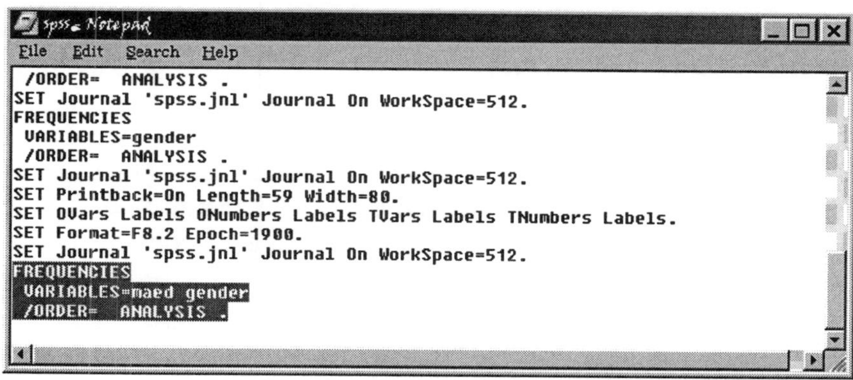

spss - Notepad
File Edit Search Help
/ORDER= ANALYSIS .
SET Journal 'spss.jnl' Journal On WorkSpace=512.
FREQUENCIES
VARIABLES=gender
/ORDER= ANALYSIS .
SET Journal 'spss.jnl' Journal On WorkSpace=512.
SET Printback=On Length=59 Width=80.
SET OVars Labels ONumbers Labels TVars Labels TNumbers Labels.
SET Format=F8.2 Epoch=1900.
SET Journal 'spss.jnl' Journal On WorkSpace=512.
FREQUENCIES
VARIABLES=maed gender
/ORDER= ANALYSIS .

Fig. I.8. Highlighting spss.jnl commands.

Running Syntax Commands

You can now run single commands, selected groups of commands, or all commands in a syntax window. See the directions on running all or selections previously given. The following options are available on the **Run** menu:

- **All**. Runs all commands in the syntax window.
- **Selection**. Run the currently selected commands, including commands partially highlighted.
- **Current.** Runs the command where the cursor is currently located.
- **To End**. Runs all commands from the current cursor location to the end of the command syntax file.

APPENDIX J

Answers to Interpretation Questions

Nancy L. Leech

Chapter 1 – An Overview of SPSS for Windows

1. a) If there are multiple people using the same data (such as in a lab classroom) it is important to print your name on your output in order to know which output is yours.
   b) Since SPSS provides very brief titles it can be helpful to include more information in the title so that it will "stand alone." In other words, a longer title helps the reader so they do not need to read the text in order to understand the table. Other information that might be included in a title would be the variable names.
   c) Putting a date on your output is helpful so that you will know when the output was created. In some situations, you might need to rerun statistical analyses. By dating your output you will know which ones were done first.

2. The Analyze menu.

3. The Transform menu.

Chapter 2 – Research Problems and Questions

1. An active independent variable is a variable that is given to the subjects during the study. An attribute independent variable is a variable that cannot be changed, given, or manipulated during the study. The similarity between an active and an attribute independent variable is that these are variables that are the predictors, antecedents, or presumed causes or influences which the researcher hopes to analyze.

2. Active independent variable.

3. The independent variable is the variable that is manipulated, or the antecedent. The dependent variable is the presumed outcome.

4. A difference question compares groups, or levels of an independent variable on the dependent variable. Difference questions are usually used with randomized experimental, quasi experimental, and comparative designs.
   An associational question associates or relates the independent variable and the dependent variable and the independent variable is usually continuous (i.e., it has many ordered levels). Statistics used are correlation or multiple regression analysis.
   A descriptive question describes or summarizes the data. Descriptive questions can be used in any type of research design.

Chapter 3 – Measurement and Descriptive Statistics

1. With categorical, ordered data the level of measurement to use would be either ordinal or scale. If the data has unequal intervals between categories or the categories are ranked it is best to use an ordinal scale of measurement. If the data are ordered and equally spaced, an interval/ratio scale of measurement should be used.

2. a) Nominal – categories are assigned a number but a category assigned the number 2 does not imply more or less than a category assigned a number 1. Nominal variables are used with data that are in categories with no order or sequence. Ordinal – categories are ordered from low to high with unequal intervals. Interval – categories are equally spaced.
   b) It is not important to distinguish between interval and ratio because it is possible to do all of the available types of statistics with interval data. The different statistics work with data with or without a true zero.

3. 34%

4. a) A z score relates to a normal curve by setting the mean equal to zero and the standard deviation equal to one. This can be done easily with SPSS.
   b) A z score equal to –3 would be interpreted as being 3 deviations below the mean.

5. Frequency polygons should not be used with nominal data because there is no necessary ordering of the points. Using a frequency polygon would not give any useful information. A bar chart would be the best chart to use to examine nominal data.

Chapter 4 – Data Collection

1. You have most likely made an error in coding the data or you have several very tall people in your class since 78 inches is taller than the national mean for height by almost a foot. If your class is composed of mostly basketball players then you might assume it is about right. If your class appears to be about average in height, you should carefully check your data set for errors.

2. It will most likely shorten the amount of time it takes to enter the data into SPSS and it allows you to check for errors.

3. It is not uncommon to drop or mix up a stack of questionnaires. This process will allow you to check your raw data even after a bad day in a windstorm. This process may also help keep the researcher from needing to use personal identifiers such as social security numbers or phone numbers, thus providing a bit more protection against violating the rights of respondents.

Chapter 5 – Data Entry and Descriptives

1. a) The term scale is used when the data have ordered categories and the frequency distribution is approximately normal. This is similar to interval or ratio data. Nominal is used when the variable is unordered categories or values. The term ordinal is used when there are categories or values but the possible values are not equally spaced.
   b) It is important to know what level of variable you are labeling so that you will be able to choose the appropriate statistics to use.

2. a) It is important to check data before entering it into SPSS to make sure subjects filled out the questionnaires correctly, check for double answers, or markings between two ratings.
   b) A way to check data before entering it is to visually look at the data (the questionnaire, etc.).

3. a) Box plots are a graphical representation of the data. It is helpful to use a box plot to understand the distribution of scores of one variable in relationship to another variable. Box plots also show any extreme scores or outliers.
   b) The line in the box plot represents the median or middle score.

Chapter 6 - Checking Data and Descriptives

1. We would look to see if any of the minimum or maximum scores in Output 6.1 were outside the ranges specified in chapter 6 and in the codebook in Appendix C. Note that algebra 1 in h.s. and geometry in high school are too high; one should be the maximum.

2. a) Gender is a dichotomous variable. There are six other dichotomous variables, math grades, algebra 1, etc., that some would consider nominal, but we think it is better just to think of them as dichotomous variables. The mean can be interpreted meaningfully. The mean of a dichotomous variable indicates the percentage of those with the higher number.
   b) At least 75 because that is the biggest *N* for any variable.
   c) 70 (valid *N* listwise)
   d) .79 = 79% took algebra 1.
   e) 2 = minimum, 10 = maximum. Yes.

3. a) 2
   b) 97.3%
   c) 34
   d) 45.3% and 46.6 valid percent were male. The percent and valid percent are different because there is missing data.

4. a) No
   b) It tells us if the assumption of normality has been markedly violated.
   c) Visually none look very much like a normal curve.
   d) The skewness calculation says that none of the variables are markedly different from normal, therefore they are approximately normal.
   e) 5.24
   f) 64.0%
   g) 12.0%

5. We recoded father's and mother's education because the education variables had a flaw; i.e., a parent with 1 week of college would get a higher score than a parent with 2 years of vocational school. *Father's education revised* for participants 2, 5, and 8 should be 2, 1, and 2.

Chapter 7 – Selecting and Interpreting Inferential Statistics

1. A between groups design is used when each subject is in one and only one condition or group.
   A within groups design is used when each subject receives or experiences all of the conditions or levels of the independent variable.

2. a) Decide whether you are asking a difference or an associational question.
   b) If you are asking a difference question, see whether it is within or between groups.
   c) Figure out what scale the dependent variable has.
   d) Decide how many independent variables are included in the question.
   e) Figure out what levels the independent variable(s) have.

3. a) There are three independent variables or factors. The first independent variable has two levels, the second independent variable has four levels, and the third independent variable has four levels.
   b) The dependent variable is not included in labeling the design.

4. a) No.
   b) There may be more than one appropriate statistical analysis to use with each design. Interval data can always use statistics used with nominal or ordinal data, but you will lose some power by doing this.

5. This signifies that the results are statistically significant at the .05 level. We then can reject the null hypothesis of no difference or no relationship. Thus, we can assume there is a relationship between the variables.

6. Pearson correlation.

7. There is a significant negative correlation between anxiety and test performance. The more anxiety one has the lower the test performance score would be. According to Cohen (1988) the effect size is medium.

8. Two-Way Factorial ANOVA.

9. Chi-Square.

10. Multiple Regression.

11. Spearman rho.

Chapter 8 - Cross-Tabulation and Chi-Square

1. a) In a Crosstabs output, the "count" describes the number of subjects which had an answer for the variable. The "expected count" is the number which one would expect by chance from the totals.
   b) The difference tells you how many more or less subjects answered compared to the number who would be expected to answer.

2. a) The (Pearson) chi-square is statistically significant ($p = .001$) using the continuity correction or $p = .001$ with Fisher's Exact Test. This means that the relationship between two categorical variables (gender and geometry in h.s.) is statistically significant. Therefore, we can be confident that males and females are different on whether or not they took geometry in high school.
   b) Yes, according to footnote b in the chi-square tests table, the expected counts in all of the cells are > 5.

Chapter 9 - Correlation

1. a) The correlation coefficients tell us the strength with which the two variables are associated or related.
   b) r squared = .113 (.336 squared) This signifies the percentage of variance in common between the two variables. In this case, it is the percentage of variance in math achievement that can be predicted from mother's education.
   c) The Pearson correlations have somewhat higher values than the Spearman correlations, but they have similar significance/p levels. Usually the Pearson r is somewhat more powerful.
   d) If one or both of the variables are clearly ordinal data, we would use the Spearman rho.

2. Two are statistically significant.
   a) There was a statistically significant correlation, r (73) = .423, $p < .001$, between visualization score and math achievement. Thus, we reject the null hypothesis of no/zero association. There is a moderate positive association between visualization score and math achievement. The effect size is small – medium

according to Cohen (1988). In general, those with a high visualization score have high math achievement; those with a low visualization score have low math achievement, and those in the middle on one variable will probably have a middle score on the other variable.

b) There was not a significant correlation, r (73) = .213, p = .067, between the mosaic pattern test score and math achievement. The effect size is small according to Cohen (1988). There is not evidence to reject the null hypothesis. In simple terms, there seems to be no association or relationship between the mosaic pattern test score and math achievement. We do not know anything about math achievement based on a student's mosaic pattern test score.

3. a) The correlation of math achievement and grades in high school, $r^2 = .25$ ($r = .5$), indicating a moderate positive correlation. There is a weak or no positive correlation, $r^2 = .05$ ($r = .21$), between mosaic and math achievement. The points scatter widely with little pattern.

   b) Scatter plots are helpful because they give the researcher a view of where all the data points fall and how near they are to the regression line. They also show us whether there are outliers and whether the best regression line might be curved.

Chapter 10 Comparing Groups

t tests

1. a) The variances for grades in high school and math achievement are roughly equal; however, the variances are significantly different for math grades ($p = .011$), which means that the assumption has been violated.

   b) The appropriate *t, df,* and *p* for each *t* test are:

grades in h.s.	$t(71) = -1.076, p = .286$
math achievement	$t(71) = 2.574, p = .012$
math grades	$t(70.81) = -2.157, p = .034$

   c) The *t* tests for math achievement ($p = .012$) and math grades ($p = .034$) are statistically significant.

   d) Boys and girls do not differ significantly in average grades in high school (5.50 vs. 5.90). However, boys scored statistically significantly higher than girls on math achievement (14.76 vs. 10.84).

   e) 95% of the time, the mean difference for grades in h.s. will fall within the range from -1.13 to .34. The difference is not significant because the signs are different; 95% of the time, the mean difference for math achievement will fall within the range from .8826 to 6.9523. Because zero is not included in the range (i.e., the signs are the same), the difference is significant.

   f) A d = .46 is a little less than a medium effect size according to Cohen (1988).

2. a) The paired samples correlation for mother's and father's education means that father's and mother's education are significantly correlated ($r = .676$). More highly educated fathers tend to marry more highly educated mothers and vice versa.

b) Even though they are moderately correlated, the fathers of these students have statistically significantly more education than the mothers ($p = .019$). We can see in the Paired Samples Statistics table that the average level of fathers' education is 4.76 while the average of mothers' is 4.17.

c) A correlation tells the strength of the association between two variables. A t test tells you is the mean of one variable is significantly higher or lower than the mean of another variable.

d) The r of .90 signifies that there is a large effect. The $t = 0$ signifies that there is no significant difference between the scores. In other words, there is a strong relationship between mother's and father's education scores. Mothers with high education tend to be with fathers with high education and vice versa.

e) An $r = 0$ signifies that there is little or no effect, or relationship, between mother's and father's education levels. The $t = 5.0$ shows that there is a significant difference between mother's and father's education scores. Mothers with high education tend to be paired with fathers with low education and vice versa.

One-Way ANOVA

3. a) The three groups of grades in high school differ somewhere on their average scores, $F(2, 70) = 4.05$, $p = .022$. Average visualization scores did not differ significantly, $F(2,70) = .67$, $p = .513$.

   b) For visualization scores, the means for the low, medium, and high father's education groups were 4.70, 5.94, and 5.46, respectively. None are significantly different from each other. For grades in high school, the group means were 5.35, 5.53, and 6.53, respectively. Because the overall F was significant, we know that there is a significant difference somewhere, but we don't know where.

4. In Output 10.4, the pairs of means that were significantly different are the grades of students with low (h.s. grad or less) and high (B.S. or more) fathers' education ($p = .018$).

Chapter 11

Factorial ANOVA

1. a) Yes, the interaction between math grades and father's education is significant, $F(2,67) = 3.46$, $p = .037$.

   b) Examining the profile plot, we note that the lines are not parallel, indicating an interaction. This plot seems to indicate that for students with high math grades (mostly A&Bs) achievement increases as education of the father increases, but for those with lower grades (less than A&Bs) math achievement does not go up as education increases. Math achievement depends on both grades and father's education.

   c) The main effect of father's education on math achievement is significant ($p < .001$). Eta squared is an index of effect size; .240 is a relatively small effect.

   d) Likewise, the effect of math grades on math achievement is significant ($p = .001$).

e) The word "effect" can be misleading by inferring that math grades "caused" the differences. We can't know that for sure because this is not a good randomized experiment.

f) Focusing on the main effect would be misleading because there was a significant interaction and the results depend on both variables.

Multiple Regression

2. a) Grades in h.s and mosaic pattern test score were identified as significant predictors of math achievement.
   b) The final multiple R is .600.
   c) The adjusted R^2 is .322 that means that 32% of the variance in math achievement can be predicted by a combination of these independent variables.

For Further Reading

American Psychological Association (APA). (1994). *Publication manual of the American Psychological Association* (4th ed.). Washington, DC: Author.

Cohen, J. (1988). *Statistical power and analysis for the behavioral sciences* (2nd ed.). Hillsdale, NJ: Lawrence Erlbaum Associates.

Gliner, J. A., & Morgan, G. A. (2000). *Research methods in applied settings: An integrated approach to design and analysis.* Mahwah, NJ: Lawrence Erlbaum Associates.

Hinkle, D. E., Wiersma, W., & Jurs, S. G. (1998). *Applied statistics for the behavioral sciences* (4th ed.). Boston: Houghton Mifflin.

Huck, S. J. (2000). *Reading statistics and research* (3rd ed.). New York: Longman.

Jaeger, R. M. (1990). *Statistics: A spectator sport* (2nd ed.). Newbury Park, CA: Sage.

Kelly, J. D. (1993). The effects of display format and data density on time spent reading statistics in text, tables, and graphs. *Journalism Quarterly, 70,* 140-149.

Merriam, S. B., & Simpson, E. L. (1995). *A guide to research for educators and trainers of adults* (2nd ed.). Malabar, FL: Krieger.

Morgan, G. A., & Griego, O. V. (1998). *Easy use and interpretation of SPSS for Windows.* Mahwah, NJ: Lawrence Erlbaum Associates.

Nicol, A. A. M., & Pexman, P. M. (1999). *Presenting your findings: A practical guide for creating tables.* Washington, DC: American Psychological Association.

Rosenthal, R. (1994). Parametric measures of effect size. In H. Cooper & L. V. Hedges (Eds.), *The handbook of research synthesis* (pp. 231-244). New York: Russell Sage Foundation.

Rudestam, K. E., & Newton, R. R. (1992). *Surviving your dissertation: A comprehensive guide to content and process*. Newbury Park: Sage.

Salant, P., & Dillman, D. D. (1994). *How to conduct your own survey*. New York: Wiley.

SPSS. (2000). *SPSS base 10.0 users' guide*. Chicago: Author.

Vogt, W. P. (1993). *Dictionary of statistics and methodology.* Newbury Park, CA: Sage.

Wainer, H. (1992). Understanding graphs and tables. *Educational Researcher, 21*(1), 14-23.

Wilkinson, L., & The Task Force on Statistical Inference. (1999). Statistical methods in psychology journals: Guidelines and explanations. *American Psychologist. 54*, 594-604.

INDEX